THE ADMINISTRATION OF JUSTICE IN ASSAM

The volume will be of immense value to the students of History, Law and Political Science.

Dr. Biswajit Baruah
Professor and Head Department of History,
Dibrugarh University, Dibrugarh, Assam

This book should fill a vacuum still existing in the administrative and legal aspects of Assam history, specially the British Assam from the time of its annexation up to its separation from Bengal.

Dr. S. Dutta
Former Dean, School of Social Sciences,
Rajiv Gandhi University, Itanagar, Arunachal Pradesh

Based on original sources, this volume is a pioneering work in the study of the growth and development of judicial administration in Assam since the beginning of the East India Company's rule in the province till it was separated from the Bengal Presidency in 1874. In view of the fact that Assam had its own laws and codes different from those of other provinces of British India, this work is unique and pioneering in its reach.

Assam was administered under non-regulation system which had its origin in the neighbouring province of Bengal and was governed by a mixed system of local and regulation laws. In the administration of civil justice, the Bengal regulations were entirely dispensed with, while in criminal administration the regulations were followed more or less. Since the occupation of the province by the Company's government till 1837 the fundamental drawback of the entire judicial administration was the want of a definite code of law, the absence of which confused the administrators in delivering justice. It was only in 1837 that rules for the civil and criminal administration, popularly known as the Assam Code, were drafted and judicial administration in the province found a sound footing.

The presentation and analysis of the laws and codes prepared by the Government of Bengal in its executive capacity in consultation with the local authorities in Assam is the most distinctive feature of this comprehensive work.

Achyut Kumar Borthakur graduated from Cotton College, Guwahati before going for his Masters from Gauhati University, Guwahati followed by a degree in law. He later obtained a PhD from Dibrugarh University. He has more than 20 published academic papers with an equal number of popular articles to his credit.

The Administration of Justice in Assam (1826-1874)

ACHYUT KUMAR BORTHAKUR

LONDON AND NEW YORK

First published 2019
by Routledge
4 Park Square, Milton Park, Abingdon, Oxon OX14 4RN
605 Third Avenue, New York, NY 10017

First issued in paperback 2023

Routledge is an imprint of the Taylor & Francis Group, an informa business

© 2019 Achyut Kumar Borthakur and Manohar Publishers & Distributors

The right of Achyut Kumar Borthakur to be identified as author of this work has been asserted by him in accordance with sections 77 and 78 of the Copyright, Designs and Patents Act 1988.

All rights reserved. No part of this book may be reprinted or reproduced or utilised in any form or by any electronic, mechanical, or other means, now known or hereafter invented, including photocopying and recording, or in any information storage or retrieval system, without permission in writing from the publishers.

Trademark notice: Product or corporate names may be trademarks or registered trademarks, and are used only for identification and explanation without intent to infringe.

Publisher's Note
The publisher has gone to great lengths to ensure the quality of this reprint but points out that some imperfections in the original copies may be apparent.

Print edition not for sale in South Asia (India, Sri Lanka, Nepal, Bangladesh, Pakistan or Bhutan)

British Library Cataloguing in Publication Data
A catalogue record for this book is available from the British Library

Library of Congress Cataloging in Publication Data
A catalog record for this book has been requested

ISBN 13: 978-1-03-265393-8 (pbk)
ISBN 13: 978-0-367-19856-5 (hbk)
ISBN 13: 978-0-429-24374-5 (ebk)

DOI: 10.4324/9780429243745

Typeset in Adobe Garamond 11/13
by Kohli Print Delhi 110 051

MANOHAR

*To the sacred memory
of my Teacher*

SWARNA LATA BARUAH

Contents

Preface   11

List of Abbreviations   19

Maps   21

1. Introduction   23

   Political Background   23
   Ahom Judiciary   30
   Evolution of English Law in India   36

2. Policy and Organizational Framework of the British Judicial Administration   49

   Problem of Administering the Brahmaputra Valley   49
   Extension of the Non-Regulation System   50
   Scott's Policies and Programmes in the
     Administration of Upper and Lower Assam   52
   Administration of Civil Justice   54
   Administration of Criminal Justice   59

3. Growth and Development of the Administration of Justice in the Early Years of British Rule   70

   Administration of Civil Justice   70
   Working of Native Courts   72
   Administration of Criminal Justice   75
   The Rebellion of Gomdhar Konwar   89
   The Rebellion of Gadadhar   91
   The Rebellion of Peali Barphukan and his Associates   91
   Appointment of Robertson as Commissioner   92
   Preparation of Civil Code   92
   The Ahom Monarchy Restored in Upper Assam   101
   Administrative Re-organization   104
   Appointment of Francis Jenkins   105
   Division of the Country Made Permanent   106

8   *Contents*

4. Judicial Administration from the Promulgation of the Assam Code till the End of the East India Company's Rule   117

    Preparation of a Code   117
    Administration of Civil Justice   118
    Administration of Criminal Justice   132
    The *Viva Voce* Examination   140
    Resumption of Upper Assam   143
    Annexation of Matak Territory   144
    Annexation of Sadiya   146
    Annexation of Cachar   146
    Annexation of Jayantia   148
    Great National Upsurge and the Administration of Justice   148

5. Administration of Justice under the Crown till 1874   178

    Extension of Codes of Civil and Criminal Procedure   178
    Peasant Uprising   182
    Raij Mel at Gobindapur   187
    Act XIII of 1859 (Workmen Breach of Contract Act, 1859)   188
    Act VI of 1864 (Whipping Act)   189
    Bengal Act VI of 1868   191

6. Judicial Agencies   193

    European Functionaries Commissioner   193
    Native Judges   200
    Honorary Magistrate   212
    Jury Trial   215
    Professional Pleaders   218
    Government Pleaders   224

7. Police Administration   234

    Powers and Duties of Police *Darogahs*   234

8. Impact of the Administration of Justice on the Life of the People   254

Procedural Law 257
Large Jurisdiction 259
Examination of Witnesses 261
Court Language 263
Concentration of Power: Justice United with
    Administration and Revenue 266
Legislation 268

9. Conclusion   271

Annexure: Assam Code   283

Glossary   319

Bibliography   325

Index   331

Preface

The British East India Company entered Assam in March 1824 to drive their foe, the Burmese out of the Brahamaputra Valley. In the war that followed, the Burmese, being defeated, concluded peace with the British at Yandabo in February 1826 and by the terms of the treaty, surrendered their claims to Assam, Cachar and Jayantia. Taking hold of this opportunity, the Company introduced its rule in Assam and gradually annexed it to its territories in India. It continued to rule Assam, as it did in other parts of the country till 1858, when India passed on from the hands of the Company to the direct administration of the British Crown. However, there was no major change in the administration of the province as a result of the change in authority. It was only in 1874 that Assam was made a Chief Commissioner's Province; earlier to that, a Commissioner under the Presidency of Bengal administered Assam.

The British brought radical changes to traditional administrative structure of Assam. The administration of justice too underwent the same fate. The pattern they introduced in Assam was in line with what they did in other parts of India, with the basic difference that the Regulations of the Governor-General were dispensed with in judicial affairs of the province. They were, however, not altogether avoided but applied or used whenever necessary. In fact, a mixed system of Regulations and local laws governed the province to the entire benefit of the imperial power. It was only after the introduction of Code of Civil Procedure and Code of Criminal Procedure or Indian Penal Code in the 1860s that the province was administered by the same system as was applicable in other parts of India.

The history of British administration in Assam from 1826-74 would remain incomplete without a thorough understanding of its system of judicial administration. But a systematic study of this subject has not yet been taken up. This study, therefore, intends to present a comprehensive and well-documented account of the British administration of justice in Assam beginning with the formal introduction of British rule in the province in February 1826 till it was made a Chief Commissioner's Province in 1874. This would help in getting a broad idea of the administrative machinery of the British as an imperial and colonial power. Every endeavour has been made to examine the growth, development and working of the judicial machinery during the period under review, covering almost all branches of the administration of justice. People's reactions to the changes and the impact of the administration of justice on their life have been analysed.

A number of works on the history of Assam have come forth since the publication of E.A. Gait's *A History of Assam* in 1906—the first authoritative work on the history of the province. A.C. Banerjee's *The Eastern Frontier of British India* (1946) discusses the policy of the East India Company towards Assam from the last quarter of the eighteenth to the first quarter of the nineteenth century. S.K. Bhuyan in his *Anglo Assamese Relations* (1949) throws much light on the earlier contracts of the inhabitants of this province with the Europeans. Bhuyan has also briefly discussed the administrative beginnings of the Company's government in Assam. R.M. Lahiri in his work *The Annexation of Assam* (1954) has focused the political developments of the period with occasional references to the administrative system including the working of the judiciary and the police. N.K. Baruah's *David Scott in North-East India* (1970) examines the different problems faced by Scott in administering the province, gives an idea about the British policies and programmes in the formative period of their rule in Assam. However, the most notable work of the period is *Assam in the Days of Company* (1963) by H.K. Borpujari. While dealing with the Company's administration in Assam, he also presents, in brief, a reliable account of the working of the judiciary, based on official records.

The indigenous chronicles or *buranjis*, which form a valuable source for the history of the earlier period, hardly contain any information regarding the working of the British administration even during its early years. *Asamar Padya Buranji*, consisting of two metrical works in Assamese by Dutiram Hazarika and Bisweswar Baidyadhipa, and edited by S.K. Bhuyan (1964) is an important contemporary work so far available, which yields fragmentary details of the administration of the period. Another contemporary work is *Sadar Aminar Atmajivani*. This being the autobiography of Harakanta Sarma Baruah, a Sadar Ameen, edited by K.C. Bordoloi (1960), the treatment of the administration of the period is rather sketchy. *Assam Buranji* by Haliram Dhekial Phukon (1829) written in Bengali gives an idea of the British judicial administration in Assam. Another Bengali work, *Aain Aru Bebastha Sangrah* (1855), titled *Notes on the Laws of Bengal* in English, is the first work to deal with the subject as such. *Orunudoi*, the first Assamese monthly published by the American Baptist Mission Society, Sib-sagar, from 1846 makes scanty references to the system of government or administrative procedure adopted by the British. *Report on the Province of Assam* by A.J. Moffatt Mills (1854) also provides vital information about the province and its revenue and judicial administration.

However, these works contain only fragmentary accounts and do not help us get a complete history of the judicial administration covering all its departments and different aspects like constitution of courts, the jury, judicial agencies, legislative authorities, police and so on. This volume is, therefore, the first attempt to make a systematic and analytic study of the judicial history of the province for the period under study covering all the important aspects of the problem. In fact, this work has grown out of my doctoral thesis 'The Judicial Administration of Assam, 1826-74', which was submitted to and approved by Dibrugarh University in May 1998.

The subject has been studied in nine chapters:

Chapter 1 is a brief study of the history of the Ahom kingdom along with a glimpse of the Ahom judiciary and the evolution of British laws and regulations in India.

Chapter 2 deals with the policy and organizational framework of the British administration of justice in Assam. It shows how the Company pursued its policy in the administration of the province immediately after its occupation by it, overcoming the manifold problems that stood on its way. It discusses how the mixed system of Regulation and locally made laws were applied in governing the province.

Chapter 3 is devoted to the administration of justice in the province in the formative period of the British rule. The working of the native courts, which actually managed the administration of justice, is elaborately examined in this chapter. It also discusses the revenue system, which was the heart of the British administration system and was intimately connected with civil justice. Cash payments of revenue in lieu of personal service were a distinctive feature of the British revenue administration, which had harmful impact on the impoverished people of the province. The new revenue system was responsible for the growth of poverty, and poverty ultimately contributed to the abnormal increase in criminal activities. The new concept of private property gave the inhabitants a right to mortgage their land and belongings in order to borrow money to pay revenue or to maintain their livelihood. This had a disastrous effect on their life, as the new legal system protected the moneylender's rights in realizing their loans. An attempt has been made to examine the law and order machinery and its workings. An appraisal of the trial of Gomdhar Konwor, the first capital trial, on charges of conspiracy against the government is also given; the condition of jails and prisoners is also discussed. This chapter further deals with the growth and development of the judicial administration after the appointment of Thomas Cambell Robertson as the Commissioner of Assam. The rules for the administration of civil and criminal Justice took written form during the commissionership of Robertson.

Chapter 4 is devoted to the study of Assam Code, i.e. the Rules for the Administration of Civil and Criminal Justice in Assam till the end of the East India Company's rule. How the courts were conducted and what procedure was followed by the courts is systematically explained in this chapter, as also the procedure of making appeals. Alongside, the rules for arbitration or compromise in order to prevent the people from going to the regular courts of law are examined. The penal law of Assam, which was a combination of Regulation laws and local customs, is looked at. The viva-voce system of trial is also discussed.

The most notable event of this period was the suppression of the Revolt of 1857, or the First War of Indian Independence. An effort has been made to analyse the impact of the mutiny on the people of the province. The trial of the Assam rebels is elaborately discussed in the chapter. The attitude of the British officers and their violation of the Rule of Law are also examined.

The Chapter 5 deals with the enactment of various codes, more specifically the Code of Civil Procedure, the Code of Criminal Procedure and the Indian Penal Code. With the extension of these codes, Assam was brought in line with the other provinces of India in the administration of justice. The changes brought about in the judicial affairs of Assam after the introduction of these codes also figure in this chapter.

Chapter 6 deals with the judicial agencies. A considerable number of courts were constituted for the performance of judicial functions. An attempt has been made here to examine how these officers discharged their duties. The powers and duties of the European officers and their nature of work are also described along with those of the native judges. Alongside a comparison of the position and authority of both the English and the native agencies in Assam with their counterparts in Bengal is made. The characteristics of jury trial, which was introduced by the British rulers since the beginning of their administration, is also examined. The Pleaders or *vakeels* form an integral part of every judicial administration. Therefore, efforts have been made to present an elaborate account of their role covering such problems, as the procedure of their appointment, and the system of examination and its usefulness in the administration of justice.

Chapter 7 is devoted to a study of police administration of the province as the police are an inseparable part of judicial administration. Without an efficient police, there cannot be any efficient criminal administration. Therefore, this chapter examines the structure of the police administration and its impact on the life of the people. Regulation XX of 1817 was the Police Law in Assam until the year 1861. In that year, the Police Act was enacted and in the very next year, it was extended to Assam. In spite of severe criticism, this act still remains valid in our country. The chapter discusses how the general inefficiency of the police affected the administration and the life of the people.

Chapter 8 studies the impact of British administration of justice on the inhabitants of the province. The people were hit hard by the sudden change of judicial administration without a corresponding change in their socio-economic conditions. They were confused by the multiplicity of laws introduced by the alien rulers in their state. The expensive legal system and complicated procedures made justice a mockery for the impoverished and ignorant masses. The new police system made the matters worse. The police, instead of being a boon, become a source of oppression for the law-abiding people. Honest attempts have been made to analyse the problem as objectively as possible.

Chapter 9 summarizes the contents of the earlier chapters and presents the findings of the study. The comments and observations of prominent contemporary British and Indian officials on the British judicial system are also assessed in this chapter.

In making this study, best attempts have been made to use and examine all the available materials relevant to the work. The work is almost entirely based on official documents preserved in West Bengal State Archives, Kolkata; National Library, Kolkata; National Archives of India, New Delhi; and Assam State Archives, Guwahati. No Xerox copies of these documents being available, these had to be studied in their original, some of which have turned brittle and some of them so faded that it was a challenge to decipher the words. Arranging these archival materials in a systematic form, therefore, required a lot of time, energy and perseverance. Scholars working on a subject pertaining to the administrative history of Assam cannot have easy access to the Bengal Political Consultations, which are still housed in the India Office Library, London. On the other hand, the records regarding Assam in the Bengal Judicial Proceedings are available in a systematic form only from the year 1834, when the jurisdiction of the Sadar Dewani and

Nizamat Adalat were extended to Assam. Therefore, one has to visit National Archives of India at New Delhi to collect information for the earlier period, i.e. from 1825 to 1834. Besides the proceedings, other official records of the Government of India, as well as of Bengal and Assam, both in manuscript and printed form containing *inter alia* administrative and law reports, tour diaries and Gazettes have also been consulted, some of which contain important information relating to the subject under study.

The sources of this work are thus mainly in their original form; secondary works have been studied only to clarify certain points and substantiate some of my ideas. To have a broad idea of the problem, the working of the British judiciary in India as a whole and in certain provinces like Bengal, Punjab and Bombay have been studied, as also in their own country, England. As the present Indian judicial system is based on the structure and pattern left by the British, a general idea of the judicial administration after 1874 and in independent India has been gathered both from primary and secondary sources.

I take this opportunity to express my sincere thanks to the staff of the West Bengal State Archives, more specifically to Chief Archivists, M.M. Biswas, Udoyan Mitra, and Ananda Mohan Bhattacharjee; Archivists, Bidisha and Sarmistha; and Volume Supplier Amal. Thanks are due to the staff and Volume Suppliers of National Archives of India, New Delhi; State Archives, Assam; Guwahati High Court Library, Dibrugarh; Guwahati University Library, without whose help and cooperation I would not have been able to collect the necessary records and information. The suggestions offered by Prof. H.K. Borpujari, Prof. Amalendu Guha, Prof. Srutidev Goswami, Prof. Sib Sankar Mukherjee of Presidency College, Kolkata, Dr. Partha Sarathi Dutta, Prof. Dambarudhar Nath, Prof. S.D. Dutta, Prof. Biswajit Baruah and Prof. Chandan Sarnah, during the preparation of my thesis were specially useful. I am deeply indebted to all of them. I owe a great deal to the renowned Advocate and the Advocate General of Arunachal Pradesh, Mr. Niloy Dutta who inspired me to publish this book. My friend and brother Prof. Uttam Duarah of Women's College, Tinsukia read the work and offered valuable suggestions, I am thankful to him. My daughters Anwesha and Anchita took great interest in the work and encouraged me in my labour. I thank them profusely. I am also indebted to my wife Anjana Goswami for her help and cooperation at every step.

I am deeply grateful to Prof. Swarnalata Baruah, Dibrugarh University, under whose supervision I worked on judicial administration in Assam, 1826-74. I received her constant advice and encouragement all through the preparation of my work. My greatest regret is that she is no more to see the publication of this book.

Tinsukia College   ACHYUT KUMAR BORTHAKUR
Tinsukia

Abbrevations

AA	W. Robinson, *A Descriptive Account of Assam*
AAR	S.K. Bhuyan, *Anglo-Assamese Relations*
AIDC	H.K. Barpujari, *Assam in the Days of Company*
AOJBI	W.H. Morley, *The Administration of Justice in British India*
AXA	R.M. Lahiri, *The Annexation of Assam*
BJP	Bengal Judicial Proceedings
BSPC	Bengal Secret and Political Consultations
CHA	(Mrs.) S.L. Baruah, *A Comprehensive History of Assam*
DAB	*Deodhai Asam Buranji*
FPP	Foreign Political Proceedings
FSP	Foreign Secret Proceedings
GP	General Proceedings
HOA	Sir Edward Gait, *A History of Assam*
MD	Benudhar Sarma, *Maniram Dewan*
RP	Revenue Proceedings
RPA	A.J.M. Mills, *Report on the Province of Assam*
SHA	S.K. Bhuyan, *Studies in the History of Assam*
TASOG	A.C. Sarma, *Tai Ahom System of Government*
TP	Territorial Proceedings

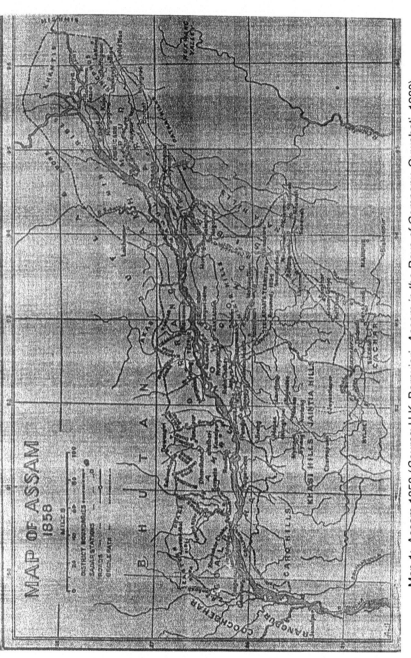

Map 1: Assam 1858 (*Source*: H.K. Barpujari, *Assam in the Days of Company*, Guwahati, 1980)

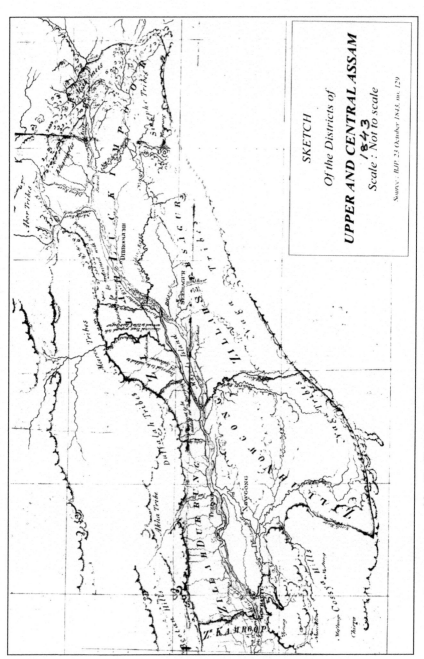

Map 2: Sketch of the District of Upper and Central Assam 1843

CHAPTER 1

Introduction

POLITICAL BACKGROUND

Assam lies in the extreme north-east frontier of India, between 28° and 24° North latitudes and 89° 86' and 96° East longitudes. Assam has been a very important historical and cultural centre since the earliest times. The reconstruction of early history of Assam is a difficult task, mainly because of the deficiency of pure and reliable historical materials. Little is known of the history of Assam before the fourth century AD. Assam was known as Pragjyotishpur and later as Kamrupa. The modern state of Assam was a part of the extensive kingdom of Pragjyotishpur or Kamrupa in ancient times, which included major portions of eastern India. The earliest known history of Assam can be traced from the rise of the Varmanas in the fourth century AD. Kamrupa during the rule of the Varmanas included considerable portion of Bengal, some portion of Bihar, Sylhet and Tripura. This territory was under the Salastambhas from the middle of the sixth century. Although there were twenty-one kings in the Salastambha dynasty, names of only fourteen are known and the regnant periods and activities of most of them barring a few, are based on mere assumptions. The Salastambhas extended their sway to Gauda, Odre, Kalinga, Kosalla and some portions in the south-west. With the fall of the Palas, who replaced Salastambhas, the kingdom of Kamrupa disintegrated. There appeared a number of independent and semi-independent kingdoms and principalities and among them the Bhuyans were the most powerful. The Palas, of course, left a good number of epigraphs, but with their fall in the beginning of the twelfth century the history of Assam again appears to be a disconnected and fragmentary account of kings and events.

Since time immemorial Assam has been bounded on the north, east and south by hills inhabited by diverse tribes, each with its distinctive manners, customs and languages. These hill tribes were the Bhutanese, Akas, Nishis, Mishings, Adis, Mishimis, Khamptis, Singhphos, Nagas, Karbis, Garos, Jayantias, and others. On the north, she is guarded by the eastern section of the great Himalayan range, where live the frontier tribes like the Bhutiyas, Akas, Nishis (Daflas), Mishings (Miris), Adis (Abors), and Mishimis. On the east lie the mountains inhabited by the Khamtis and Singphos. This region, as a whole, except the part inhabited by the Bhutiyas, now forms the state of Arunachal Pradesh. The Patkai range on the south-east, which forms the natural boundary between Assam and Burma (Myanmar), is inhabited by the Nagas and merges itself into the mountains of Burma. To the south of the Brahamaputra Valley, beginning from the extreme south-west, the mountain chains take the name of Garo hills, the Khashi and the Jayantia hills, the North Cachar, Mikir hills and the Naga hills. This mountain system is collectively known as the 'Assam Range', which with the exception of the North Cachar, the Mikir hills and Naga hills, forms the state of Meghalaya. The Naga hills, together with the eastern portion of the Patkai range, created the state of Nagaland. The North Cachar and the Mikir hills (the Karbi Anglong) forming two districts remain within the present State of Assam. To the south of the Assam Range lies the Barak Valley or Surma Valley, which includes the present district of Cachar. To the south of Cachar and Nagaland lie the states of Mizoram and Manipur. To the south-west of Cachar is the state of Tripura and to the west of Cachar is Bangladesh. Assam's relations with the neighbouring hill states of Arunachal Pradesh, Nagaland, Manipur, Mizoram, Meghalaya and Tripura has been from time immemorial very close.

The early part of the thirteenth century saw major events in the history of Assam; one was the beginning of a series of invasions from the west led by the Turko-Afghan rulers of Bengal, and the other was the foundation of a kingdom by the Tai Shans, who came to be known as 'Ahom', in the south-eastern part of the Brahmaputra Valley. The former appeared as raiders with an irrepressible zeal for territorial aggrandizement, the latter as agricultural settlers in search of land. Whereas the rulers of Kamrupa were losing their hold and authority over their possessions due to internal dissensions, they were finally overtaken by a small group of Tai Shans who later became lords of the Land, and also became one with the indigenous people in their fight against invaders from the west. They successfully repulsed the invaders in a series of battles which lasted more than one hundred years. With the establishment of their power, the centre of gravity in Assam's political life shifted from the western to the eastern part of the Brahmaputra Valley. The Ahoms, during their glorious six-hundred-year rule, extended their power and authority as far as to the river Manaha in the west.

The right to dispense justice comes with the acquisition of sovereignty. Before entering into the history of the administration of justice in Assam, it is necessary to begin with the origin and development of British sovereignty in this province.

Mention has already been made about the Ahoms, a member of the Shan branch of the great Tai or Thai family of South-East Asia. Their leader Sukapha en route from his homeland Maulung in Upper Burma to the Brahmaputra Valley defeated all the opposing tribes and thereafter the Nagas living between the Daikham and the Patkai hills by a policy of blood and rapine. In the Brahmaputra Valley, however, he pursued a policy of peace and conciliation against the Morans and the Barahis, the first tribes to be subjugated by him. But those who challenged him were ruthlessly killed.[1] In AD 1228 Sukapha laid the foundation of the Ahom kingdom in Assam with its capital at Charaideo, a place 25 miles south from the present town of Sibsagar. Sukapha's successors established firm control over the area from River Dihing in the east to river Dhansiri in the west. In the course of the next three centuries the Ahoms reduced to submission the Chutiyas, Kacharis and Bhuyans. The territorial expansion of the Ahoms towards the west led them to a direct confrontation with the Koches, who were interested in expanding their territory towards the east in the sixteenth century. Though initially the Koches overpowered the Ahoms, the latter soon recovered their position.

However, the most formidable power the Ahoms had to face in the western frontier of their kingdom were the Mughals. The Ahom conflict with the Mughals covered almost the whole of the seventeenth century. The Mughals after occupying the Koch kingdom attempted to conquer Assam. The western division of the Koch kingdom called Koch Hajo or Kamrupa, covering the territory between Sonkosh in the west and Barnadi on the north bank and Asurar Ali on the south bank in the east formed a bone of contention between the two powers. Consequently this part of the kingdom was ruled intermittently by both the powers. From 1616 to 1658, it was under Mughal occupation, when the Mughal system of administration was introduced here. It is to the credit of the Ahoms that they could resist the repeated attacks of the Mughals successfully, except on one occasion in 1662-3, when Mir Jumla, the great general of Emperor Aurangzeb occupied the Ahom capital, Gargaon and forced the Ahom king to flee to Namrup. But the success cost the general his life and Assam shook off Mughal allegiance which lasted barely a few months. Aurangzeb then sent Raja Ram Singh of Amber to recover the lost hold but the Ahom general Lachit Barphukan inflicted a crushing defeat on the Mughals in the famous naval battle at Saraighat in 1671. King Gadadhar Singha finally expelled the Mughals after defeating them in the battle of Itakhuli in 1682. The river Manaha remained the western boundary of the Ahom kingdom from the battle of Saraighat till the British occupation of the kingdom in 1825.

The Ahoms resorted to different policies of stratagem, peace overtures, spreading rumours, threating and so on in dealing with their enemies including the Mughals. They subjugated the Kacharis mainly by a policy of stratagem. They successfully deceived the Koches, when they were not ready for a war with them. Knowing that the Koch royal family were orthodox Hindus, the Ahom king sent his soldiers garbed as Brahmanas, who rode on the back of cows, prominently exhibiting their sacred lines in their foreheads and raising their sacred threads up on their ears. An attack under such circumstances would mean slaughter of both cows and Brahmanas. The Koch generals, therefore, retreated without fighting. Often they deceived the Mughals by making exaggerated statements about their military strength.

The Ahom rulers described Assam as *Sonar Saphura* or 'casket of gold', which must not be opened to foreigners.[2] They were, therefore, determined to repulse any foreign attack with the last drop of blood in their veins. But curiously enough, the Ahom kings, who could successfully meet the challenges of the great Mughals, could not defend their kingdom from the rebellion of their own subjects. This was due to the fact that after the end of the Mughal wars, the Ahom royalty and aristocracy gradually got alienated from the people. They became intriguing, pleasure-loving, and indolent and consequently oppressive. The result was the rebellion of the Moamaria (1769), the first popular challenge to the Ahom monarchy.[3] The internal troubles created a situation in which the Ahom king Gaurinath Singha (1780-95) had to seek the help of the East India Company and, thus, himself opened 'the casket of gold' so dearly preserved by his predecessors, to the white foreigners.

In response to Gaurinath's appeal for help, Lord Cornwallis, the then Governor-General of Bengal sent Captain Welsh to Assam (1792-4) with a contingent of 360 sepoys. Welsh recovered the Ahom throne from the possession of the Moamaria rebels and brought about an amicable settlement between the Ahom king and the rebellious Raja of Darrang, after which he returned. But the Moamarias revolted again. They were finally won over in 1805 by the astute Ahom prime minister, Purnananda Buragohain, by ceding to them a territory which roughly covered the present districts of Dibrugarh and Tinsukia. This territory came to be known as Matak country.

In the meantime, the Burmese were becoming very powerful in the eastern frontier of Assam. The conflict between premier Purnananda and Badan Chandra, the Barphukan or Viceroy of Guwahati, gave the Burmese an opportunity to invade Assam. On Badan Chandra's advice, they first invaded Assam in 1817 and again in 1819 and 1821 and continued to rule Assam as *de facto* rulers keeping the puppet king Jogeswar Singha on the throne.

The establishment of Burmese authority in Assam and later in Cachar was viewed by the British government as a serious menace to the security of the British territories in Bengal. David Scott, the Joint Magistrate of Rangpur, pointed out to the Government of

Bengal the vulnerability of entire eastern frontier suggesting that the policy of non-intervention which had so long been the watchword towards the north-east frontier should be definitely discarded and that it was highly expedient to support and encourage the Assamese and the frontier tribes to resist and shake off the Burmese yoke.

Early in 1824, when the Burmese converged on Cachar from three directions on the plea of restoring the rightful claimant to the throne, Lord Amherst, the Governor-General of India had no alternative but to resort to arms. The British government issued a formal declaration of war on 5 March 1824.

The war actually broke out in three regions: Assam, Arrakan and Rangoon. The force under Colonel Macmorine occupied Guwahati on 28 March 1824. In January 1825, the British forces occupied Jorhat and advanced towards Rangpur. After offering some resistance, the Burmese garrison at Rangpur asked for truce, and they were permitted to leave Assam on the condition that they would not commit any ravages on the road or forcibly carry away any of the inhabitants. The fall of Rangpur practically completed the conquest of Assam and by the treaty of Yandabo on 24 February 1826 the Burmese surrendered their claims to Assam, Cachar and Jayantia.

Lord William Bentinck, the Governor-General of British India (1828-35) admitted that 'there must have been something intrinsically good in the constitution of the Ahoms'[4] due to which they could enjoy uninterrupted sovereignty for six centuries. One of the intrinsic goodness lay in their ideology of government, which was a form of benevolent paternalism. According to Ahom legends, their two progenitors Khunlung and Khunlai, at the time of their departure from heaven to rule over this earth, were advised by their grandfather Lengdon, the god of heaven thus: 'Just as a man loses his wife if he quarrels with his father-in-law or brother-in-law, and just as a mother bird guards her nestlings with her wings and protects them from rain and storm and rears them up by feeding them herself, so you two brothers should protect your subjects and desist from quarreling with your friends and supporters.'[5] The Ahoms believed in utopia and their kings were encouraged to rule in a way so that the noble principles of Utopia could be realized. In the Satya Yuga or Golden Age, love was the order of the time. Men used to take food in the same dish like sons of the same mother and nobody entertained any jealousy or hatred towards any other person.[6] A descend of Khunlung is said to have ruled his kingdom in accordance with this ideology, which set an example to his successors. During his rule, the sufferings of the people came to an end and they became happy as before. He governed his subjects as his own sons. There was no taxation in his time. He lived a righteous life, according due punishment to every guilt and rewards and honour to virtue and merit.[7]

The ideology of the Ahom government was, therefore, justice, benevolence and equity. An efficient and benevolent king was highly honoured. One such was King Pratap Singha (1603-41). When he fell ill at the age of ninety, one hundred of his subjects offered to sacrifice their lives before the Goddess Kesaikhati (eater of raw flesh) of Sadiya[8] if by so doing they could save the aged monarch. The earlier Ahom kings beginning with Sukapha mixed freely with the subjects without any air of superiority. Any indolent or oppressive king had to suffer deposition or death. Disuse of these noble practices towards the end of their rule ultimately caused the decline of the Ahoms.

The Ahom government was both monarchial and aristocratic. The aristocracy, originally of three *dangariyas* or cabinet ministers the Buragohain, the Bargohain and the Barpatragohain acted as a strong deterrent to the king exercising arbitrary power. The Gohains, if united, could make and unmake a king. With the extension of Ahom territory the cabinet was expanded to five members, the new entrants being the Barbaruah, the Chief Executive, and the Barphukan, the Viceroy of Lower Assam.

The pivot of the Ahom administration was the *paik* system. In this system, all adult males within the age group of sixteen to fifty years were termed as *paik* and were made liable to work for the state as labour in normal times and as soldiers in war time. The Brahmanas, the members of the nobility and the royal family were exempt from performing this job. The members of the gentry, called *chamua*, by paying commutation money of rupees three per head per annum could claim exemption from rendering forced manual labour. Four *paiks* (later three) formed a unit called *got*. Every five *got* or twenty *paiks* were placed under the charge of an officer called *bora*, every hundred under a *saikia* and every thousand under a *Hazarika*. The *paiks* were also organized into *khels*, both functional and territorial. Important functional *khels* having about six thousand *paiks* were placed under a class of officers called the *phukan*. Those of smaller size were placed under the control of *baruas*.

The *paik* system was the backbone of Ahom revenue and military organization. There was no regular land tax as tax was levied in the form of compulsory manual labour from all adult males. The officers were also paid in the form of service of the *paiks*. The *paik* system kept a huge army at the disposal of the king. It was obligatory on the part of all officers, high or low, to bring forth the *paiks* under their respective control to the battlefield, whenever a notice to that effect was issued by the king. This, therefore, served the purpose of a regular militia. All officers again administered justice within their respective jurisdiction. There were also frontier governors like Marangi Khowa Gohain, Sadiya Khowa Gohain, and Salal Gohain, who governed the frontier areas named before their designations. In judicial matters they had the same authority as the cabinet ministers. Another class of officers called *rajkhowas* governed small territorial units like *bacha, salaguri*, and so on. They had also their courts and exercised judicial powers.

AHOM JUDICIARY

In the Ahom administration, the king was the highest judicial authority and the fountainhead of justice. As such, the king's court was also the highest court of appeal which tried cases of rebellion and civil and criminal suits.[9] The king was assisted by the chief justice called Nyay Sodha Phukan. Normally, the cases involving nobles or high officials were only put up before the king. No mercy was shown if they were found guilty of any crime. Important cases, especially, the records of trials involving offences of commoners which justified death sentence, had to be submitted to the king for final verdict and, he alone could sanction death penalty which required the shedding of blood.[10]

Other than the king's court there were also tribunals of justice. These the courts of the three *dangariyas*, the Barbaruah and the Barphukan. Next to the king's court, the courts of these officers occupied prominent position in the Ahom judicial administration. The three *dangariyas* exercised independent jurisdiction in their respective areas. The right to award capital punishment, which did not involve shedding of blood, was reserved to the three *dangariyas* and the Barphukan only.[11] The verdict of the *dangariyas* was always final and binding and no further appeal was allowed.

The Barbaruas' court exercised both original and appellate jurisdiction. As the head of executive, the Barbarua wielded wide powers. His court tried all important civil and criminal cases. All disputes pertaining to men under his command were settled by him. The decisions were usually arrived at with the help of assessors. Severe punishments like amputation and mutilation, could be inflicted by the Barbarua's court, but the king's consent was necessary for inflicting capital punishment, especially, on senior officials. The Barbarua received appeals from subordinate or inferior courts.

Another important court was that of the Barphukan. This court had excersied both original and appellate jurisdiction. It had jurisdiction over a large part of Lower Assam. This court could inflict all kinds of punishment including death sentence. But the nature of capital punishment had to take a form in which blood was not shed. Appeals from inferior courts of Lower Assam came to the Barphukan's court.

There were also the courts of the Phukans, the Rajkhowas and the Baruas. Each of these courts had original and appellate jurisdiction. The decisions of any of these courts could be challenged in the court of the Nyay Sodha Phukan and also in that of the Barbaruah. Appeal against the verdicts of the frontier governors could be made to the king.

At the village level, petty cases were decided with the help of a village assembly. The judicial work of the village assembly was usually entrusted to a small body of influential persons or village elders. They were mainly authorized to settle disputes pertaining to their own village. The village assembly was the main instrument of civil justice. The emphasis was on amicable settlement of disputes. The *satra* institutions had brought into existence the village *namghars* or prayer halls, which served as village courts, where criminal and minor civil cases of the village were dispensed with by the *mels* or village councils.[12] The decision of such *mels* were arrived at unanimously. However, in case of any disagreement, the opinion of the majority prevailed. Their decision was binding on the parties to the dispute. Complicated cases were referred by them to the superior court.

In Kamrup, the *parganas* were placed under a *chowdhury* and he decided petty cases, usually with the aid of *mels* or council of village elders. The *parganas* were further divided into *taluks* which were placed under *talukdars*, who also had judicial powers.

Nothing like modern legislation or a written code of laws existed during the Ahom period. The king himself constituted the law-making agency. In the earlier period of their rule, the judges administered justice according to the customs and traditions of the country and their own standard of right or wrong. In the latter period, when they came under the influence of Hinduism, the Hindu law as expounded by the Brahmanas were followed in civil matters.[13] On the other hand, the Muslims who settled in Assam permanently retained their laws of marriage, testamentary and intestate succession sanctioned by the Islamic faith.[14]

There was no distinction between civil and criminal cases and the same court tried both. No regular set of procedures was followed in the trial of cases. No record was kept in criminal trials, but in civil cases, a summary of the proceedings was drawn up and given to the winning party.[15] This proceeding was called *Siddhartha Patra*.[16] The principle of justice, equity and good conscience played an important role in the disposal of cases.

The accused was usually kept in prison guarded by *teckela* or *chowdang* till the completion of trial. The practice of releasing a person on bail or on sureties was prevalent. During the trial, if an accused was treated as innocent, he could move freely without any sort of harassment or humiliation. The criminals of distant places were lodged in well-guarded stations and they were led to the court under proper escort.[17]

In case of complaints of minor nature, witnesses were examined and written documents were received in evidence. The witnesses were examined in an open court in presence of the plaintiff and defendant and an enquiry of investigation was ordered to elicit the truth.

It might not be out of place to discuss how far representation of a party by his agent or pleaders in judicial trial was allowed in the Ahom period. Although the contemporary works are silent on this point, it would be wrong to conclude that there was nothing like modern lawyers or pleaders in the Ahom judicial system. At least we have some reference of government pleaders took part in judicial proceedings. Khargharia Phukan and the Choladhara Phukan acted as public prosecutors during criminal trials that took place in the reign of *swargadeo* Lakshmi Singha (1769 to 1780 AD).[18] They interrogated the accused in the trial before the king or *swargadeo*. From the above, it appears that the procedure of recording the contents of a decree in the Ahom rule, namely, statement of the parties, the points for decision, the particulars of the evidence, the decision of the court and the name of the officials present and their remarks were almost same as the present procedural code. It is also interesting to note that the contents of a decree, as enjoined by the high official bear striking similarity with those of the *roobkaris* of the Indian courts during British rule, prior to the earliest code in 1859.

The Ahom penal code was quite severe. Trials for crimes were characterized by extreme sternness. Severity and relation were the guiding principles of the penal code. Rigorous punishment, death and mutilation of limbs were frequently awarded. Offenders were inflicted rough and ready punishment, such as slitting of throats, impaling, grinding between two cylinders, sawing asunder between two planks, starving to death, scourging, etc. The common punishments were extraction of eyes and knee-caps, slicing off of noses and ears, blowing, slapping, beating with sticks, and so on. The penalty for rebellion was various forms of capital punishments, such as, starvation to death, flaying alive, impaling and hanging.[19] The death penalty was often inflicted in case of libel not only on the guilty but on all the members of his family.[20] In most cases punishments for criminal offences were governed by the principle of retaliation—tooth for a tooth and eye for an eye.

Almost all the Ahom kings paid attention to the maintenance of law and imparted equal justice to all. They took care that the influential or the strong should not prey upon the low or the weak. Prior to the Moamaria disturbances, the administration of justice was said to have been speedy, efficient and impartial.[21] Normally, no consideration of official rank or even royal kinship prevented the king from mete out condign and even severe punish-ment to the culprit. Credit must be given to the Ahom judiciary for dispensation of quick and inexpensive justice. The procedure observed in the court was also simple and not hedged in with numerous formalities or technicalities. The king generally followed the opinion of his advisers in conducting trial. He also discussed with his cabinet ministers before awarding sentences to culprits, especially in case of treason or sedition.

The Ahom administration of justice, however, was not entirely free from shortcomings. The concept of an independent judiciary separated from the executive was non-existent. The king was the head of the judiciary, the executive and the legislature. The vesting of judicial powers in the hands of the executive led to misuse of powers, especially in the later part of Ahom rule. There were no precise or elaborate rules of appeal. Lack of judicial books in the country created confusion for the judicial authorities. Further, mutual relations among the different courts were not smooth and their working and scope were not clearly defined. In the absence of proper system of evidence, there were sometimes arbitrary decisions. During the later part of their rule, the distinction between so-called high-born and low-born appeared in the Ahom judicial system, perhaps due to the influence of the Brahmanical religion. There was also the influence of the queen mothers, royal priests and religious adversaries in judicial decisions. However, such cases were rare and uncommon. In spite of all these shortcomings, the king and the royal officials made sincere efforts to make justice inexpensive and popular. Due to their constant supervision and guidance, the inferior tribunals imparted informal, speedy and inexpensive justice. As a result, the Ahoms could provide order and security to their subjects. The fact that the Ahom rule continued for six hundred years speak highly of the efficiency of their administration of justice.

The method of inflicting punishment to the guilty during the Ahom period was severally criticized by historians, especially the British. They described the Ahom Penal Code as barbarous and uncivilized. But judging by the contemporary standard this cannot be termed so. Most monarchial governments of the period practised such punishments as deterrents against crime. When the occasional barbarity of the Ahom punishment is emphasized, one should remember that in England, the law which condemned murderesses to be burnt alive was not repealed until 1790 and such horrible sentences continued to be executed as late as 1726. Queen Anne, the wife of King Henry VIII (1509-47) was found guilty of the charge of adultery and she was executed by burning alive.[22] Boiling to death or poisoning was practiced during the reign of Henry VIII. There are several instances of persons suffering such horrible and lingering death. The punishment for high treason was most inhuman and barbarous in England. The offender was dragged to the gallows; he was not allowed to walk. There, he was hanged by the neck and his entrails taken out and burnt while he was yet alive. His head was, thereafter, cut off and his body truncated into four parts. After the completion of this savage feat, the head and the quarters were placed at the king's disposal.[23] Until the early 1820s, England's penal code, was anachronistic compared to those of the Ahoms, providing death penalty even for pick-pocketing, sending threatening letters and stealing fish. This criterion of justice in the country of those who began to rule in India in the later half of the eighteenth century must be borne in mind while examining the state of contemporary judicial administration in Assam or other states of India. Humanitarian value about justice developed only with cultural enlightenment in the modern times.

The Ahom government was primarily military in nature. Its

main function was to guard the kingdom against foreign invasion and internal rebellions and give security to the subject population. These functions kept the king and his officials occupied. In the latter part of their rule, rebellions broke out as frequently as they were suppressed. It was more vital a function of the government to apprehend a refractory *raja* or an absconding claimant to the throne than to catch an offender to the law. It was likewise considered more essential to use the *paiks* for military service than for safeguarding the peace and tranquillity of the kingdom. The functions of maintaining law and order and the protection of life and property of the common men were generally entrusted to the village councils, without proper supervision. The village system worked satisfactorily so long as the Ahoms were able to maintain a general state of order and peace in the kingdom. But after the death of Rajeswar Singha in 1769 when the central authority began to decline, lawlessness broke out in many parts of the provinces. Starting from 1769 until 1824, the Moamaria rebellion and successive Burmese invasions impoverished the government and made it unstable. The internal administration of the province went into a complete state of disorder only to be marginally restored in 1826 after the coming of the British.

EVOLUTION OF ENGLISH LAW IN INDIA

Reference has been made above to the chaos and confusion prevailing in Assam since the latter part of the eighteenth century due to internal disorder and the Burmese invasions. The British appeared as a saviour at this hour of worst peril for Assam. Naturally therefore, the Assamese people hailed them with unbounded joy and extended them the most loyal cooperation.

Initially there was some confusion about the disposal of Assam. In 1828 the British finally decided to retain Lower Assam permanently under their occupation. However, it took more than eight years to take a final decision about Upper Assam. In 1833, Upper Assam was assigned to an Ahom prince, but on the plea of misgovernment, the British removed the prince and the tract was annexed to their territories in India in 1838.

Thus, the English became the sovereign in Assam by conquest. They exercised sovereign authority since their arrival in Assam, though the entire province formally passed into their hands only after the conclusion of the treaty of Yandabo on 24 February 1826.

The occupation of a country by an alien power is necessarily followed by the imposition of the legal system of the victors. The new rulers exercised power in accordance with laws, customs and administrative practices with which they are familiar in their own country, subject to local exigencies and political expediency. Moreover, they usually looked upon their new subjects as inferior and who would be benefited by the replacement of their indigenous legal system, representing a higher stage of political development.

No wonder, therefore, that the British East India Company brought radical changes to the traditional administrative structure of the province. Such changes also found their way into the administration of justice. They abrogated most of the existing laws and judicial institutions and introduced English laws and institutions in their place subject to local circumstances and practices.

In order to have a clear comprehension of the system of British administration of justice in Assam, it is necessary to inquire into the history of the system and the nature of the laws administered by the British in other parts of India, more specifically in Bengal.

When the Englishmen came to this country, they brought with them their own laws for the settlement of disputes among themselves. With the rise of their factories, English law came to be recognized as the law of the Company's settlements. Indian residents in the factories were, however, allowed the privilege of their own laws in such matters as inheritance and marriage.

The first authority for the introduction of British law in India was granted by Charles II, who, by a Royal Charter dated the 3 April 1661 gave the Governor and Councils of the several places belonging to the Company in the East Indies power 'to judge all persons belonging to the said Governor and Company, or that should live under them in all causes whether civil or criminal, according to the laws of the kingdom, and to execute judgment accordingly'.[24] The Company's legislative and judicial authority was to be exercised over its servants with a view to strengthening its disciplinary control. Such authority derived from the British Crown could not be exercised over the inhabitants of its factories and trading settlements in India. The Crown could not confer legal authority on the Company in any part of India other than Bombay Island.[25] This was because Bombay was indisputably British territory and hence they were empowered to make laws, orders, ordinances and constitution for the good government there. In fact, 'Bombay was the first place in India where British justice was administered to native inhabitants by a special court of judicature'.[26]

The year 1726 marked the beginning of an important era in the evolution of laws and courts in India. The Charter passed this year vested in the local authorities in the three Presidencies of Madras, Bombay and Calcutta authority to make by-laws and ordinances and to impose reasonable pains and penalties in case of beach upon all persons.[27] But such bye-laws, rules and ordinances as also the pains and penalties imposed by them were not to be repugnant to the laws of England. Mayor's courts were established in three Presidencies with a regular system of appeal from these courts to the Governor and Council of the Presidencies and thence to the King in-Council.

Under the charter of 1726, a Mayor's Court was established in each Presidency town. These were the courts of the King of England and not of the Company, though the king had at the time no claim of sovereignty to any part of India except Bombay. This charter introduced into the Presidency towns of India, the law of England, both common and statutory as it stood in 1726. It was not, however, the whole of the English law that was so introduced but only so much of it as suited the conditions of India.

The charter of 1726 was amended suitably by the charter of 1753. This latter charter retained the Mayor's Court in Madras, Bombay and Calcutta, but they were limited in their civil jurisdiction to suits between persons not natives of these towns, and suits between natives were directed not to be entertained by the Mayor's Court, unless by consent of the parties.[28]

After the Battle of Plassey, the Company became supreme in Bengal. Had the Company desired, it could have taken over the

Governance of Bengal, Bihar and Orissa directly into its own hands. But the Company did not do so and placed its nominee Mir Jafar on the Nawabship of Bengal. Mir Jafar could not continue as Nawab for long and was replaced by Mir Kasim. Mir Kasim was again replaced by Mir Jafar in 1763. With every change in the Nawabship, the power of the company increased and slowly the real authority had passed into its hands.

In 1765 Shah Alam, the Mughal emperor granted to the East India Company the Dewani of Bengal, Bihar and Orissa. With the acquisition of Dewani, the East India Company became responsible for the collection of revenue, and directly or indirectly for the proper administration of civil and criminal justice in the region. Nevertheless, the administration for the most part of the revenue and still more of civil justice was conducted through the native agency, till the year 1771.

Meanwhile in 1771, the Directors of the Company issued orders to the President and Council in Bengal 'to stand forth as Dewan' and by the Agency of the Company's servants to take upon themselves of the entire care and management of the revenue. By this they did not mean mere collection, but wider functions of government, which would have to be administered with the revenue realized and by the agency of their own officers.

Warren Hastings was sent out in 1771, to give shape to the new plan of administration. Hastings' Regulations of 1772 were the principal steps for the assumption of wider powers of government, particularly in the field of administration of justice. He assumed complete control of the civil judiciary. The previously existing machinery, howsoever it might have been functioning, was completely replaced by courts presided over by European officers both at the district headquarters and at the Presidency. These were called Mofussil Dewani Adalats; and over them was the Sadar Dewani Adalat consisting of the President and two members of his Executive Council. The European officers who presided over the Mofussil Dewani Adalats in the district were the same persons who were in charge of the administration of revenue. The personal laws of the inhabitants were not sought to be interfered with, and it was definitely enjoined that in all suits regarding inheritance, marriage, caste, and so on, the laws to be followed were to be the laws of the Koran in case of Muslims and those of the Shastras in case of the Hindus.

On the criminal side, the change effected was less radical, though substantially effective control was assumed. In the districts, irregular administration of criminal justice by the zamindars and other persons of local influence was sought to be replaced by a better reorganization of the Mughal system of *kazis* and *muftis*. Such persons with proper credentials from the authorities were to hold courts at the district headquarters and pass judgement; but their proceedings were to be under close supervision of a European Supervisor or Collector. In the Nizamat Adalat at the Sadar, the officer to preside was to be appointed with the chief *kazi*, the chief *mufti* and four capable *maulavis*. Their duty was to see the proceedings of the Mofussil Foujdari Adalat.

The Regulating Act of 1773 empowered the Crown to establish, by charter or letters patent, a Supreme Court of judicature at Calcutta on the ground that the charter of 1753 did not sufficiently provide for the administration of justice in the Presidency of Calcutta which it then required. The Supreme Court was independent of the Governor-General and his Council and distinct from the Sadar Dewani and Nizamat Adalat establishment at Calcutta. The judges were appointed by the king and hence this court also came to be called the, 'Kings Court' to distinguish it from the Sadar Dewani and the Nizamat Adalat established by the Company. The Supreme Court was to have jurisdiction in all civil matters over all European and British subjects' resident in Bengal, Bihar and Orissa and over persons who, either at the time of bringing the action or at the time the action occurred, were employed or were directly in the service of the Company. The charter further laid down that the Supreme Court was to have jurisdiction to try action or suit against all other persons, inhabitants of India residing in Bengal, Bihar or Orissa upon any contract or agreement in writing with any of the king's subjects, where the cause of action should exceed the sum of 500 current rupees, and when such inhabitants should have agreed in the said contract, that in case of dispute, the matter should be determined in the said Supreme Court.[29]

The Regulation Act, however, left wholly untouched the question of the nature of the law to be administered in the Supreme Court. The Supreme Court had been created on the foundation of the Mayor's Court which administered English law. It, therefore, followed that the Supreme Court was also to administer English law.

Thus, there were two parallel tribunals to administer justice in the Bengal Presidency, viz., (1) the Sadar Dewani and Nizamat Adalats with their subordinate provincial and district courts administering the Hindu and Muslim laws and procedures, as adopted by the rules of the various regulations, and (2) the Supreme Court established by the Parliament administering English law and procedure. Such a system continued without any change throughout the period of Company's administration in India. It was only in the year 1861 that the British Parliament enacted the Charter Act, 1861 establishing High Courts of Judicature in India and the two system of courts amalgamated. With this the existence of two separate courts for the Rulers and the Ruled discontinued.

The Regulating Act authorized the Governor-General-in-Council to frame rules, ordinances and regulations for 'the good order' and civil government of the settlement at Calcutta, other factories and subordinate places. They were to be just, reasonable and not repugnant to the laws of England. The rules, ordinances and regulations were not to be valid unless they were duly registered in the Supreme Court.

Doubts and difficulties arose with regard to the provisions of the Act of 1773 and the charter issued under it. It became difficult to carry on government due to conflict and mutual suspicion between the executive and judiciary. There arose 'unfortunate contentions between the Governor-General-in-Council and the Judges of the Supreme Court at Calcutta, which, whoever may have been in the wrong, were certainly very discreditable to both parties'.[30] The complicated situation was relieved eventually by the Regulating Act of 1781. The most important feature of the Act was the recognition by the Parliament of the civil and criminal provincial courts existing independently of the Supreme Court. The Act also authorized the Council to frame regulations for those Provincial Courts independently of the Supreme Court.

The Acts of 1773 and 1781 thus constituted the authority for the Regulations promulgated by the Company up to February 1834. An Act of 1833 vested in the Governor-General-in-Council extensive powers of legislation, and the laws passed thereafter were called 'Acts' and not 'Regulations'. A considerable number of Regulations were passed up to the year 1793, when most of them, with modifications and elaborations were consolidated in the series of Regulation promulgated on 1 May 1793. The celebrated Regulation XLI of 1793 (A Regulation for forming into a regular code all Regulations that may be enacted for the internal governance of the British territories in Bengal) inaugurated the system of Regulation laws.

Regulation XLI of 1793 laid down that all Regulations should be numbered, and bound up into a regular code. They were also required to be printed and translated for wide circulation amongst the officers, courts and the public. An Act passed in 1797 endorsed the plan in the Regulation of 1793, and to give it the stamp of parliamentary authority, repeated the provision in the Regulation of 1793 that all Regulations which would be issued and framed by the Governor-General-in-Council, affecting the rights, persons, or property of the natives or of any other individuals amenable to the Provincial Courts of Justice, should be registered in the Judicial Department, formed into a regular code and printed with translations in the country languages; and that the 'grounds' of each Regulation should be prefixed to it.

Before 1833 each of the three Presidencies, viz., Calcutta, Madras and Bombay enjoyed equal legislative powers, though the Governor-General-in-Council possessed a right of veto over the legislations of the subordinate presidencies. However, the legislative competence of subordinate presidencies was far from absolute, for all Europeans and British subjects and the Presidency towns were generally beyond their scope. But the whole system of revenue and judicature which the Company enforced throughout each Presidency had been amended and expanded by the 'Regulations', framed and passed by the Governor-General or Governor and the Council of the three Presidencies. On the passing of the Charter Act of 1833, one Legislature was established over the whole of

British India with authority not over Indians only, but also over Europeans and others. Thus the Act of 1833 took away the legislative powers from the Presidencies of Bombay and Madras and made the Governor-General-in-Council in Calcutta the supreme legislative authority.

In 1833 the attention of the British Parliament was directed to three leading defects in the framework of the Indian government. The first was in the nature of the laws and regulations. The second was in the ill-defined authority and power from which these various laws and regulations emanated. The third was the anomalous and sometimes conflicting judicatures by which the laws were administered. In other words, the defects were in the laws themselves, in the authority who made them and in the manner of executing them. In the debates which preceded the passing of the Act of 1833, Thomas Babington Macaulay said 'I believe that no country ever stood so much in need of a code as India'[31] and added that there never was a country in which the want might be so easily supplied. The Charter Act of 1833 considered these views and the Parliament opened its minds more explicitly in section 53 of the Act, which recommended provisions for a special arrangement of a general system of judicial establishment and police, as local circumstances might require, to which all persons—Europeans as well as natives might be subjected, and this should be established in the same territories at an early date. Section 53 of the Charter Act of 1833 (3 & 4 Wilm. IV C 85) was the legislative mainspring of law reform in India as regards policy, though principles and ideas were still to be evolved.[32] It laid down that it was expedient that 'such laws as may be applicable in common to all classes of the inhabitants of the said territories, due regard being paid to the feelings and peculiar usages of the people, should be re-enacted and that all laws and customs having force of law within the same territories should be ascertained and consolidated, and as occasion may require amended'.[33] In order to carry out the objectives of section 53 properly, the parliament required the Governor-General to appoint a Law Commission to formulate proposals for the overhauling of the judicial and police machinery and for the codification and revision of the Indian law. Thomas Babington

Macaulay was the guiding spirit of the Commission, which was instituted in 1834.

The First Law Commission provided a means for collection and consideration of existing laws and customs of all kinds applicable to any part of the territory of India and to any class of Indians. The members of this commission under the instruction of the local government, employed themselves in the first instance in the preparation of a draft of a Penal Code.[34] On the basis of this draft were prepared the Indian Penal Code, the Code of Civil Procedure and Criminal Procedure Code and other codes of substantive and procedural law, which now form part of the Indian statue book in its original or amended form. But the working of the First Law Commission received a series of setbacks after Macaulay's return to England.

The Second Law Commission was appointed in November 1853 under the provisions of the Charter Act of 1853. Its main purpose was to examine and consider the proposals of the First Law Commission and to make recommendation for the reform of court procedures and laws in India.

The Second Law Commission submitted four reports, one of these being most important because it contains the recommendations of the Commission regarding the ground on which the future work of codification of the substantive law in India was to proceed.

The Second Law Commission in its other reports submitted a plan for amalgamation of the Supreme Courts and the Sadar courts, for uniform Code of Civil Procedure Code as well as Criminal Procedure applicable to all the courts of British India. The recommendations of this commission resulted in important legislations both in the Parliament and the Legislative Council of India.[35] The Indian Penal Code which had been drafted in the time of Lord Macaulay was revised and enacted into law in 1860. A Code of Civil Procedure was passed in 1859 followed by a Code of Criminal Procedure in 1861.

In December 1861 a fresh commission was constituted (the Third Law Commission), as the life of the Second Law Commission was expressly restricted to three years. The Third Law Commission was directed to frame a body of substantive civil law, in the preparation of which the Law of England was to be used as a basis. The commission submitted various draft bills on succession, contracts, negotiable instrument, evidence, transfer of property and insurance besides making suggestion for revision of the Code of Criminal Procedure of 1861. Of these drafts, only the first, namely the one on succession, became law in 1865 and all the rest became laws only after the institution of the Fourth Law Commission.

In August 1861, the British Parliament passed the Indian High Courts Act with the object of amalgamating the two rival judicial systems—the Crown Courts and the Company's Courts—and bringing uniformity into the laws to be administered.

The Act merged the Supreme Court in the Presidency towns with the Sadar Courts and created in their stead new courts called the High Courts of Judicature. Each High Court should consist of a chief justice and not more than fifteen other judges.

With the enactment of various codes, the Regulations issued by the Governor-General-in-Council were entirely repealed or replaced. Only 45 of these Regulations out of about 675 continued to remain in force in Bengal and of these again, a good many in much amended forms.

Certain areas under different Presidencies were exempted from the regulations promulgated by the Governor-General-in-Council, because a refined and elaborate system of law was considered to be unsuitable to such territories and their populations. To a greater or lesser extent the people of these areas were allowed to follow their own customs; introduction of Regulations there was to be gradual and tentative. Legislative needs of these areas were attended to by the executive government. To administer such provinces, special rules were made to suit their circumstances or meet the exigencies of the situation of the province so governed; such a province was called a Non-Regulation province.[36]

The earliest reference to such a policy has been found in the orders of 14 June 1782 and in the Regulation of 1796 by which the hills situated to the south and west of Bhagalpur was exempt from the purview of the General Regulations.

In the year 1822 the same policy was adopted in areas of the north-east frontier of Rangpur inhabited by the Garos. By Regulation X of 1822, the tract of country lying within the jurisdiction of the *thanas* of Goalpara, Dhubri, and Karaibari in the district of Rangpur were separated from the said district and the entire administration of these *thanas* was declared to be vested in an officer appointed by the Governor-General-in-Council, denominated as the Civil Commissioner for the north-eastern part of Rangpur.[37] The said officer was to conduct the administration agreeably to the principle and spirit of the existing Regulations, subject to the restrictions and such other alterations as might be ordered by the Governor-General-in-Council. David Scott, Commissioner in Cooch Bihar and Joint Magistrate at Rangpur was appointed the Civil Commissioner of the north-east parts of Rangpur in 1822. Scott's power and jurisdiction was enhanced on 15 November 1823 to meet the emergency arising out of the Anglo-Burmese conflict and he was made the Political Agent to the Governor-General in the North-East Frontier of Bengal and Civil Commissioner of Rangpur. With this extension of David Scott's jurisdiction, Non-Regulation system imperceptibly got extended into Assam.*

The province was governed by a mix of local and Regulation laws throughout the Regulation period. Only after the extension of the Code of Civil Procedure and Criminal Procedure Code, the Indian Penal Code, the Police Act and other important codes, the system of Non-Regulation ceased to exist. Assam was administered, thereafter, by the same laws and by the same procedures prevailing in other parts of the British India.

* Non-Regulation Provinces under the Lieutenant Governor were of three classes, viz., (i) New conquest or cession to which the Regulation was not extended. (ii) Tracts of country formerly subjected to the General Regulations, but which were removed in consideration of the people inhabiting them not being sufficiently advanced in civilization to benefit by a refined code of laws. (iii) Semi-independent and tributary estates administered in the political department. Assam was placed in the first category'. (BJP, December 1870, No. 13, see Appendix A, Memorandum)

Introduction   47

How far was Assam judicially administered as a Non-Regulation province? Was it essential or desirable to extend Non-Regulation system into Assam? Were the people benefited by the introduction of English law and procedure? The answers to these questions will be found in the subsequent chapters.

NOTES

1. *A Comprehensive History of Assam*, p. 222.
2. *Studies in the History of Assam*, pp. 150-1.
3. For details of the rebellions see S.L. Baruah's *Last Days & Ahom Monarchy*, chapters III & IV.
4. *Studies in the History of Assam*, p. 150.
5. *Deodhai Asam Buranji*, p. 2.
6. Ibid., p. 96.
7. Ibid., 97.
8. A noted centre of Shakti worship was the Tamreswari Temple of Sadiya, where the goddess in her Kesaikhati form was propitiated with sacrifices even of human beings (see *Asom Buranji* by Hara Kanta Baruah, p. 43).
9. *Tai Ahom System of Government*, p. 215.
10. *Studies in the History in Assam*, p. 131.
11. *A Comprehensive History of Assam*, p. 400.
12. Ibid., p. 401.
13. Ibid., p. 400.
14. *Tai Ahom System of Government*, p. 332.
15. *History of Assam*, p. 241.
16. See Captain T. Welsh's Report on Assam 1794. Reproduced in Alexander Mackenzie's *History of the Relations of the Government with the Hill Tribes of the North-East Frontier of Bengal*, Home Department, p. 380.
17. *Tai Ahom System of Government*, p. 213.
18. For details see article—'A Criminal Trial of Swargadeo Lakshmi Singha's Regime on Studies in the History of Assam', pp. 116-23.
19. *History of Assam*, p. 241.
20. Ibid., p. 241.
21. Ibid., p. 241.
22. H.P. Dubey, *A Short History of the Judicial System of India and some Foreign Countries*, pp. 14-15.

23. Blackston's commentaries on the laws of England, pp. 87, 88 as quoted in Dubey, ibid., pp. 14-15.
24. *The Administration of Justice in British India*, p. 5.
25. The island of Bombay became in 1661 British territory by cession under marriage treaty with Portugal and was transferred in 1668 to the Company.
26. S.C. Fawcett, *The First Century of British Justice in India*, p. 2.
27. A.B. Keith, *A Constitutional History of India 1600-1935*, Methuen & Co., London, 1936; rpt. Central Book Depot, Allahabad, 1961, p. 18.
28. *Administration of Justice in British India*, pp. 7-8.
29. Ibid., pp. 9-10.
30. Ibid., p. 11.
31. Ibid., p. 25. See *A New Forward by Mangal Chandra Jain Kagzi*, University of Delhi.
32. Ibid., p. 26.
33. Ibid.
34. B.K. Acharayya, *Codification in British India*, p. 63.
35. Ibid., p. 65.
36. *Aain Aur Babyastha Sangraha* (*Notes on the Laws of Bengal*), p. 14.
37. BJP, 19 September, 1822, no. 4.

CHAPTER 2

Policy and Organizational Framework of the British Judicial Administration

PROBLEM OF ADMINISTERING THE BRAHMAPUTRA VALLEY

After the retreat of the Burmese from the Brahmaputra Valley, a question arose as to whether the newly-occupied territory would be administered by the civil administration or by marital laws. The matter was referred to the Governor-General-in-Council who decided that the country must continue to be considered as an 'enemy country' merely occupied by the British army and not subject to the ordinary rules of civil and criminal justice as administered in the British territories elsewhere in India.[1] However, efforts were made to invest David Scott, the Civil Officer, with a great if not greater amount of power and authority. So, a dual administration was inaugurated during the interim period (1824-8).

After the capitulation of Rangpur on 31 January 1825, the whole of the Brahmaputra Valley was practically cleared of the Burmese and, as a result, it became necessary to devise a comprehensive plan for the temporary administration of its internal affairs. As a provisional arrangement, Scott and Col. Richards, a military officer, were appointed Joint Commissioners for Assam. While Scott was to hold civil charge of western Assam, commonly known as Lower Assam, Col. Richards was to hold charge of the area east of Biswanath, commonly known as Upper Assam.

The respective duties of Col. Richards and Scott were clearly defined and demarcated from the very beginning to avoid possible disputes and entanglement. Scott was forbidden from interfering with matters of purely military nature and he was asked to afford most cordial and zealous support to the Officer Commanding on all questions of general interest. The general management of the area was entrusted to Scott, whose jurisdiction had in the meantime been extended to the whole of the North-East Frontier.

EXTENSION OF THE NON-REGULATION SYSTEM

Reference has already been made to the extension of Non-Regulation System into Assam. Its principal feature was the union of executive and judicial functions in one individual, the office of judge being added to that of magistrate and collector.[2] The instruction was that the spirit, not the letter, of the Regulations was to be followed. The province was to be governed in arude and simple fashion: 'by an executive composed partly of soldiers, and partly of civilians, upon a mixed system, into which the spirit of the Regulations is infused in such a manner as to cause it to harmonize and blend itself with all that is good in the spirit of native institutions, and to be respected in the local usages of the country'.[3] In criminal matters, the Regulations were practically followed, but in civil matters, they were entirely dispensed with and the court was conducted on simple and natural principles suited to the country and its people. The Company's servants, both civil and military, were equally eligible for administrative work but most of the administrators were military men. All functions of executive, revenue and judiciary were concentrated in the same person. Scott enjoyed wide powers and he had the liberty to devise suitable means to dispose civil suits. Under the Non-Regulation system, the province escaped from the elaborate procedures of the Bengal law courts.[4]

A question arises as to why the Non-Regulation system was extended to Assam. It is interesting to note that there was neither any declaration nor any notification to that effect. The system which had its beginning in the neighbouring district of north-east Rangpur was imperceptibly extended into Assam. Here we must remember that the system which was the result of the Regulation X of 1822 clearly stated that the 'operation of the existing Regulations was to be suspended except in cases of subjects other than the Garos and other hill tribes'.[5] The preamble of the Regulation observed that 'with a view to promote the desirable object of reclaiming these races (the Garos), to the habits of civilized life, it seems necessary that a special plan for the administration of justice of a kind adopted to their peculiar customs and prejudices should be arranged'.[6] The extension of such a system to the people of the Brahmaputra Valley was, therefore, neither desirable nor essential. The people of Assam were not savage marauders or extremely backward so that for reclaiming those to the art of civilized life such a system was to be applied. Still they allowed the Non-Regulation system to continue because it had afforded to the Company certain obvious advantages.

Assam had been widely devastated because of the Moamaria rebellion and the Burmese invasion. Its institutions were completely disorganized and the population had been thinned and reduced to utter destitution. In this situation, the Non-Regulation system, unfettered from the letter of the laws, might well be adopted. Besides, owing to their imperfect knowledge of the affairs of Assam, the Supreme government could not furnish any instruction to the man on the spot to administer the areas.[7] Again, the system of land revenue in Assam was not a simple one and it bore little resemblance to the Bengal system. Scott had prior knowledge about the land revenue system and he rightly anticipated the problem of assessing and collecting land revenue by applying Bengal land revenue regulations. Therefore, Scott, who was the author of Regulation X of 1822, favoured the application of that Regulation to the plains of the Brahmaputra Valley to devise suitable arrangement for its revenue administration. Further, with the extension of Regulation system the employees having adequate experience in Regulation laws would have to be appointed. As a result, all posts of native judges and *omlahs* would have gone to the Bengalis and north Indians. Since the beginning of hostility towards the Burmese, Scott was in favour of annexing Lower Assam permanently to the British dominion. But he could not convince the Supreme government until 1828, as the government rejected Scott's proposal for extending British authority over a widely extended area of doubtful value. They held that 'the amount of revenue too would not be commensurate with the risk and responsibilities involved'.[8] The Burmese war had taxed heavily upon the Company's exchequer and its debts had mounted up. Under such circumstances, Scott was bound to minimize the cost of the administration, if at all he desired to retain Lower Assam. He, then, discarded the costly Regulation system which required an elaborate system of establishment. Further, application of a refined legal system might confuse the simple and ignorant population. He favoured, instead, the Non-Regulation system which was less expensive and in which the administration would be highly centralized giving him wide and discretionary authority as the officer supervising. In Regulation provinces, all the revenue and judicial matters were regulated by published laws, the rights of the government were defined and limited and it could exercise no arbitrary power in individual cases. This gave the people adequate safeguard against arbitrary action of government officials. Thus, being governed by Non-Regulation system, people of Assam were subjected to an oppressive and despotic system of government. Interestingly, Goalpara or northeast Rangpur was governed as a Regulation district where Bengal Regulations were followed in the administration of justice.

SCOTT'S POLICIES AND PROGRAMMES IN THE ADMINISTRATION OF UPPER AND LOWER ASSAM

In the administration of Lower Assam, it was thought expedient to keep more closely to the rules observed in the judicial department in other British possessions. The annexation of this division to the Company's possession would present no difficulty, as Lower Assam was never amalgamated with the rest of the Ahom territory. Being under the Mughal rule for a considerable length of time, the people in this part were accustomed to the administrative system of the Mughals, which the British followed immediately after their occupation of the country. Hence the people would prefer to be ruled by the British than their former masters, the Ahoms,'who were reported to have humiliated and heaped upon them all sorts of indignities'.[9] Scott made all arrangements and organizations in Lower Assam keeping in view this possibility of integrating this division permanently to British possessions.

Scott was directed in early April 1825 to devise a provisional system of police and rules for arbitration and adjustment of civil disputes for Lower Assam. He appointed many people in the native establishment of the Commissioner's office. It was inevitable that when the system and its officers were so unfamiliar with the Ahom tradition, the posts should be filled by experts already trained in the Regulation system of Bengal.[10] The organizational framework of the offices was closely modeled on the system which prevailed in the other districts of the Bengal Presidency, and like them still bore the Persian titles taken over by the Company from their Mughal predecessors.

In Upper Assam, Scott's policy was to establish the simplest laws and procedures conforming as far as possible to the native customs and institutions. It was expected that by this policy, the objections that the erstwhile Ahom nobility and other influential classes of the state were likely to have against the permanent introduction of British Government, could be met with and made acceptable to them. Scott believed that this could be done, especially, by continuing to employ the leading men of the country in the discharge of the duties of their hereditary offices subject to such control by the local European officers as experience might suggest.

Scott thought it expedient to restore Ahom monarchy in Upper Assam, 'with a constitution designed to eliminate the weakness of the old regime and the need for any detailed British interference'.[11] Such a restoration, Scott believed, would relieve the Company of the financial burden of administering an impoverished, devastated country, and would help the British government in obtain the loyalty and confidence of the native people, and thereby removing a major cause for unrest and rebellion.

Although Scott was aware of the incompetence of the old nobles to work in the new administration, he thought it wise to employ their services as, according to his calculations, restoration of the old monarchy was bound to take place at a near date. Scott believed that some purpose at least would be served by grooming the future monarch and his nobles for their rule. In judicial matters too, Scott followed the same policy of keeping the old practices, institutions and offices as far as possible and giving employment to the Ahom officials. He thus sought to use native juries and native judges for both civil and criminal suits. His scheme of administration was to share power and authority with the natives of India. He might well have penned Malcolm's letter to Whynne, quoted by Stokes, saying: 'With respect to raising natives both in the fiscal and judicial lines, I am of the same sentiments as Sir Thomas Munro. . . . I desire the Aristocracy of office with the natives of India.'[12] Scott was fully aware that the native states had their strengths as well as their weaknesses, and that their traditional institutions, if properly supported, could be made to work very well. Scott entertained high opinion about the intellectual capacity of the natives. He was animated by the noblest motives in proposing this arrangement; conceiving that to give the people a share in their own government was the most direct mode of elevating them in their estimation.[13]

If the government desired to retain Upper Assam under its direct management, a large number of Assamese officers would have to be removed and replaced by Europeans. On the other hand, Scott also believed that the time had come, when the British government could no longer recede from its responsibility of providing proper administration, whether native or European. At the same time he argued, 'an imperfect British administration must be worse than a native one, which even if it wants in integrity, at least possesses a perfect knowledge of the laws, customs and prejudices of its subjects and an intimate acquaintance with their peculiar revenue system'.[14]

Until June 1828, the government adhered to its original plan of restoring Upper Assam to a native prince. This was clearly stated in a joint letter from Scott and Col. Richards dated 25 May 1825, while taking charge of the Office of the Commissioner in Assam. All the arrangement made in that division of Assam were formed with relation to that event, no alterations in the ancient system having been adopted, except in such cases as were likely to tend to the better administration of justice.[15]

ADMINISTRATION OF CIVIL JUSTICE

For the administration of civil justice, Lambodhar Barphukan, a brother-in-law of the former king, Chandra Kanta Singha, was appointed in May 1825. The Barphukan was a man of talent, character and considerable wealth. Janardan Barbaruah, a man of rank and substance, who was entrusted with the management of revenue in Upper Assam, was to be co-adjudicator with the Barphukan. The Barbaruah was paid, as in the previous regime, in the form of lands and *paiks*, while the Barphukan received a salary of Rs. 300 per month, besides the service of fifty lickshows.[16] The composition of the native judicial establishment with their respective salaries for Upper Assam proposed in May 1825 is displayed in Appendix 2.1.[17]

The entire civil or *dewani* business in Upper Assam was carried on by the courts of the Barphukan and the Barbaruah. Any appeal on special grounds lay to the Political Agent of Upper Assam and subsequently to the Agent to the Governor-General, N.E. Frontier.[18] Some Surasuree Panchayats consisting of former pundits were also instituted to decide summary suits of minor importance.[19] The Kheldars were authorized to try civil cases up to Rs. 100.

In Lower Assam, Senior Commissioner Scott was empowered to try all civil suits. His position was similar to that of the Barphukan, the Viceroy of Guwahati under the previous regime. In administering civil justice Regulations were dispensed with and the court was conducted on simple and natural principles, suited to the province. Scott also had the authority to devise suitable means to dispose of civil cases subject to the approval of the Governor-General-in-Council. The existing machinery of civil justice was kept unaltered, and, in practice, the Ahom form of administration of justice continued with minor changes. The respective salaries and expenditures proposed by Scott for the native establishment of Lower Assam in May 1825 is displayed in Appendix 2.2.[20]

In Lower Assam the *chowdhury* of the *parganas* were authorized to try civil suits up to Rs. 100. They usually decided these petty civil cases with the aid of *mel* or panchayats. The *rajas* (tributary chiefs of Lower Assam holding small territories under the Ahom king) and other revenue officials were also allowed to continue their judicial authority in disposing minor civil disputes in their respective jurisdiction.

Scott always tried to make justice affordable, expeditious and impartial. Armed with purity of intention and firmness of purpose, he hoped to clear the judicial agency of all anomalies and incompetence and to impart to it maximum honesty and efficiency. But despite his sincere efforts, the system did not work according to his expectations. It proved physically impossible on the part of the Commissioner and Major. White, the only Assistant at Guwahati, to dispose of civil suits of landed property involving conflicting rights and tenures with promptitude to meet the ends of speedy justice.[21] Scott himself admitted,as much as was possible,

> of the most complete access to his person: his kutchery was at all times crowded; indeed, to a great degree which would have rendered it impossible for persons of an ordinary strength of constitution to have transacted business at all. The most unlimited freedom of petitioning was allowed without expense to the complainants. A large box was placed in the Kutchery into which the petition could be thrown. To ensure detpatch of business, they were limited to 25 to 30 lines, but no stamp tax or other restrictions existed.[22]

Towards the end of 1826, the Commissioner found at the court of Guwahati 1,500 petitions requiring immediate decision.[23] Alarmed by such a state of affairs, Scott provisionally instituted three native courts without obtaining approval from the government. These native courts were to be presided over by Assamese officials having experience of judicial work. Of these, the first consisting of a Rajkhowa and three assessors would try civil suits to the extent of Rs. 150; the second with one Barphukan and three assessors would decide civil cases up to Rs. 1,000 and hear appeals from the first tribunal; and the third, with the same composition as the second, would have the additional authority to decide criminal cases of minor consequence. The third and highest court had the power to receive appeals from the *rajas, chowdhury* and other *mulguzars*.[24] The second court was presided by Ghinai Barphukan while the third and highest court was presided over by Bapuram Barphukan.[25]

The composition and the monthly expenditure of these courts are displayed in Appendix 2.3.[26]

A Mofussil Panchayat court was also instituted to deal with the cases originating in any of the nine Southern Doars of the Khasia hills.[27] The members of this court were the *rajas* of the several

Duars, three of whom had to attend to form a court. They received no salary or other remuneration for their attendance, which was considered to be a 'duty annexed to the tenure of their Raj'.[28] Appeal against their decisions could be made to the Commissioner at Guwahati.

Scott further instituted Mofussil Panchayat courts in the populated areas of Darrang and Nowgong in Central Assam. These Mofussil courts decided civil disputes of minor importance but their decisions could be challenged at the court in Guwahati by way of appeal. The members of the panchayat were elected generally by the people of the locality and were remunerated as under the former government, with a number of *lickshows* and *paiks*, who were bound to serve them and on that account they were exempted from the payment of taxes.[29] One such court at Darrang was presided by Mookand Narayan,[30] with one pundit and four assessors. This panchayat court, according to the *roobkari* of the Revenue Department dated 14 October 1828, could keep a person in confinement for a term not exceeding fifteen days.[31] If they found it necessary to keep any one in confinement for a longer period than fifteen days, he/she was sent to the Assistant at Guwahati. The property of such persons was to be made over to the *tahsildar*, who was to realize the amount of the decree by the sale of the same. The Dewani or the civil court of Raha (Nowgong) consisted of the respectable people of that locality. But they did not receive any salary and appear to have been left to do just as they pleased.[32] Till 1828 this court was managed by the *tahsildar* of Nowgong.

To deal with the summary suits regarding rent, Scott set up Summary Suit Court at Guwahati. The president of this court received a salary. The remaining members were selected from among the *chowdhuries* 'who received a deputation allowance of eight *annas* each per diem while sitting in the courts'.[33] The Summary Suit Court had jurisdiction over all the country in disputes between the *ryots* and the *chowdhury* without limitation as to the amount. No appeal lay against its decision; parties aggrieved of its decision had their remedy in a regular civil suit.[34]

In consequence of a great number of summary suits instituted and the inability of the panchayats to dispose them of with the expedition that was desirable, Scott instituted in 1828 another court for the speedy cognizance of summary cases.[35] The expense attending this arrangement had hitherto been defrayed from the fines levied upon persons convicted of extortion. This court was of urgent necessity 'to afford speedy relief to the ryots from a source of grievances beyond comparison, the most serious of any to which they are subjected'.[36]

In course of time, some minor alterations were made in the power and limits of these courts. The gradation of courts dealing with civil suits in Lower Assam by 1832 was as follows:

1. Commissioner's court tried civil suits above Rs. 1,000 and hear appeals from inferior courts.
2. First Panchayat Court Sadar having original jurisdiction to the amount of Rs. 1,000. It also received appeals from the decision of Second and Third Panchayat Sadar.
3. Second Panchayat Sadar having jurisdiction to try civil suits up to Rs. 200.
4. Third Panchayat Sadar having jurisdiction to try civil cases up to Rs. 200.
5. First Mofussil Panchayat had jurisdiction over cases up to the amount of Rs. 1,000, originating in any of the Nine Doars (Passes through which hill people maintained contact with the plains people).
6. Second Mofussil Panchayat having jurisdiction in cases not exceeding Rs. 200. An appeal against its decision could be made to the First Panchayat Sadar at Guwahati. This court sat at Darrang within which province alone it had jurisdiction.
7. Third Mofussil Panchayat having jurisdiction to try civil suits up to Rs. 100. An appeal against its decision went to the First Panchayat Sadar at Guwahati. This court sat at Nowgong,
8. Sadar Summary Suit Court to try summary suits of rent. It had jurisdiction over all the country and without any limit as to the value of the suit.
9. Mofussil Summary Suit Court consisted of two individuals who had served as superannuary members of the Sadar Panchayat at Guwahati. The members received a salary of Rs. 300. Their

area of jurisdiction overlapped with that of the Sadar Summary Suit Court to clear off the arrears accumulated. This court was ambulatory and had the discretional power of proceeding to any quarter, where the number of summary suits were understood to have accumulated.[37]

ADMINISTRATION OF CRIMINAL JUSTICE

The administration of criminal justice was founded upon the correspondence[38] between the local government and the Government of Bengal. In Upper Assam criminal cases were tried by the Junior Commissioner and later by the Political Agent of Upper Assam. The Barphukan was also authorized to hear criminal cases and empowered to pass sentences of thirty stripes, imprisonment for six months or a fine not exceeding Rs. 50.[39] Trials of heinous offences were held before the juries with the Barphukan as the president. The decision of this court was to be submitted to one of the commissioners, who could award punishment according to his own judgement.

After the British occupation of Lower Assam all cases not involving capital punishment were tried by the Senior Commissioner, Scott. In that capacity he was empowered to pass sentences of fifty stripes, imprisonment with or without labour and transportation for life.[40] The Commissioner occupied the position formerly held by the Barphukan or Viceroy of Guwahati. Under Regulation X of 1822, the Commissioner was also em-powered to perform all the functions and exercise the authority of a Magistrate with respect to apprehension and trials of persons charged with offences. He was also authorized to hold trials and pass sentences to the extent permitted by the Regulation to a Judge of Court of Circuit established under Regulation IX of 1793 (see Regulation IX in M.N. Gupta's *Analytical Study of Bengal Regulations*). In exercise of the powers and authority conveyed to the Commissioner, he should ordinarily conform to the principles and spirit of the Regulations. He was bound further to conform to any special rules or orders that might be issued from time to time by the Governor-General-in-Council. The trial and punishment of heinous offences were left in the hands of the Officer Commanding. A tribunal was instituted under Col. Richards to try heinous offences requiring sentences of death. However, owing to technical difficulties, the tribunal could not be assembled even on one occasion. Therefore, a large number of suspected criminals had to be kept confined for their trial. Added to this problem was the increasing rate of mortality in Guwahati Jail. In his letter of 30 December 1826, Scott reported that the number of prisoners in confinement never exceeded 400 at any period, but the number of deaths in 1825 and 1826 amounted to 266 and 261 respectively.[41] In view of the alarming mortality at the Guwahati Jail and on account of the increase in heinous crimes, the Commissioner recommended in early 1826 that Lower Assam should be placed under the jurisdiction of Nizamat Adalat. In the event of delay in complying with his recommendation, Scott solicited permission to institute a Bar Panchayat or a Court for the trial and disposal of heinous cases. The Bar Panchayat was to be constituted of three native judges of experience to be aided by two *pundits* and six assessors.[42] In a subsequent dispatch on 28 March 1828, Scott informed the Government of Bengal that the provisional native courts set up by him primarily to deal with the civil cases had already proved a tolerably efficient and satisfactory instrument. As such, the business of the criminal department, even in capital cases, did not appear to involve any difficulty which they were incapable of coping with.[43]

Scott spoke highly of the efficiency and sincerity of the native judges and informed the Bengal government that the native judges were capable of discharging every duty assigned to them. Substantiating his recommendations, he pointed out that in recent times only 50 decrees were appealed against out of a total of 756 that were decided by Assamese judges.[44]

In May 1828, the government informed Scott that 'after the fullest consideration the Governor-General-in-Council had concluded that in the present state of the country, it would be premature and inexpedient to extend the authority of the Nizamat Adalat into Lower Assam under provisions analogous to those of Regulation X of 1822'.[45] It further informed Scott that an efficient system for the dispensation of criminal justice in Assam, generally, would be best provided for by using to the full those tribunals and institutions which Scott had 'very judiciously revived and put in action'.[46] The government also considered Scott's plan for judicial administration as a novel and interesting experiment. The government accordingly approved as an experimental measure, the machinery of civil and criminal justice already instituted and subsequently proposed by the Commissioner, subject to the supervision of the Political Agent, Upper Assam and the Assistant to the Commissioner, Lower Assam as the case might be by Stirling's letter of 2 May 1828. Accordingly, in the administration of criminal justice, an Assistant was authorized to perform the functions of a magistrate, and to commit offenders to trial before panchayat to be presided over by them. The panchayat gave a decision as to the guilt or innocence of the accused, and in all cases not involving a severe punishment than the magistrates were competent to award, he passed the sentence.[47] The assistants as officiating magistrates were empowered to award imprisonment up to three years. Later the magistrate's power was increased for the cases decided in Lower Assam for imprisonment up to four years.[48] In cases of heinous offences, the proceedings of the panchayat, with the opinion of assistant thereon, were to be forwarded to Scott for final decision. Scott was empowered to pass the death sentence for crimes of murder and robbery attended with murder.[49] Scott fulfilled the functions of Nizamat Adalat in approving or disapproving of the proceedings.[50] For offences committed in Upper Assam, which required the awarding of punishments beyond the power of a magistrate, Scott passed sentences. But in Lower Assam, persons apprehended on charges or offences which were beyond the power of a magistrate to punish, committed to trial before Scott at sessions in the mode prescribed in the Regulation provinces.[51] For the guidance of the assistants and native courts the Commissioner Scott issued from time to time Regulations in the native languages, as required.

Trifling criminal cases in Upper Assam were tried by the revenue officers and those of Lower Assam by the *chowdhury* and the *rajas*. In Darrang trifling criminal cases were tried by Raja Bijoynarayan. Later Rajas Mookandnarayan and Raja Bijoynarayan tried petty cases, both sitting together. Thieves, however, were to be taken to Guwahati to the magistrate.[52]

Later, Scott found that the magistrates and the members of the panchayat did not dispose off the cases promptly. The proceedings in their trials had been exceedingly prolix and although the cases were selected as being of a simple nature, they took an inordinately long time to complete. This caused much trouble to the official magistrate with whom a number of cases had been accumulating. As such Scott made minor modifications in the administration of criminal justice.[53]

Accordingly, the magistrate and commissioner had to exercise respectively the powers of the Bengal magistrate and the judge of Circuit,[54] either singly or with the assistance of a panchayat, when the nature of the cases might render their advice desirable.

The commissioner was further empowered to decide, as at present, all cases not requiring capital punishment but referable by a Court of Circuit to the Nizamat Adalat. Second, all cases of capital sentence had to be tried before the officiating Magistrate and a panchayat under the rules already prescribed and where the commissioner and the magistrate might concur in disagreeing with the verdict of the panchayat; a new trial might be ordered to take place, to be similarly conducted before a jury consisting either of the same members of the panchayat or of other individuals and their verdict was to be final. Third, the rules with regard to Upper Assam remained in force as originally promulgated with the like provisions for a new trial.

The natives of the province exercised considerable influence as member of panchayat in the administration of criminal justice. Scott wished that respectable persons should come forward as jurymen but very few did so. Consequently, the panchayats were composed members of the native civil courts, and in fact, they were assessors rather than jurymen.[55] Like other parts of India, in Assam too, the natives had less share in the judicial posts involved in the dispensation of criminal justice. However, they were not wholly excluded from it. In February 1832, Haliram Dhekial Phukan, belonging to a noble family of Assam was appointed Assistant magistrate at Guwahati.[56] He was empowered to pass sentences from six months to two years imprisonment. Under the rules framed for the guidance of the assistant magistrate, he was required to prepare a list of 310 inhabitants of Guwahati capable of serving as jurymen. The vacancies, if any, were to be filled up monthly. Whenever a jury might be wanted, the assistant magistrate would prepare a list the day before the trial and would ask the selected persons to attend his Kutchery the following day at 9 a.m. Absentees without good and sufficient cause would be fined two rupees. Five persons would be chosen by lot from those who might attend and would give verdicts on the trial for the day. But if any individual was related to the plaintiff or the defendant within three degrees he would be rejected and another name would be drawn. The jury was to select its foreman, who would deliver the verdict of the majority without specifying any individual opinion. Each juryman who might deliver one or more verdict would receive 8 *annas* per diem. Should the assistant magistrate be of opinion that a verdict of guilty was in contradiction to evidence, he could remand the prisoner and report the same immediately to the commissioner, whose decision would be binding. However, a verdict of acquittal by a jury was final. The assistant magistrate had to take care not to commence a trial without reasonable expectation of coming to a decision on the same day, but in cases of necessity, the trial could be postponed for another day.[57] The native machinery restored by Scott worked very badly. Instead of being affordable it became expensive due to the immensity of the loss which its inefficiency had occasioned.[58]

The judicial system was evolved as a result of trial and error and was subjected to experimental schemes. The government's indecisiveness about the restoration of Upper Assam compelled Scott to depart from pursuing a particular policy. At the same time, there had been a scarcity of European agency employed in Assam, which affected administration, causing misery to the people.

When Robertson took charge of this province in 1832, he felt that grave injustice had been done to this much-neglected province by reposing its responsibilities entirely on a single functionary, the Agent to the Governor-General, N.E. Frontier and Commissioner, over-burdened as he was with multifarious duties.[59] Robertson said in May 1832 that 'in the whole country of Arracan from which about six European Officers are allowed does not equal in extent the province of Lower Assam which constitutes the jurisdiction of a single assistant'.[60] He admitted that nothing could succeed in Assam without effective supervision by European officers, for the system of 'Native Agency' had utterly failed even though it had received the fairest possible trial under the supervision of 'a man of great talents and great knowledge of native character'.[61] Pointing out the advantages of both native and European administration, Robertson observed:[62]

In a purely native administration, the unscrupulous rigour with which faults are visited with the cruelest punishments tends by diffusing a dread of detection to correct the propensity of every native agent to abuse of Power.

In a purely European system, on the other hand, such as obtained in our Regulation provinces very flagrant abuse is prevented by that knowledge of their rights which men acquire by living under its influence by the limited powers imparted to natives and the certainty of redress in every clear case of wrong that can be brought to the cognizance of the European assistant.

But the system hitherto followed in Assam had been something of a middle character in which European principles of Government are brought into action without the aid of European integrity to carry them into practice and the consequence has been that the native agent relieved from the dread of prompt and fearful punish-ment which hangs over them under a native Government and vested with a power never entrusted to them under a European rule have wanton in an almost undisguised excess of extortion and abuse.[63]

Conceiving, therefore, a middle course to be the worst kind of administration, Robertson recommended that it be forthwith abandoned and one or the other of the systems mentioned above established instead. In other words, he strongly recommended the retention of Upper Assam as an integral part of the British dominion, if the government was prepared to spare an adequate number of European officers and provide for the ruling families; failing which he was decidedly in favour of making over the territory to a native prince.

NOTES

1. Secret Proceedings, 28 May 1824, no. 20, quoted in AXA, p. 17.
2. G. Campbell, *Modern India*, p. 251.
3. John William Kaye, *The Administration of the East India Company: A History of Indian Progress*, p. 433.
4. Surya Kumar Bhuyan, *Anglo-Assamese Relations 1771-1826*, p. 571.
5. Bengal Judicial Proceedings (Civil), 19 September 1822, no. 4.
6. Ibid.
7. H.K. Barpujari, *Assam in the Days of the Company*, p. 23.
8. Ibid., p. 18.
9. Bengal Secret and Political Consultations, 5 April 1828, no. 27 quoted in ibid., p. 19.
10. Nirode Kumar Barooah, *David Scott in North-East India 1802-31: A Study of British Paternalism*, p. 134.
11. Ibid., p. 131.
12. Ibid., p. 236.
13. Major Adam White, *A Memoir of the Late David Scott*, p. 5.
14. *David Scott in North-East India 1802-31*, p. 152.
15. Foreign Political Proceedings, 10 June 1831, no. 50, Scott to Swinton, 18 May 1831.
16. Hiteswar Barbaruah, *Ahomar Din*, p. 334.
17. *David Scott in North-East India 1802-31*, p. 158.
18. Foreign Political Proceedings, 23 July 1832, no. 70, Robertson to Swinton, 30 June 1832.
19. Barpujari, *Asssam in the Days of the Company*, p. 31.
20. *David Scott in North-East India 1802-31*, p. 158.
21. Barpujari, *Assam in the Days of the Company*, p. 31.
22. Major Adam White, *Memoir of the Late David Scott*, p. 2.
23. Bengal Secret and Political Consultations, 16 February 1827, no. 2 quoted in *Assam in the Days of the Company*, pp. 31-2.
24. Surya Kanta Bhuyan, *Anglo-Assamese Relations 1771-1826*, p. 558.
25. Ibid., p. 568.
26. *Davd Scott in North-East India 1802-31*, pp. 233-4.
27. Foreign Secret Proceedings, 1830, 12 March, no. 21, Scott to Swinton, also see Bengal Judicial Proceedings (Civil), 25 October 1836, no. 18, Robertson to Macsween, 5 August 1833.
28. Ibid.
29. Ibid.

30. Foreign Political Proceedings, 30 May 1833, no. 83, Robertson to Secy., 4 Febraury 1833.
31. Ibid.
32. Territorial Proceedings (Revenue) 1 July 1833, no. 3, Robertson to Macnaughten. Extracts from the proceedings of the Governor-General, 6 June 1833.
33. BJP (Civil), 25 October 1836, no. 18, Robertson to Macsween, 5 August 1833.
34. Ibid.
35. Foreign Secret Proceedings, 12 March 1830, no. 22 Scott to Swinton, 3 October 1828.
36. Ibid.
37. Bengal Judicial Proceedings (Civil), 25 October 1836, no. 18, Robertson to Macsween, 5 August 1833.
38. From Scott, 25 May 1825, 2 March 1826, 29 April 1826, 30 December 1826, to Secretary, Bengal and BJP, December 1870, no. 2, Agnew to Secretary Bengal, 18 August 1869.
39. Hiteswar Barbaruah, *Ahomar Din*, p. 334.
40. H.K. Barpujari, *Assam in the days of the Company*, p. 32.
41. Bengal Secret and Political Consultations, 16 February 1827, no. 2, quoted in *Assam in the Days of the Company*, p. 33, see fns.
42. Ibid.
43. Bengal Secret and Political Consultations, 2 May 1828, no. 11-13, quoted in *Assam in the Days of the Company*, p. 33.
44. Surya Kumar Bhuyan, *Anglo-Assamese Relations 1771-1826*, p. 569.
45. Barooah, *David Scott in North-East India 1802-31*, pp, 235-6.
46. Ibid., p. 236.
47. Bengal Judicial Proceedings, December 1870, no. 2, Agnew to Secretary Bengal, 18 August 1869, also see letters received from Government of Bengal, no. 253.
48. Foreign Political Proceedings, 23 July 1832, no. 70, extracts from a private letter from White to Governor-General, 28 May 1832.
49. Bengal Judicial Proceedings, December 1870, no. 2.
50. Foreign Political Proceedings, 23 July 1832, no. 70.
51. Bengal Judicial Proceedings, December 1870, no. 2.
52. Foreign Political Proceedings, 30 May 1833, no. 83.
53. Foreign Secret Proceedings, 12 March 1830, no. 19, Scott to Swinton, 2 October 1828.
54. The constitution of the Courts of Circuit were embodied in Bengal Regulation IX of 1793. Four Courts of Circuit were constituted in Bengal

Presidency for trial of the serious criminal cases which were committed to them by the magistrate of the districts. The judges were to move from districts to districts periodically.
55. Foreign Political Proceedings, 23 July 1832, no. 70, White to Governor-General, 28 May 1832.
56. Ibid., 19 March 1832, no. 81, Crocroft to Swinton, 21 February 1832.
57. Ibid.
58. Ibid., 23 July 1832, no. 70, Robertson to Swinton, 30 June 1832.
59. Ibid.
60. Ibid.
61. Bengal Political Consultations, 30 May 1833, no. 93, quoted in *Assam in the Days of the Company*, p. 74.
62. Foreign Political Proceedings, 30 July 1832, no. 92, Robertson to Swinton, 5 July 1832.
63. Ibid.

APPENDIX 2.1: THE COMPOSITION OF THE NATIVE JUDICIAL ESTABLISHMENT WITH THEIR RESPECTIVE SALARIES FOR UPPER ASSAM

Barphukan	300
Roobkari	60
Mahafiz	40
2 Mohurers	60
2 Assamese Mohurers	50
Nazir	40
Mohurer	20
Jemadar	12
15 Peons	90
Duftari	6
Gangajollia	6
Korani	6
Interpreters	30
Assamese Pundits	30
Boats for records and Omlahs	70
Boats for Nazir and Prisoners	70
Stationery	20
Total Sicca Rs.	910

APPENDIX 2.2: NATIVE ESTABLISHMENT OF LOWER ASSAM

Serishtadar	100
Roobkari	60
Mahafiz	40
3 Mohurers	90
2 Assamese Mohurers	50
Nazir	40
Mohurer	20
Jemadar	12
15 Peons	90
Duftari	6
Gangajollia	6
Korani	6
Interpreters	30
Assamese Pundits	30
Boats for records and Omlahs	70
Boats for Nazir and Prisoners	70
Stationery	20
Total Sicca Rs.	740

APPENDIX 2.3: NATIVE COURTS

Court No. 1	A Rajkhowa	Narayani Rs.	60
	Three Assessors	Rs.	102
	Establishment and Contingencies	Rs.	72
		Rs.	234
Court No. 2	Barphukan	Rs.	150
	Three Assessors	Rs.	102
	Establishment and Contingencies	Rs.	72
		Rs.	324
Court No. 3	Barphukan	Rs.	150
	Three Assessors	Rs.	102
	Establishment and Contingencies	Rs.	72
		Rs.	324
	Bengali Mohurer Two Sheristadars for preparing Monthly reports	Rs.	72
	A Nazir and Peons	Rs.	25
		Rs.	97
	Narayani	Rs.	979
	Or Sicca	Rs.	616

CHAPTER 3

Growth and Development of the Administration of Justice in the Early Years of British Rule

There was total suspension of administrative business in Assam for several years antecedent to its annexation by the British. The British authorities in Assam, therefore, had to go through long and weary process in order to find solutions to the problems that confronted them in the administration of justice. After numerous experiments, some definite principles were formulated towards the close of 1837 and these formed the basis of the administration of justice which we see around us today.

The administration of justice was classified under two heads: (a) civil and (b) criminal.

ADMINISTRATION OF CIVIL JUSTICE

In the administration of civil justice the British initially preserved the traditional form, 'well suited to the peculiar conditions of its society and people'. Attempts were made to revive the efficiency of the ancient system with modifications aimed at removing the glaring abuses or inconvenient practices, so that the changes led to better administration of justice to the people as well to the government.

Following the Non-Regulation System, it was not considered desirable to hamper the courts by introducing elaborate laws, which the judge and the people were incapable of grasping. In practice, however, instances of following the Bengal Regulations in the absence of any proper code of law and procedure, were not uncommon. Scott issued rules of practice, mostly prepared from local customs and Regulations of Bengal for the guidance of the Assistants. Much attention was given to the *lex-loci* or the local customs and prejudices. It was necessary for the judge to know the basic principles of European jurisprudence as well as the Regulations and local laws. In matters relating to succession, inheritance and marriage the general principle was that the personal laws of the party—Hindu or Muslim—were to be followed. However, when the plaintiff was of a different religious persuasion from the defendant, the decision was to be regulated by the laws of the latter. However, it was recognized that in special circumstances, deviations were justified on grounds of 'justice, equity and good conscience'. On matters such as contracts, sales, and mortgage, Scott laid down principles borrowed either from Bengal Regulations or from local customs and practices.

The changes in the system of revenue administration brought about corresponding changes in the administration of civil justice. The British government created a new land system based on private property and introduced money economy. A uniform system of law had to be evolved to maintain and regulate the new land relations and contractual transactions, such as, purchase, sale and mortgage of land. The abrupt change from a demand of the revenue in kind to an exaction in cash fell pressingly on the *ryots*, who were unfamiliar with such kind of payments and for which the economy was yet to be developed. Such a drastic change prepared grounds for extortion and oppression leading to enormous increase of civil suits relating to rent and monetary transactions.

Suits concerning dispossession of land, restitution of conjugal rights, adoption, extortion, attainment of majority age and so on, also were not less frequent. The recovery of money expended in the ceremony of betrothal, claims on simple bond-debts and balances of accounts constituted three-fourths of the suits in the province. The character of civil litigation was generally very simple and the suits were mostly of small value.

The administration of civil justice was almost entirely in the hands of the panchayats or native courts composed of the local gentry. There was no written code to regulate the decisions of the panchayats. They were guided by their views of justice, which were, no doubt, in conformity with the principles of the law (Hindu or Muslim) governing the parties, instructions issued by the local authorities or the Government of Bengal and the accepted customs of the country. Scott set up three native courts at Guwahati and three in the mofussils. Besides, he authorized the revenue officers of the mofussils to exercise their jurisdiction on trifling civil suits. The judges in these courts had held similar appointments under the Ahoms; and therefore, Scott was of the opinion that their recruitment not only provided them subsistence but had also given the government knowledge about the local system of judicial administration.[1]

WORKING OF THE NATIVE COURTS

In spite of the best of intentions, the native courts could not dispose of the civil suits with promptitude. Cases inevitably accumulated in their files and the machinery could not keep pace with the everincreasing business which was partly due to the period of prolonged confusion preceding the British rule.

Table 3.1 shows the number of civil suit disposed of by the native judges or the panchayats of Assam between the years 1827 and 1832.

The civil litigations seem to have been increased phenomenally since 1827 as Table 3.1 shows. All these cases were tried by the native courts at Guwahati, the Mofussil and the Tahasildars' Summary Suit Court at Guwahati and Nowgong. Large numbers of cases were pending in different courts every year bringing untold hardship to the litigants. Moreover, there existed the practice of deciding petty civil cases by written pleadings and depositions, which were not intelligible to the people, more than 90 per cent of whom were illiterate. Lack of experience of the native judges in the British mode of conducting business, general inefficiency of the *mohurers* and the slothful and irregular habits of the peons serving in the courts also contributed to the arrears of civil cases. Likewise, ignorance and irresponsibility of the *tahsildars*, *chowdhuries* and other revenue officers were instrumental in the miscarriage of justice in the interiors of the country.

TABLE 3.1: NUMBER OF CIVIL SUITS DISPOSED OF BY THE PANCHAYATS (1827-32)

Year	Cases depending on 1 January	Cases admitted during the year	Total no. of case	Total no. of cases disposed	Cases pending at the end of the year
1827	106	2,116	2,222	1,168	1,054
1828	1,054	2,684	3,738	3,061	677
1829	677	3,413	4,090	2,988	1,102
1830	1,102	3,466	4,568	3,244	1,324
1831	1,324	2,992	4,316	2,907	1,409
1832	1,409	2,527	3,936	3,322	614

Sources: FSP, 12 March 1830, no. 21; ibid. no. 29; FPP, 14 May 1830, no. 32; ibid., 3 June 1831, no. 71; ibid., 6 August 1832, no. 61; BJP (Civil), 25 October 1836, no. 19.

The native courts or the panchayats had no trained judge, *omlah* or uniform laws and procedures. The only law in force in the province was rules of practice laid down by Scott under 'the principle and spirit of the Bengal Regulations'. As a result, the work of these courts was carried out in a dilatory manner and cases were decided most carelessly. The same was true of the mofussil courts. Some cases remained pending there for years. A petty case that could be disposed of easily kept hanging in the highest tribunal.

The government was no less responsible for the failure of the native courts. The commissioner was required to exercise general superintendence over the working of all these courts and to attend their proceedings. He was also to see whether the judgements passed were fair and impartial. But he hardly could afford time to supervise all these. Consequently, the native courts, especially in the mofussils, were left practically to themselves. 'In civil cases', admitted Robertson, 'the only control they are liable to is that of a remote supervision by a superior so overwhelmed by other duties as the Governor-General's Agent.'[2] The Governor-General's Agent had been virtually the judge, magistrate and collector of Lower Assam, besides managing other offices of the superintendent of police, executive engineer, post master, etc. It was utterly impossible for a single human being to look into so many affairs. Moreover, the very nature of the British administration was such that an officer was to be praised or condemned based on his services in the revenue department. Obviously, the judicial business suffered, as officers were more concerned with their revenue duties. Scott visited Nowgong once and Darrang thrice during his tenure as Commissioner of Assam.[3] An inference can be drawn from a report of A. Bogle, Assistant at Guwahati on the working of panchayats and the inadequacy of government supervision over them. He reported:

The necessity for the *Panchayats* being more strictly looked after is very great but whilst appeals be from them to the Commissioner and the Officer-in-charge here has not the power of interfering, it occurs to me that their proceedings cannot be efficiently checked as from all the circumstances connected with the office of the Commissioner, it seems more than probable that a decision cannot be given for a considerable time that the parties must incur considerable expenses and some vexation.[4]

The assistant-in-charge of a district could not interfere with the working of the native court even if he observed that there was miscarriage of justice. Were it placed entirely under his control, all cases decided by the courts could have been appealed and the assistant could have had the authority to supervise the functioning of these courts. But that was not permitted because the government did not want to take the sole blame for any failure, which they could now put directly on the shoulders of the natives. 'On the whole', said Bogle, 'I consider the Panchayats only valuable when acting on clearly defined rules of practice and under the immediate control of superior authority. Those which were formed in the interior possessed neither of this essentials.'[5]

There were also allegations of corruption against the members of the panchayat. 'The Sadar Panchayat', said Robertson, 'are generally reported to be venal in the extreme, while the Mofussil Panchayats are, as I have had proofs before me, mere engines of abuse and extortion.'[6] Even the agency for serving summons was reported to be corrupt, exacting and oppressive. As a result, the people lost faith in the working of the native courts or the panchayats. 'The experiment of making natives exclusively the judge of the first resort,' observed, the Court of Directors, 'an experiment which we have not yet thought safe to try even in those of our provinces which have been long accustomed to a regular administration of justice, must be considered to have been tried in Assam under most unfavourable circumstances, and in a very imperfect manner and the result has been the most complete failure'.[7]

These observations made by the British Officials may be exaggerated but there were, in fact, persons amongst the natives who used their power to their own advantage and did not hesitate to extort from their own people.

ADMINISTRATION OF CRIMINAL JUSTICE

In the administration of criminal justice, the rules prevalent in Assam were quite close to the Bengal Regulations. Only minor modifications were made maintaining the spirit of these Regulations, to suit the circumstances of the province. Thus, the local laws followed in the tracing of criminals, and enforcing the responsibility of the revenue officers for the maintenance of peace and stability within their jurisdiction prior to the British occupation of Assam, continued to remain in force. The maintenance of law and order was considered in those days to be a joint responsibility of the people, and in the event of their failure to detect and apprehend criminals requiring thereby the deputation of a regular force, the expense for the same was realized by a collective fine on the inhabitants of the disturbed area.

Important reforms were made in the administration of criminal justice ever since the days of Scott. The inhuman punishments of the previous government, such as the cutting off of nose, ears, extracting eyes, and other forms of mutilation were discontinued. Heinous cases were tried by the commissioner and his assistants with the assistance of a jury or a body of assessors. These assessors were generally Assamese-speaking public officers of the civil courts. However, respectable natives unconnected with the government were also encouraged to apply for permission to sit on these trials like the members of the Dewany Court. In criminal trials, their opinion was of great importance in counting the merit of the evidence.

The number of crimes was low in Upper Assam. This might be due to the fact that changes in Upper Assam in the early years of British rule were somewhat limited and the traditional bonds of communal unity still remained strong there. It being the place of habitation of majority of the erstwhile nobility, lawsuits in this area were more concerned with property than with injuries to persons.

On the other hand, number of crimes was very high in Lower Assam, which compared to Upper Assam, was much thickly populated and where changes in the new settlement had been drastic, because the Company adopted an instant decision to annex this part of the province to its territory. Apart from usual burglary, theft, and cattle-stealing, cases of highway robberies, murder and decoity—previously uncommon in Assam were of frequent occurrence. Table 3.2 reveals the extent of crimes in the early years of the British rule in Lower Assam.

TABLE 3.2: EXTENT OF CRIMES IN EARLY YEARS OF BRITISH RULE IN LOWER ASSAM

Year	Wilful Murder	Highway Robbery	Decoity	Burglary & Theft	Cattle Stealing	Other Crimes	Total
1825	5	X	29	17	2	X	53
1826	3	2	56	48	6	X	115
1827	6	X	39	52	15	X	112
1828	13	2	87	670	94	59	925
1829	9	2	35	766	116	169	1,097
1830	2	2	21	533	140	32	730
1831	3	1	39	1,044	195	18	1,300
1832	1	3	39	846	160	19	1,068

Sources: FSP, 12 March 1830, no. 83; FPP, 28 May 1830, no. 78; BJP (Criminal), 20 October 1835, no. 40.

Crimes increased abnormally after 1828. Cases of decoity were predominant in the years immediately following British occupation, while cases of burglary, theft and cattle stealing became rampant after 1828. The prevalence of crime of such magnitude became a serious subject to deal with for the English officials. The fear of imprisonment had little or no effect in deterring people from committing crime.[8] The British officials attributed this to the continued disuse of inhuman corporal or capital punishment practiced by the previous rulers. But this was only an attempt to conceal the reality. Demand for taxes, extreme poverty, and immoderate use of opium and absence of police to protect lives and property were the main factors responsible for increase in the intensity of vices. The British revenue policy impoverished the people and poverty ultimately contributed to the abrupt increase in crimes. It is thus necessary to have a clear understanding of the revenue policy and its impact on the native population before analysing the state of criminal justice in these early British years.

The advent of the British in Assam, as stated earlier, was hailed with joy by the inhabitants with the sanguine expectation of peace and happiness from this rule, after several years of chaos, disorder and devastating warfare. But the people were soon disillusioned as they realized that the British had come not as their deliverers but as exploiters, with plans to oppress them in multiple ways. They found that the Company officials were only interested in the collection of revenue and doing little civic duty. For many years after the introduction of the British rule, the province remained in a deplorable state and its condition in many respects deteriorated. Hard pressed from several quarters, many starving inhabitants left the country to seek shelter in the jungles or in the no man's land near the border of Bhutan.

Under the new revenue system, the inhabitants had to pay revenue in the form of a definite sum of money to the government every year. The people were unaccustomed to money payments, as the previous government realized revenue in the form of personal service and articles of produce and only a small part in cash. The British government replaced this with a fixed amount of cash payment, without bothering about the amount of produce of an individual. The scarcity of cash occasioned by very limited trade and poorly developed manufacturing industry in the province rendered it difficult for the inhabitants to pay their tax in cash.[9] There was hardly any consideration shown by the government for non-payment of revenue due to failure of crops on account of floods or droughts. More often than not, the inability to pay revenue drove the peasants to borrow money at high rates of interest from the moneylenders. The moneylenders charged high rates of interest and through cunning and deceit, got the peasant deeper and deeper into debt until he parted with his property. Taking advantage of the illiteracy and ignorance of the village folk, some ambitious and rich persons conspired with the revenue officers and sometimes took illegal possession of the properties of the poor, innocent villagers. Consequently, difficulties and disputes arose, the courts were appealed to, and the litigations began, the losing parties being generally the cultivators.

The moneylenders exploited the provisions of the new legal system and the revenue policy to their advantage. On the other hand, the rights given to the cultivator under the new legal system to mortgage his properties placed him at the mercy of the moneylender and eventually made him a slave of the latter.

The rich moneylender had an advantage over the poor cultivator since litigation was expensive. The moneylender could hold out even if the suit dragged on; on the other hand, the poor *ryot* who could hardly maintain himself on his income, failed to take the benefit of the costly legal service. Further, the literate and shrewd moneylender exploiting the ignorance of the illiterate *ryot*, could twist the complicated legal procedure in his favour. The result was a large-scale impoverishment of the peasantry. The high and arbitrary rate of revenue was another source of evil. Heavy assessment based on imperfect data contributed largely to the growth of poverty among the people and deterioration of agriculture.

The situation was worst in Lower Assam, more specifically in its central part. Table 3.3 exhibits the rate of cash revenue in the district of Darrang which went on increasing oppressively since the days of the Burmese rule in the district.[10]

An inference could easily be drawn about the plight of the *ryots* under such an exorbitant rate of assessment. Table 3.3 shows that the revenue, increased only moderately by the Burmese, was raised

TABLE 3.3: RATE OF CASH REVENUE IN DARRANG DISTRICT OF LOWER ASSAM

In the time of the Assam king previous to Burmese Rule	Amount of Tax Extracted by the Burmese	Amount imposed by Scott & *bundhbust* with Raja Bijoy Narayan 1824/5	Second year with Raja Bijoy Narayan 1825/6	Third year with Raja Bijoy Narayan 1826/7
Cash 10,000	Cash 15,000	Cash 32,000	Cash 36,000	Cash 54,749

Source: FPP, 30 May 1833, no. 83.

exorbitantly by the new conqueror. In spite of the most stringent measures, it was impossible to realize revenue due from the *ryots* and as a result, arrears kept accumulating every year. 'It is sufficient to state,' Robertson observed, 'that the settlement hitherto formed in Assam have been in a manner conjectural resting rather upon what people would offer than on what the *Parganah* could yield.'[11] The result of such a system was necessarily fluctuating, causing unnecessary embarrassment to the government and untold miseries to the people.

The complex list of revenue to be paid was a problem of great magnitude. Even persons of intelligence would be puzzled to calculate, how much a *ryot* had to pay to the government; to the unfortunate peasant, the account must have been wholly incomprehensible.[12] There was no end to government demand. Levying of *Barangani* or extra cess, *soroo* or hearth tax, commission for revenue agents, over and above the usual taxes, brought untold hardships to the people. The whole system of keeping the mofussil establishment of police and *tahsildari* by *barangani* or extra cess on the *ryots* afforded grounds for extortion. The police establishments were only nominally paid by the government. They, therefore, maintained themselves mainly on plunder.[13] On the other hand, the *soroo* in most instances bore heavier on the poor than the rich, the tax being levied on the cooking place, because '8 or 10 persons of same caste, if cooking and eating on the same hearth, only pays which one poor man is subject to, if he has no chums'.[14]

Growth and Development of the Administration of Justice 81

Apart from the rate of assessment and the kind of taxes, the system or machinery of collecting taxes was also oppressive. Hosts of revenue collectors were engaged to realize revenue from the people. These collectors sometimes collected as much as they could and deposited to the government whatever they pleased. With an object of enriching government's coffer, David Scott permitted the ex-Khangia Phukan to make a *peol* or census of the *bhoggonia* or runaway *paiks* of Upper Assam at Nowgong and to collect taxes from them.[15] Similar privilege was granted to one Madhoram Baruah in Darrang. Both of them were authorized to collect taxes disregarding the normal practice of granting *sunnud* or authorization from the commissioner's office at Guwahati. These officers and their subordinates, 'collected where and from whom they could, paying what they pleased of their collections to the Government',[16] stated Rutherford, assistant at Central Assam.

In Kamrup, the *paraganas* were placed under a set of unprincipled men, the *chowdhury*. They extracted without any limit and sans any effective machinery to check their oppression. The mode of assessment had been shown to consist of a number of items, many of them being illdefined, and the effects caused by it were declared to have been 'productive of greatest evil'. The process of selection of *chowdhury* was vested with the *ryots* themselves, who voted him by ballot. In practice, the former bribed off the latter with promise, even with money to get elected. The *chowdhury* again had to bribe the *omlah* at Sadar station for which a considerable amount had to be spent. These expenses together with the cost of revenue and profit for himself were afterwards extracted from the ryots. Further, moved by the fear of not being re-elected, the *chowdhury* extracted through all possible ways before his term came to an end. 'Sometimes 5 or 6 times of the real revenue of rent have been collected'[17] said Rutherford. To realize the arrear of revenue from the *ryots*, *chowdhury* employed the *kuruk sezwals*, who forced the *ryots* failing to clear revenue payments to abandon their homes and to take shelter in the lawless region of Bhutan. The *chowdhuries* were compelled by the circumstances to indulge in such extraction because they, in their turn, had to face prosecution if they failed to clear their dues to the government in time. Still there was no dearth of application for *chowdhuryship* because the mere name of *chowdhury* was attractive in the eyes of the natives, even when the field of extortion was somewhat barren.

The administration, therefore, felt that 'an error was committed in not allowing the country to continue under the erstwhile system, after so long a period of misrule, instead of proceeding to levy taxes at once, on imperfect date'.[18] The country was originally over-assessed and the evils of over-assessment were aggravated by the new system of realizing the revenue in cash. No remission was ever granted; on the contrary, extra cess were levied for a variety of purposes, when even the stipulated revenue could not be collected.[19] As the governments demand was never reduced even when land was lying vacate due to the emigration of inhabitants, who formed the basis for the estimate of revenue, the estimate itself soon became fictitious. Admitting those facts, Rutherford was constrained to remark, 'dreadful extortion (by the farmers of revenue) had beggared the *ryot* and rendered a large portion of the country waste (in) which, up to our conquest, such a thing as jungle was hardly to be seen'.[20]

The miserable state of things went on for a number of years. When the people found their resources drained away by repeated exactions, they had no other alternative but to flee away in hundreds or to mortgage themselves as slaves and bondsmen. 'It is astonishing to find', reported Rutherford, 'the number of people who from the pressure of rent have sold themselves for trifling sum and become bondsmen with their wives, families and descent until the original sum which they can never have the means of repaying is obtained'.[21]

Unable to meet the bare necessities of life the people were compelled to resort to crime for their subsistence. The punitive measure of imprisonment for a short period and a few stripes by criminal courts did not have any effect on the people, when the question was their survival. Thus, the new situation drove out the *ryots* either to the street to beg or to the prison bar.

Immoderate use of opium since about the third decade of nineteenth century was also contributing towards the growth of poverty and wretchedness among the people. Although opium was used in

Assam ever since Captain Welsh's expedition in 1792-4, it was confined to a limited few. With the cultivation of opium at Beltola near Guwahati after Welsh's expedition, the use of this harmful drug was steadily taking on an alarming proportion. The Company's government made no sincere attempt to prevent the use of this drug and totally ignored the moral and social aspect of its effects. When the economic condition of the people was somewhat better, they could afford to purchase the drug, but when their condition deteriorated, it was impossible for them to buy it. The people who were addicted to opium could not live without it, and hence they even took to stealing.[22]

Maintenance of law and order depends upon an efficient police system. But there was no proper police administration in Assam in the early years of the British rule. During the Ahom period, the functions of maintaining peace and order were generally the concern of the *kheldars* and the individual *kheldar* was the unit of police administration. The *kheldar* was also the pivot of the social and economic life of the people and, security being a vital part of people's life, it was his responsibility to protect his subjects from disturbances, robberies and theft. After the introduction of the British rule, *thana* establishment superseded this system. But the new police establishments were grossly inadequate for the prevention of crimes. For a considerable period, its effective operation was confined to a certain distance around the Sadar station. 'The police system, I regret to say,' said Neufville, Political Agent, Upper Assam, 'is imperfect and introduction of a perfect or even tolerably efficient police in a country like Assam is altogether out of our power.'[23]

The magistrate, who was also the head of the police, was unable to exercise adequate supervision in maintaining law and order due to the multiplicity of his duties. The police in the interior areas acted independently without any control that could check their abuse of authority. Instead of seeking protection from the police, people therefore regarded them as a source of intolerance, vexation, and oppression. In the process of seeking justice, people were obliged to pay the *teckela* or *peada* who were in charge of serving summons to the defendants and in practice 'the exhibition of a complaint becomes more injurious than putting up with the original loss'.[24] The victim, therefore, preferred to conceal his injury than to seek redress from the police, which would invite additional extortion. The result was obvious; the criminals roamed about the country unchecked and people lacked security of life and property.

With the increase in crimes, there arose the problem of holding the trial of the criminals. The paucity of courts and their inaccessibility for the people of the interior areas created a lot of inconvenience to the under-trials as well as to the law-enforcing agencies. The cases that were to be tried by session judge not taken up for trial in time, and even when taken up, dragged on for months together, with the result that the accused were tried long after the crime had been committed. The accused had to remain in jail all throughout this period. The condition of Guwahati Jail was miserable. The detainees hardly came out of it after completing sentences or on acquittal in good health. Within a span of five years, from 1825 to 1829 more than 500 detainees lost their lives in jail or just after their release. 'It is impossible to shut one's eye', said Scott, 'to the undeniable fact that the deaths of the greater portion of the prisoners are as much occasioned by the sentence of the law as if they were executed on gallows.'[25] In the year 1829 alone, 166 deaths were reported of a total of 600 prisoners. Being the only session judge of the province, it became difficult for Scott to hold session trials in appropriate time. As a result, jail deliveries were greatly delayed. On one occasion it was delayed for more than two years and on another occasion all the prisoners, witnesses, etc., had to be summoned to Goalpara.[26] where Scott was stationed. These show the inconveniences and hardships the people had to undergo in facing trials.

It has been stated that the Ahom institution of law and justice constituted the basis of the Company's administration of justice in the formative years of its rule in Assam. The indigenous courts were revived and reconstructed to serve the judicial requirements of the Company's government. At the same time, the British abrogated those laws and judicial institutions then existing, which were against their imperial or colonial interest and not suited for the working of their administration. They substituted them with

English law and English judicial system. Of course, the English law was not hurriedly thrust upon this province, because justice being a very sensitive issue, the British had to proceed with caution and tact. Scott could feel that the Assamese people still venerated the authority of the Ahoms, though the substance thereof had long passed and only its shadow remaining. Scott kept in mind all those factors while introducing the British administration in Assam. He intended to create a new class of officials loyal to the Company and to minimize cost of his administration too. Scott believed that the laws and procedures to be used should be of the simplest kind, and as far as possible, based on native custom and institutions. Such a policy required the involvement of the most influential and respected classes of society, who afforded great assistance to the British in their struggle against the Burmese. Scott found the service of these people worthwhile in the effective discharge of his administration. These classes ultimately secured all the prized posts available to the native population, and extended to the British their most loyal cooperation. Along with these classes, there appeared another class of fortune-seekers from Bengal who subsequently occupied the most dominant positions in the administration of Assam.

Scott's policy of employing natives in the administration of justice, however sound in theory, proved disastrous in practice. The native officials were found to be no less oppressive than the Burmese. In the sphere of revenue administration, their oppression on the people crossed all limits. In course of time, it was established that these classes proved themselves wholly incompetent in discharging their duties in revenue and judicial administration. On the other hand, 'their presence caused great labour and trouble to European functionaries'.[27] Complaints of extortion and oppression against these officers became a regular feature. The revenue officials were permitted to exercise judicial function with the avowed object of placing them in a position of influence over the tenantry, so that they could realize rents more easily. But in practice, they applied their judicial authority to oppress the *ryots* to the extreme. Having lost everything to the Burmese, these officials were, 'anxious to make up for what had previously been extracted from them'.[28] During the first eight years of the British rule in this province, the administration of justice conducted by these officials had created confusion as there was no adequate authority to supervise their workings. Therefore, an error was committed in entrusting to the natives, the greater part of the administration of justice without any provision for repressing the abuse of their power. 'The general laxness', observed Capt. Bogle, assistant at Guwahati, 'and delay in their proceedings, more specially in serving processes and enforcing decrees and the want of confidence in the honesty of the members is only what most of the poorer classes in Assam feel towards their superiors who for generations have been famous for their disregard to all interest but their own.'[29] Owing to the difficulty of obtaining qualified persons trained in the British system of administration, it was necessary to employ *omlahs* convicted of bribery and refuse (persons who were not allowed employment in different districts of Bengal because of bad records) of other zillahs[30] and the result was that these villains maltreated the people at their pleasure. Not only the officials from Bengal but almost every one, whether Assamese or non-Assamese, never failed to exploit the situation, whenever had an opportunity presented itself. In the words of Scott, 'The improvement of the general administration of justice and the police which could only be effected by the appointment to the chief revenue and other offices, real men of business of inferior ranks; in lieu of the indolent nobles whom it had hitherto been our policy to employ'.[31]

The police officers were no less corrupt and were equally inefficient. They were wholly incapable of preserving the life and properties of the people. As the *thana* establishment was centred only in Sadar stations, the functions of the police in the interior areas were left to the *chowdhuries, rajas* and other revenue officials. In Nowgong, the police was under Ghinai Barphukan.[32] while in Darrang it was under Raja Bijoy Narayan.[33] For police duties in Upper Assam, Capt. Neufville, the Political Agent appointed Juggorram Kharkhoria Phukan.[34] But almost all the inferior police officials were outsiders and mainly Bengali adventurists who were inefficient and corrupt. Their mode of functioning received condemnation from both the people and the government. It was found that in the year 1828 four police officials, all from Bengal, were sentenced to imprisonment on charges of extortion and bribery.[35]

The native officials alone, however, could not be blamed for all these confusions and mismanagements. Most of the native officers were unfamiliar with the British method of administration. Further, as literacy was not a prerequisite to become an officer, few of them were able to read and write and they were in the habit of transacting all business through the medium of *kakotis* or writers. Added to this was the astonishing number of civil cases, mostly of land boundaries and debts. One could easily comprehend, if the records of civil and criminal cases in the early part of British administration are consulted, the inconvenience the officials had to face with an inadequate agency for making investigation, servicing summons and enforcing services.

When the Court of Directors was apprised of the situation prevailing in Assam, it appeared to it that the arrangement made for governing Assam demonstrated want of foresight on the part of the Company's servants in India. 'From whatever cause', observed the Court of Directors, 'we have hitherto governed Assam extremely ill, evils are natural consequences of the system which pursued.'[36]

The system so far followed in the administration of the province was entirely conceived in Scott's mind. Therefore Scott could not be absolved of the blame for its mismanagement. He was the man on the spot and as the head of a non-Regulation province; he enjoyed wide powers and authority. Most of the arrangements he proposed were approved by the government at Fort William without modification. But the absence of financial authority created inconvenience in carrying his schemes to successful conclusion. Further, indecisiveness on the part of the Supreme government about the disposal of Upper Assam caused a lot of confusion in his plans for the administration of the province. Added to this was the inadequate European agency to administer a country of nearly 400 miles in length and about 65 miles in breadth with a population of 8,30,000 people. Scott had the assistance of only one European assistant till 1830 to govern the province which suffered from prolonged confusion and disastrous effects of internel trouble and external aggression. The two officers, therefore, had no alternative but to carry on the administration through the native officers who had no experience of the new procedures. In fact, the native officers had been entrusted with the work of judicial administration 'without any adequate provision for repressing the abuse of their power'.[37] As a result, affairs rather retrograded than improved.

The introduction of the British administration of justice, it must be admitted, is one of great importance, having far-reaching consequences. It could not, therefore, be without some benefits, which were essential for modern values and principles. The British inaugurated a new system of dispensing justice through a hierarchy of civil and criminal courts. They removed some of the glaring evils of the erstwhile judiciary and also some social abuses and inhuman punishments. Although the full benefit of English law was not extended in the early part of their administration and even thereafter, yet the infrastructure of the British Indian judiciary was laid during that period.

Equality before law was one of the most outstanding features of the new administration of justice. Previously, the administration of justice took heed of caste distinction and had differentiated the so-called high-born from the low-born. Under the new system, same the punishment was to be awarded to a person found guilty, Brahmin or non-Brahmin for the same offence. For instance, in the year 1825, one Maheswar Gosain along with a few others committed a murder. The case was tried in 1828 by a panchayat assembled under orders of the government on 2 May 1828. The accused Gosain was awarded light punishment, as he was formerly a *rajguru* or royal priest. Scott reversed the decision of the panchayat and the accused Gosain was imprisoned for life.[38] This was in contrast to the customary law prevalent in pre-British Assam which discriminated between caste and caste, community and community. This was due to the fact that the customary law was governed by religion which sanctified the hierarchically graded castes and their privileges.

The protection of an individual against arbitrary rule and imprisonment, the right of the individual to seek and obtain justice, whether against the state or against the rich and the powerful were other privileges guaranteed to the people.

If we take a broad view of the first eight years of the administration of justice in Assam, the first thing that attracts our attention is the increase in litigations. The courts were flooded with civil and criminal cases. While poverty and distress of the people and inadequate police service had contributed to the rise of criminal suits, the concept of private property had contributed in the increase of civil suits. It was a period of experiments, good in principle, but as yet producing no satisfactory result. There was security against foreign aggression, but theft, robbery and other crimes were rampant causing insecurity to the lives and properties of the people. The judiciary had not yet become an efficient instrument of impartial and speedy justice, while the police served as an agency of oppression rather than protection.

The early enthusiasm and expectations of the enlightened section of the Assamese society were giving way to disillusionment and despair, while the common people, full of misery and discontent, bided their time in sullen resentment, marked by occasional outbursts of violence.

THE REBELLION OF GOMDHAR KONWAR

The first to raise the standard of revolt against the British East India Company was Gomdhar Konwar, son of Phena Konwar, a scion of the Ahom royal family. Gomdhar entered Assam from Burma in the year 1828 and fomented trouble in collaboration with the Khamtis. He entered into correspondence with the principal functionaries at the headquarters of the Political Agent of Upper Assam and particularly with Dhanjoy, an ex-Borgohain. Gomdhar was enthroned with all formalities. He was invested with the white shoes and the umbrella, the insignia of royalty.[39] The *bailungs*—the royal priest—also performed the necessary rituals on the occasion.

After making necessary preparations for the seizure of Rangpur, Gomdhar advanced in the last week of November 1828 towards

Mariani, 12 miles from Jorhat. He was intercepted by the Company's army under Lieutenant Rutherford, at Mariani. After a feeble resistance, Gomdhar fled to the Naga hills. After roaming a few days in the jungles and completely abandoned by his adherents, the fugitive prince ultimately surrendered himself to Rutherford.

Gomdhar was tried by the Sadar Panchayat, which was held on 14 December 1828 at Jorhat.[40] The panchayat was assembled and the trial conducted as per the instructions laid down in Secretary Starlings letter of 2 May 1828 employing *Patra Mantrees* as jury. Gomdhar was found guilty of taking up arms against the state and was 'declared liable by the laws of Assam to suffer death'.[41] Considering Gomdhar's tender age and the fact that he had become a mere tool in the hands of other scheming people, the Agent to the Governor-General, commuted his sentence to imprisonment for seven years in banishment from Assam.

The following paragraphs give the proceedings of the criminal court held by the Agent and Commissioner of Assam on 14 March 1829 at Guwahati.[42]

David Scott, Agent to the Governor-General North-East Frontier and Commissioner of Assam, who was present and presided over the trial.

A letter from political agent, Upper Assam dated 14 December 1828 was read together with the proceedings held on the Trial of Gomdhar Konwar charged with Rebellion against British government and the verdict delivered by the Panchayat assembled under orders of government dated 2 May 1828.

The Court ordered Gomdhar to suffer imprisonment for 7 (seven) years in banishment from Assam, but execution deferred pending reference to government.

> Signed duly by David Scott as the Presiding Officer

Among his other accomplices, Dhanjoy was found guilty of abetting and aiding the rebellion for which he was given death sentence; but he managed to escape to the Naga hills. The Khamti Borgohain who was accused of high treason was sentenced to death at the first instance, but it was later commuted to seven years of imprisonment.[43]

THE REBELLION OF GADADHAR

Hardly a year passed since the suppression of the revolt of Gomdhar Konwar, when an Assamese prince named Gadadhar roused the people to fight the invaders and proposed assassination of the British officers. Later, he attempted to win over the British regiment at Sadiya by diplomatic means, which was thwarted by Zalim Singh, the Subedar of the regiment, who handed him over to the Agent to the Governor-General at Guwahati.

THE REBELLION OF PEALI BARPHUKAN AND HIS ASSOCIATES

A fresh attempt to put an end to the British occupation of Assam had been made in 1830. Dhanjoy Borgohain, the leader of the first abortive attempt of 1828, who subsequently made his escape to the Matak Country, had been organizing another grand attack. He was assisted by his two sons, Harakanta and Haranath and his son-in-law Jeoram Dulia Baruah. Within a short time, Dhanjoy could collect a large following, the most prominent among whom were Peali Barphukan, son of Badan Chandra Barphukan, Rupchand Konwar, Deoram Dihingia Baruah and Boom Singhphos. Emissaries with secret letters were sent out to the chiefs of the Moamaria, Khamtis, Khasis, Garos, Manipuries and the Nagas calling upon their aid to expel the British from Assam and the neighbouring territories.

The rebels, however, failed miserably in forming an effective alliance and a section of them even betrayed their cause. The rebellion was suppressed easily and most of the leaders were arrested. Peali, Jeoram, Haranath, Roopchand and Boom Singhphos were tried by the panchayat at Jorhat and all of them, found guilty of treason and rebellion, were sentenced to death.[44] Peali was said to have made a heroic speech in which he announced that attempts to liberate one's own motherland should not counted as a treasonable offence. The proceedings of the panchayat together with the opinion of the Political Agent was referred to Scott for revision. The criminal court held in Cherrapunji under his presidentship reviewed the proceedings of the panchayat and confirmed the death sentence passed on Peali and Jeuram. The death sentence on the other rebels was commuted to banishment for fourteen years with confiscation of their properties. Scott ordered execution of both Peali and Jeuram without waiting for the approval of the Supreme government. Although he had the authority to do so as the head of a non-Regulation province, it was normal practice to seek confirmation from the Supreme Government in such cases where the question of convicting the members of the erstwhile nobility or ruling family was concerned. This time Scott acted politically, not judiciously, 'since deterrent punishment was considered absolutely necessary to stop reoccurrence of similar uprising'.[45]

APPOINTMENT OF ROBERTSON AS COMMISSIONER

In October 1831 T.C. Robertson was appointed as Agent to the Governor-General, North-East Frontier and Commissioner of Assam.[46] W. Crocroft, who was officiating since David Scott's death in August 1831 was relieved of his duties by Robertson on 25 April 1832.[47] A nobleman of high rank and approved talents, Robertson laid the foundation of civil and criminal justice in Assam. The problem which confronted the new commissioner was twofold: to reform the administrative mechanism, both executive and judiciary, in which corruption was rampant, and to redress the grievances of the people, who were the sufferers of the new revenue administration established by the British. Robertson tried his best to solve the problem in a very efficient manner.

PREPARATION OF CIVIL CODE

The most notable contribution of Robertson was the preparation of a written code for the administration of civil justice in Assam. The rules of practices laid down by Scott were thoroughly revised and re-arranged with such additions and modifications as his own experience had suggested. These rules were prepared from the various orders of Scott lying scattered among voluminous Bengali proceedings.[48] These he attempted to arrange into a code for the future guidance of the civil court of Assam. Robertson found it very difficult, owing to the state of records, to ascertain precisely what rules of practice were laid down by his predecessor. His work was only partially accomplished as he was removed to Fort William, being appointed as the judge of Sadar Court. However, he was successful in preparing a set of General Rules of Practice to be observed in the institution of trial and decision of civil suits for the districts of Lower Assam. These rules were circulated amongst the Assistants for their guidance and also amongst the people for their information making them effective from 1 January 1834.[49]

CONSTITUTION OF COURTS[50]

The first Panchayat Court was vested with the powers of deciding original suits of real and personal property from Rs. 500 to 1,000 and to hear appeals from the decisions of the Second Panchayat and Munsif's Court.

The Second Panchayat Court was to investigate all suits from Rs. 100 to 500, whether real or personal property.

The Munsif's Court was vested with the power to investigate all cases of movable or immovable property not exceeding in value an amount of Rs. 100.

All suits for property exceeding in value the sum of Rs. 1,000 as well as special appeals or appeals from the decisions of the First or Senior Panchayat were declared to be cognizable only by the commissioner.

PROCEDURE TO BE FOLLOWED[51]

All petitions of plaints as also of ordinary and special appeals were to be presented to the assistant. He would then refer them to such courts which according to the rules of practice were competent to proceed upon. All petitions in cases cognizable by the commissioner were to be submitted to his court and he would then issue orders deemed necessary. No petitions of plaints were to be received by the panchayat courts except those referred to it by the Assistant in charge of the district. Munsif's Court was however authorized to receive petitions of plaints which were within their competency to decide.

APPOINTMENT OF VAKEEL[52]

No vakeels were permitted to practice in the Munsif's Court. The parties had to attend in person or depute a relative or *muktear* to plead for them. In the Commissioner's Court as well as in the Courts of First and Second Panchayats, the parties might plead in person or appoint a vakeel. But the vakeel had to be selected from amongst those attached to the courts and the parties had to deposit to the treasury the usual fees of 5 per cent of the property litigated.

INSTITUTION FEES[53]

Robertson regulated the fees and expenses attended on all original suits and appeals (Table 3.4).

In case of disputes for land, the value of the property sued for was to be calculated at the amount of its gross annual proceeds. The introduction of fees on suits and appeal, however, deferred due to objection raised by the Court of Directors of the East India Company.[54]

TABLE 3.4: ROBERTSON INSTITUTED FEES AND EXPENSES ON SUITS AND APPEALS

Rs. 1-10	8 *annas*
Above Rs. 10 to 20	1 Re.
Above Rs. 20 to 50	2 Rs.
Above Rs. 50 to 100	3 Rs.
Above Rs. 100 to 150	4 Rs.
For every Rs. 50, above Rs. 150 one additional rupee	

Source: BJP (Civil), 25 August 1934, no. 16.

REFORMS IN CIVIL JUSTICE

The immediate task of Commissioner Robertson was to restore the confidence of the people in the native courts. There were constant complaints against the inefficiency and partiality of panchayat courts. Robertson proposed to abolish the Moffussil Panchayat courts as complaints against these courts vindicated by the assistants in charge of district. The panchayat courts were to be replaced by the courts of Sadar Ameen and Munsif courts. In fact, Robertson was in favour of following a system that was established and guided by the Regulations, because, departure from the Regulations was as practicable to be avoided. 'We should, he said, adopt them (Regulations) for our guide in the proposed arrangement at Guwahati'.[55] He was, however, not in favour of immediate abolition of panchayat courts at Guwahati, as the proceeding of the panchayat courts that came before Robertson in appeal did not confirm their total inefficiency. 'On the contrary', he said, 'I have found cases to all appearance well tried and the decisions sound and impartial.'[56] But he reduced the number of panchayat courts in Lower Assam from three to two terming them as senior and junior panchayat courts.

The establishment along with respective salaries proposed by Robertson and subsequently sanctioned by the government for these two courts is given in Table 3.5.[57]

Bapuram Barphukon was the president of the Senior Panchayat while Preeo Nath Parbatia Phukon was the president of Junior Panchayat.

The Mofussil Panchayat courts were to be abolished. He also proposed detailed arrangement for the disposal of civil cases in Lower and Central Assam, which was separated from Lower Assam in October 1832 (see Appendix 3.1). The Mofussil Panchayat courts in Lower Assam were abolished and cases tried by them were transferred to Guwahati courts.

Capt. Bogle, Assistant at Guwahati, differed with Commissioner Robertson on the constitution of native courts in Lower Assam. Bogle did not want to retain panchayat courts and was in favour of complete abolition of panchayat courts in Lower Assam as the institution fixed no individual responsibility and greater delay in conducting business. 'The conviction in my mind,' said Capt. Bogle, 'that were the courts to consist of one person and to be under the supervision of the officer-in-Charge of the district to whom appeal should lie, the revision of proceedings would follow to speedily,

TABLE 3.5: STRUCTURE OF AND SALARIES OF OFFICERS IN THE SENIOR AND JUNIOR PANCHAYATS

SENIOR PANCHAYAT		
President		100
2 Members @ 40		80
1 Duftery		4
1 Sidhanta Patra Novis	Rs.	10
Contingencies		9
1 Assamese Mohurer		28
1 Assamese Mohurer		20
2 Assamese Mohurer @ 12		24
		Rs. 275

JUNIOR PANCHAYAT		
President		60
2 Members @ 30		60
1 Duftery		4
1 Sidhanta Patra Novis	Rs.	10
Contingencies		9
1 Assamese Mohurer		24
2 Assamese Mohurer @ 12		24
		Rs. 191

Source: TP (Revenue), 12 August 1833, no. 2. Also see FPP, 30 May 1833, no. 94.

and irregularities, delays or erroneous judgment be directly brought home to the individual in error.'[58] Robertson took into consideration the views of the local people before taking any decision on the recommendations of Capt. Bogle. After having intensive discussions with people he changed his own views on the subject and observed, 'My own opinion did certainly incline to the court as it now stands but all the Assamese with whom I conversed on the subject gave the opinion so decidedly in favour of the single judge i.e., of the court of Sadar Ameen and Munsif, that there can I believe remain little doubt of such being the judicature which they will prefer'.[59] He was, however, apprehensive of the efficiency of munsifs, permanently established in the mofussil without any adequate supervision and opined that such munsif might carry litigation rather than carrying justice to the poor men's door. Robertson suggested that munsif courts that were to be established should be ambulatory in character, accompanying the assistant in his tour of the province and deciding on all such cases falling within his cognizance as he could get through on the spot and bringing the remainders back to be disposed of in the Sadar Station. But before he could take any final decision on the subject of complete abolition of panchayat courts and the constitution of Sadar Ameen and munsif courts Robertson was moved to Calcutta to take up his new assignment of being a Judge of Sadar Court.

The subject of the substitution of courts of Sadar Ameen and munsif for those of the panchayats in Lower Assam was not resolved during the brief tenure of Commissioner Robertson. The matter dragged on and there was complete absence of judicial business at the mofussils. The people living in the interiors of a district had to travel to the Sadar Station to decide every petty dispute in the senior or panchayat courts which were still functioning at Guwahati. The new Commissioner Captain Francis Jenkins immediately on taking charge brought the attention of the Government of Bengal to the subject of introducing single-judge courts in place of panchayats in Lower Assam. The Government of Bengal after voluminous correspondences approved the constitution of Sadar Ameen and munsif courts in Lower Assam and the abolition of panchayat courts as suggested by the local authorities. The government also directed the commissioner to forward the names of experienced native officers for the post of Sadar Ameen and munsif. The Sadar Ameen and munsif were to exercise the same powers and authority as enjoyed by the officers of the same grade in Regulation provinces. The commissioner, however, had discretionary powers as head of a non-Regulation province, giving him the power to make local variations as he deemed fit and proper.

Another post of munsif was sanctioned for six *parganas* in Kamrup with a monthly salary of Rs. 40 and an establishment allowance of Rs. 32.

The newly-appointed munsifs were to be stationed at Guwahati under the immediate control and observation of the assistant in charge of Lower Assam for a period of one year. The assistants were

TABLE 3.6: THE COMPOSITION OF THE SADAR AMEEN
AND MUNSIF COURTS IN LOWER ASSAM
IN APRIL 1835[60]

1. Sadar Ameen Salary		150
Establishment, stationery & contingencies	Rs.	55
2. 3 Munsif Salaries @ Rs. 40		120
Establishment, Stationery & Contingencies @ Rs. 32		96
Total		Rs. 421

Source: BJP (Civil), 14 April 1835, no. 7.

directed to assess their proceedings during the period of their probation and to correct them 'when they feel at a loss or fall into error'.[61] At the end of the probation period the assistant would prepare a report on the conduct and efficiency of the munsifs and detach any of the munsifs to the mofussil and to exercise the full functions allowed therein by the Regulations.

POWERS OF SADAR AMEEN AND THE MUNSIF[62]

The suits for personal or real property up to an amount of Rs. 300 would be cognizable by the munsifs and of Rs. 100 by the Sadar Ameen under the orders of government, but with advertence to the number of small suits and the fear of a large amount, the assistant-in-charge of the district would be pleased to use his discretion in occasionally referring to the Sadar Ameen suits below Rs. 300 and limiting the munsifs to suits below Rs. 200 in amount with a view to an equitable distribution of work amongst the native judges.

Appeals from the courts of munsifs went to the assistant's court, but in case of pressure of other business and the accumulation of appeals the assistant might refer some of the appeals to the Sadar Ameen or to his junior assistant. The appeal that referred to the junior assistant had to be decided with the assistance of assessors as per Regulation VI of 1832.[63]

The decisions of assistants or junior assistants and of Sadar Ameens on the appeals of the decision of munsifs would be final, if they were in conformity with the previous decisions. In case of disagreement a special appeal could be made to the Commissioner's Court.

Appeals on the decisions of the Sadar Ameen had to be tried by the assistant if presented within thirty days and a special appeal would be to the Commissioner's Court if there were disagreements. All suits for sum of money or amount of property above Rs. 1,000 would be cognizable by the Assistant only. In all suits for amounts not exceeding Rs. 500 assistant had the discretionary power to decide such suits with or without the assistance of assessors. But in all cases above Rs. 500 it would be incumbent upon the assistant to avail himself of the assistance of respectable natives.

Appeals on the decisions of assistants were taken up by the Commissioner's Court with a special appeal to the Sadar Dewani Adalat.

In normal circumstances the Sadar Ameen and the munsif were debarred from executing their own decrees. But the assistant was authorized to refer the execution to the Sadar Ameen and the munsif at his discretion.[64]

With the abolition of panchayat courts at Guwahati all its three members were transferred to Darrang since its separation from Lower Assam on an experimental basis as Central Assam. Munsif courts were set up in Central Assam even before the formal constitution of Sadar Ameen and munsif courts in Lower Assam. These munsifs were, however, not functioning as single judges. Instead, they decided civil cases sitting together, exactly in the same manner as panchayat courts. The panchayat courts of the mofussil in Central Assam, however, continued to function as usual till 1835 and in southern part of Central Assam till 1834. However, with the creation of the district of South-Central Assam in July 1833 a munsif court was established at the Sadar Station of Nowgong with panchayat courts in the mofussils. Later the Panchayat court in South-Central Assam was replaced by single-judge Mofussil Munsif Court in 1834. Sadar Ameen was appointed in Lower Assam in the year 1835 while at Darrang and Nowgong in the year 1837. By 1837 all the districts which were under the direct occupation of the British East India Company in Assam, viz., Goalpara, Kamrup, Darrang and Nowgong had Sadar Ameen and munsif courts.

CHANGES IN THE CRIMINAL JUSTICE

Robertson laid down specific rules for the guidance of magistrates in the trial of criminal cases. In all cases of unaggravated burglary, theft, robbery, assault or other crimes of a less aggravated nature, the magistrates were to try the parties accused in the usual manner and to pass sentence to the extent allowed by Regulation XII of 1818, as in similar cases within the Regulation districts. The magistrates had the discretion to pass sentences of imprisonment for a term not exceeding four years, when a person should be convicted simultaneously of two distinct offences.[65]

In all cases of theft and other crimes of aggravated nature, the magistrates were authorized to hold trial themselves without a panchayat, transmitting the proceeding to the commissioner for final orders.[66]

Under the new rules, theoretically, the principal assistant was to exercise the same authority as the magistrate of Bengal; but in practice, he was vested with more extensive powers than a magistrate in the Regulation provinces.

Petty criminal cases were tried by the officiating magistrate without a panchayat as had been the practice. Magistrate could sentence a criminal to an imprisonment for a term not exceeding four years. But in case of murder, the aid of a panchayat was obligatory.

In cases of a more heinous character, like murder or robbery with attempted murder, the magistrate would, after making the necessary preliminary enquiries, fix a date for the trial of the accused. If the merit of the case required a jury, this would be empanelled consisting of not less than three persons for hearing of evidence for the prosecution and defences. All the proceedings of the hearing were to be recorded in the Bengali language. The magistrate would then call upon each member of the jury to give his opinion in writing. Thereafter he would transmit the entire proceedings along with an abstract of the evidence and his own comments on the merit of the cases to the commissioner's office.[67] In all cases of crimes demanding a more severe punishment than imprisonment of fourteen years, the magistrate instead of trying the offenders himself, was to commit the offenders, after investigation, to the Court of Circuit for trial.[68]

At the end of every month, the magistrate would send a statement in a prescribed form in Persian or Bengali language of all prisoners punished by him under the provisions of this rule.

THE AHOM MONARCHY RESTORED IN UPPER ASSAM

In October 1832, it was resolved to assign Upper Assam experimentally to a member of the Ahom royal family who might be considered fit to conduct the administration on the principles of the former government and to the satisfaction of the people. The question then arose as to who was to be raised to the Raj. There were two principal claimants—the former Raja Chandra Kanta, and Purandar Singha. Purandar's claim to succession had been held superior to that of Chandra Kanta in view of his descent from King Rajeswar Singha (1751-69), son of Rudra Singh (1696-1714), whereas the latter descended from a collateral line, viz., Lechai, the Namrupia Raja. The issue was ultimately settled in favour of Purandar Singha. Robertson on behalf of the British East India Company entered into an agreement with Purandar Singha at Guwahati in March 1833 and recognized him as the Raja of the country lying between the Dhansiri and the Dihing in the south bank and Biswanath and Sadiya on the north bank, commonly known as Upper Assam. The main provisions of the treaty were as follows: [69]

- 'The Company made over to Raja Purandar Singha the portion of Assam lying on the south bank of the river Brahamaputra to the east of the river Dhansiri and on the northern bank to the east of a small river near Biswanath.'
- 'The *raja* promised to pay to the East India Company an annual tribute of Rs. 50,000.'
- 'The *raja* bound himself in the administration of justice to abstain from the practices of the former *rajas* of Assam, as to cutting off ears and noses, and extracting eyes or otherwise mutilating or torturing, and that he would, generally, assimilate the administration of justice in his territory to that which pre-

vailed in the Company's possession. Further, he would not permit the immolation of women by *sati*'.
- 'He also agreed to listen with attention to the advice of the Political Agent, Upper Assam, or to that of the Agent to the Governor-General.'
- 'He further promised to surrender on demand from the British officials any fugitive from justice who might take refuge in his territory; and he was to apply to those officers for the arrest of any individuals who might flee from his territory into the Company's or of any other states.'
- 'It was distinctly understood that the treaty invested the *raja* with no power over the Moamaria country of the Barsenapati'.
- 'In the event of Purandar's continuing faithfulness to the terms of the treaty, the British government agreed to protect him from foreign aggression, but if he should in any way depart from a faithful adherence to the same and be guilty of oppressing the people of the country entrusted to his charge, it was reserved to the East India Company either to transfer the said territory to another ruler, or to take it into its own immediate occupation.'

Purandar made necessary changes in the administration of justice in the territory under his jurisdiction. The lowest courts in the administration of civil justice in Purandar's territory were those of *kheldars*, who were empowered to try civil suits up to Rs. 10.[70] They were also authorized to investigate complaints or irregularities or exaction of the *omlahs*. The Court of *Gram Adhikars* or District Judges were set up at Rangpur, Majuli, Uttorpar (north bank of the river Brahmaputra, i.e. in North Lakhimpur), Bassa and Dayang. Besides having authority to enquire into cases of extortion or oppression by public officers, they had the jurisdiction to decide 'cases up to one hundred rupees and to hear appeals against the decisions of Kheldar's Court'.[71] At the capital two panchayats were instituted to deal with petty cases and also to hear the proceedings of the lower courts. The Barbarua's Court was vested with the power of deciding civil suits to the extent of Rs. 1,000. At the helm of the administration of civil justice stood the Supreme Court consisting of the *raja* as the president and three judges to try civil cases above Rs. 1,000. No written pleadings or depositions were allowed in the local or district courts. The *kheldars* were empowered to try criminal cases involving a penalty not exceeding imprisonment for six months and with power to inflict punishment of fifteen stripes or a fine of Rs. 20. The Barbarua's Court was authorized to try criminal cases with a power to award sentences of imprisonment to the extent of three years.[72] The heinous crimes of decoity and homicide were to be tried by the *raja*, who could award a sentence of imprisonment to the extent of fourteen years.

Raja Purandar Singha made adequate efforts to improve the administration of justice. He took prompt measures to remedy the evils of the European system of judiciary established by the Company's government and to make justice within easy reach of all. The judicial system was thoroughly reorganized by the efforts of the *raja*. Regular courts began functioning in his territory with defined jurisdiction and powers.

Despite the *raja's* complete control, the judicial machinery was obviously not working according to his expectation. There was, of course, some mismanagement in the judicial department. The principal complaint was against the corrupt *omlahs* in the departments of both civil and criminal justice. The *omlahs* and the *darogas* were stated to have been, 'in the habit of protecting robbers, concealing theft and other malpractice common to *darogas* of the period'.[73] Allegations were made of vexatious interference of the magisterial police in taking cognizance of complaints of abuse, assaults and trifling thefts—all these under the new arrangement were to have devolved upon the heads of the villages. In other respects, the administration of justice was found to be tolerably efficient. On the whole, admitted Major White, Political Agent, and Upper Assam. 'The Faujdari department had not been so pure or efficient when the province was under the British rule . . . it has not fallen much short of it.'[74] White also admitted that the raja's *dewani* decisions had given satisfaction to the *ryots* than those of this European predecessors.

ADMINISTRATIVE RE-ORGANIZATION

Robertson realized that scanty European officers employed in Assam and inadequate supervision were mainly responsible for the mismanagement of the province. To effectively control the native officials and to extend considerable relief to the people of the interior, Robertson in October 1832, entrusted Lieutenant Rutherford with the responsibility to look after Central Assam independently.[75] In fact, he separated Central Assam from Lower Assam without even obtaining approval from the Government of Bengal.[76]

After deciding to restore Upper Assam experimentally to *Swargodeo* Purandar Singha, Commissioner Robertson proposed in February 1833 to divide Assam into four districts excluding Goalpara as under (1) A small district called Biswanath on the north bank of the river Brahmaputra having a boundary from Biswanath in the east to the River Bharalee in the west and on the south bank from the river Dhansiri in the east to Raha in the west along the hill; (2) Central Assam including the provinces of Chardoar, Darrang, Nowgong and Raha with their dependencies; (3) Lower Assam, consisting of 20 *parganas* of the large province of Kamrup including Nine Doars on the south bank of the river Brahmaputra; and (4) Six *parganas*, comprising six western *parganas* of Kamrup.[77] The native establishments as proposed by Robertson were sanctioned by the Government of Bengal in May 1833. Arrangements were also being made for the European establishments of this province. The table in Appendix 3.1 gives an idea of the judicial establishment and corresponding expenditure incurred under Robertson gives an idea of of the British occupied areas of the province.[78]

In each district there would be a European officer designated as principal assistant to the Commissioner of Assam. The Supreme government accorded their approval for the above measures as proposed by Robertson with some modification. Accordingly, Major White was to retain his present office and allowances as Political Agent, Upper Assam ordinarily stationed at Biswanath. Captain Davidson was to be principal assistant at Goalpara. Lower Assam was to be placed under Lieutenant Matthie. Captain Bogle was appointed as the principal assistant at Biswanath with a sphere of authority extending to Darrang. The Six-Parganas, which was under Captain Bogle, was to be transferred to be placed under Goalpara jurisdiction. Lieutenant Rutherford, junior assistant ordinarily stationed at Biswanath but now deputed to Nowgong to look after the southern part of the Central Assam had a sphere of authority extending to Dharampur.[79] Following Lieutenant Matthie's sojourn in Cherrapunjee due to bad health some changes had to be made in allotting several districts to the European functionaries. Captain Bogle was asked to take charge of Lower Assam, while Central Assam was placed under Lieutenant Rutherford. Rutherford had already served in the areas of Desh Darrang (Darrang), Chardoar, Nowgong and Morung in Central Assam as junior assistant under Lieutenant Matthie. In July 1833 Central Assam was experimentally divided into two districts North-Central Assam and South-Central Assam.[80] Hamilton Vetch, a Junior Assistant, was appointed to assist Lieutenant Rutherford in the areas of Nowgong, Raha, Dharampur and Jomnamokh of the South-Central Assam leaving Rutherford exclusively in charge of the northern division.[81] Lieutenant Matthie joined to his duties recovering from illness and Lieutenant Rutherford handed over the charge of North-Central Assam to James Matthie on 18 December 1833.[82] He was posted at North-Central Assam without disturbing Captain Bogle. At the beginning of the year 1834 the five districts of Assam were as follows:[83] (1) Goalpara under Captain Alexander Davidson, (2) Six-Parganas under the charge of Junior Assistant Captain Cathcart with the head stationed at Barpeta, (3) Lower Assam under Captain Archibald Bogle, (4) North-Central Assam under Lieutenant James Matthie, and (5) South-Central Assam under Henry Rutherford, besides a small district was maintained at Biswanath under Captain Adam White, Political Agent, and Upper Assam.

APPOINTMENT OF FRANCIS JENKINS

In January 1834 the Supreme government abolished the office of the Political Agent to the North-East Frontier of Bengal and Commissioner of Rangpur, and in its place created the distinct office of the Commissioner and Agent to the Governor-General for Assam and north-east Rangpur. On 28 February 1834, Captain Francis

Jenkins relieved T.C. Robertson of his duties as Agent to Governor-General and Commissioner for Assam and north-east Rangpur.[84]

The new commissioner's administrative reforms built a superstructure whose foundation had been laid by T.C. Robertson and thus gave to this province the basic administrative set-up that continued for long without major changes.

Jenkins introduced important changes in the administration of civil justice. The civil panchayat set up by David Scott and retained by Robertson in Guwahati was overburdened and struggled with accumulated arrears. The judicial procedure followed in these courts was cumbersome and often resulted in delays and uncertainties. Jenkins abolished these courts, transferring their duties to the Sadar Ameen and munsif under the supervision of assistant-in-charge of Lower Assam.

The Sadar Ameen and the munsif were invested with the same powers that their counterparts possessed in the Regulation provinces under the provisions of Regulation V of 1831 and the Regulation VII of 1832. Hence, they were to be guided by the spirit of those regulations.[85]

In October 1834, Assam was placed under the jurisdiction of Sadar Dewani and Nizamat Adalat in all matters connected with civil and criminal administration of the province.[86]

DIVISION OF THE COUNTRY MADE PERMANENT

The experimental division of Central Assam by Robertson was found to have worked well. This arrangement was made permanent and all the districts were placed under one principal assistant. On the other hand, attempts to relieve the principal assistant at Kamrup from excessive duties by separating Six-Parganas from it did not yield the desired result, because the officer-in-charge of that area had to remain at Guwahati instead of Barpeta to assist the principal assistant there. The *parganas* were, therefore, reannexed to the district of Kamrup. The district and the officer in-charge are given in Table 3.7.[87]

Besides, each officer in-charge was to be aided by a junior assistant or sub-assistant in the discharge of his duties. Capt. H. Ruther-

TABLE 3.7: OFFICERS-IN-CHARGE OF VARIOUS DISTRICTS OF ASSAM

Districts	Name of the Officer	Designation	Salary
North-East Rangpur	Capt. A. Davidson	Principal Assistant	1,000
Lower Assam	Capt. A. Bogle	Principal Assistant	1,000
North-Central Assam	Capt. J. Matthie	Principal Assistant	1,000
South-Central Assam	Capt. H. Rutherford	Principal Assistant	1,000

Source: BJP (Criminal), 23 February 1835, nos. 48-50, Jenkins to Macnanghten, 23 January 1835. Also see BJP (Criminal), 17 February 1834, no. 63.

ford, junior assistant at north-central Assam was promoted to the post of principal assistant. Later, acting on the suggestion of Capt. Jenkins, the Government of Bengal made alterations in the designations of the divisions which were unknown to the natives. Accordingly, noth-east Rangpur was to be called as the division of Goalpara, Lower Assam as Kamrup, north-central Assam as Darrang and southern-central Assam as Nowgong.[88]

NOTES

1. BSPC, 2 May 1828, no. 11, Scott to Swinton, 29 March 1828 quoted in S.K. Bhuyan, *AAR*, p. 569.
2. FPP., 23 July 1832, no. 70, Robertson to Swinton, 30 June 1832.
3. FPP, 30 May 1833, no. 83, Robertson to Secretary Bengal, 4 February 1833.
4. TP (Revenue), 22 September 1834, no. 9, Bogle to Robertson, 1 August 1833.
5. Ibid.
6. FPP, 23 July 1832, no. 70, Robertson to Swinton, 30 June 1832.
7. RP., 9 June 1835, no. 6, Extracts from a letter from the Court of Directors no. 14, 3 December 1834.
8. FPP, 28 May 1830, no. 76, Scott to Swinton, 22 April 1830.
9. FPP, 30 May 1833, no. 87.
10. FPP, 30 May 1833, no. 83, Robertson to Secretary Bengal, 4 February 1833.
11. TP (Revenue), 9 December 1833, no. 12, Robertson to Macsween, 29 October 1833.
12. RP, 9 June 1835, no. 6, Extracts from a letter from the Hon'ble Court of Directors, no. 14, 3 December 1834.

13. TP (Revenue), 1 July 1833, no. 3, Robertson to Macnaughten. Extracts from the proceedings of the Governor-General in Council, 6 June 1833.
14. TP (Revenue), 11 August 1834, no. 5, Matthie to Robertson, 10 January 1834.
15. FPP, 30 May 1833, no. 83, Robertson to Secretary Bengal, 4 February 1833.
16. Ibid.
17. FPP, 23 July 1832, no. 70.
18. Ibid.
19. RP, 9 June 1835, no. 6.
20. Ibid.
21. TP (Revenue), 1 July 1933, no. 3, Rutherford to Robertson, 28 March 1833.
22. FPP, 23 July 1832, no. 70, Major Adam White to Governor General's Agent, 28 May 1832.
23. FPP, 10 June 1831, no. 58, Neufville to Scott, 29 April 1830.
24. TP (Revenue), 1 July 1833, no. 3
25. FPP, 16 September 1830, no. 47, Scott to Swinton, 29 July 1830.
26. BJP, December 1870, no. 2, Agnew to Secretary Bengal, 18 August 1869.
27. BPC, 10 June 1831, no. 50, quoted in AIDC p. 49.
28. FPP, 23 July 1832, no. 70.
29. TP (Revenue), 22 September 1834, no. 9, Bogle to Robertson,1 August 1833.
30. Bengal Political Proceedings, 23 July 1832, nos. 70-1, quoted from AIDC p. 65.
31. FPP, 10 June, no. 50, Scott to Swinton, 18 May 1831.
32. TP (Revenue), 1 July 1833, no. 3, Extracts from the Rt. Hon'ble the Governor-General in Council in the political department under date the 6th June 1833.
33. FPP, 30 May 1833, no. 93, Robertson to Secretary Bengal, 21 March 1833.
34. BJP (Civil), 14 April, no. 5.
35. FSP, 12 March 1830, no. 31.
36. RP, 9 June 1835, no. 6.
37. Ibid.
38. FSP, 12 March 1830, no. 32.
39. AIDC, p. 52.
40. FSP, 12 March 1830, no. 17, Neufville to Scott, 27 December 1828.
41. Ibid., no. 15, Scott to Swinton, 14 March 1829.
42. Ibid., no. 16.

43. Srutidev Goswami, *Gomdhar Konwar's Rebellion: A Reprisal*, p. 190 Proceedings of North-East India History Association, 1990.
44. AIDC, p. 57.
45. Ibid.
46. TP (Revenue), 8 Novemver 1831, no. 10, proceedings of the Council, 1 November 1831.
47. FPP, 7 May 1832, no. 26.
48. BJP (Civil), 25 October 1836, no. 18, Robertson to Macsween, 5 August 1833.
49. BJP (Civil), 25 August 1834, no. 16.
50. Ibid.
51. Ibid.
52. Ibid.
53. Ibid.
54. The introduction of stamps in Assam at the time of instituting a suit, as proposed by Commissioner Robertson in Section V of his brief code, received the consent of the Government of Bengal with modification. The rate was reduced by the Government of Bengal in their letter to Commissioner Jenkins no. 1414, dt. 7 July 1834: BJP (Criminal), no. 12, 7 July 1834. The revised rate would be 8 *annas* for all original suits and appeals involving an amount not exceeding Rs. 150. The Court of Directors, however, expressed its displeasure with the decision of the local authorities in introducing stamps in Assam in spite of their clear direction on the subject. In October 1834 the Supreme government asked the Government of Bengal to convey to the Commissioner of Assam that Section V of the proposed rules was cancelled and a provision inserted in lieu thereof to the effect that no fee should be levied on the institution of a suit in any court of justice within the province of Assam. BJP (Criminal), no. 53, 3 December 1834, Macnaghten, Officiating Chief Secretary, Government of India to Macsween, Sec. Bengal, dt. 9 October 1834.
55. BJP (Civil), no. 9, 10 November 1834, Jenkins to Secretary Macsween, 27 October 1834.
56. FPP, 30 May 1833, no. 93, Robertson to Secretary, 21 March 1833.
57. TP (Revenue), 12 August 1833, no. 2, also see FPP, 30 May 1833, no. 94.
58. BJP (Civil), no. 9, 10 November 1834, Captain Bogle to Jenkins, 4 October 1834.
59. BJP (Civil), no. 20; 25 August 1834, Robertson to Secretary Macsween, 28 February 1834.
60. BJP (Civil), no. 7, 14 April 1835, R.D. Mongles, Secretary Government of Bengal to Commissioner of Assam, 14 April 1835.

61. BJP (Civil), 26 May 1835, no. 3, Jenkins to Captain Bogle, 8 May 1835.
62. Ibid.
63. Ibid.
64. BJP (Civil), no. 4, 26 May 1835, Secretary R.D. Mongles, 26 May 1835.
65. BJP (Criminal), 20 October 1835, no. 55, see rules for the guidance of Magistrate in Assam in the trial of Criminal Cases issued on 28 July 1834.
66. Ibid.
67. Ibid.
68. On 3 December 1828, Commissioner Scott was selected by the Government of Bengal for appointment as Commissioner of Revenue and Circuit of Assam with special powers under Regulation I of 1829. He was to hold sessions of Gaol delivery with the same powers as for the judges of the previous Courts of Circuit, see M.N. Gupta's *Analytical Survey of Bengal Regulations*, pp. 129-30.
69. BPC, 30 May 1833, no. 91 quoted in AIDC, pp. 82-3.
70. AIDC, p. 116.
71. Ibid., The Annexation of Assam, also, p. 194.
72. Ibid.
73. AIDC, p. 127.
74. Ibid., p. 128.
75. FPP, 26 November 1832, no. 82.
76. BJP (Criminal), 1835; 20 October, no. 50.
77. FPP, 30 May 1833, no. 86, Robertson to Secretary Bengal, 7 February 1833.
78. TP (Revenue), 12 August 1833, no. 2, also FPP, 30 May 1833, no. 94.
79. TP (Revenue), 12 August 1833, no. 2, extract from a letter to the Agent to Governor-General, N.E. Frontier, 30 May 1833.
80. BJP (Criminal), 20 October 1835, no. 51.
81. Ibid., 12 August 1833, no. 52.
82. FPP, 3 January 1834, no. 116.
83. TP (Revenue), 18 August 1834, no. 1.
84. BJP (Criminal), 10 March 1834, no. 69, Robertson to Macsween, 28 February 1834.
85. BJP (Civil), 26 May 1835, no. 3, Jenkins to Bogle, 8 May 1835.
86. BJP (Criminal), 25 August 1834, no. 28, Resolution of the Vice-President-in-Council, Governor-General's minute recorded on 18 January 1834.
87. BJP (Criminal), 1835; 23 February, nos. 48 & 50, Jenkins to Macnaugten, 23 January 1835, also BJP (Criminal), 17 February 1834, no. 63.
88. BJP (Criminal), 23 February 1835, no. 49, Macnaughten to Jenkins, 23 February 1835.

APPENDIX 3.1

LOWER ASSAM

FAUJDARI ESTABLISHMENT

Designation of Officers	Salary/Expenditure in Rs.
Sheristadar	60
Report Novis	30
Mahafiz	30
2 Assamese boys learning*	6
2 Mohurers @ 20	40
2 Mohurers @ 15	30
2 Mohurers @ 12	24
Persian Mohurer	25
Nazir	30
Mohurer to Nazir	10
Treasure's Mohurer	15
2 English Writers	75
Duftery	6
Koranee	10
Gangajollia	10
Jamadar	10
4 Chaprasies @ 6	24
Contingencies	10
	445

JAIL ESTABLISHMENT

Darogah	25
Mohurer	10
2 Duffadars	16
20 Barkandozes @ 5	100
Jamadar	10
Contingencies and Stationery	4
	165

* Owing to the unavailability of trained local people to work as *mohurer* (clerk) in the administration, Commissioner Robertson decided to attach in his court and also in district courts a few local boys as trainee *mohurer* in the year 1833. The practice, however, was discontinued in August 1862.

The Administration of Justice in Assam

HAZUT JAIL ESTABLISHMENT

Designation of Officers	Salary/Expenditure in Rs.
6 Borkandozes @ 5	30
8 Teckelas @ 2/8	20
	50

DEWANI ESTABLISHMENT

Designation of Officers	Salary/Expenditure in Rs.
Head Mohurer	30
Persian Mohurer	25
Bengali Mohurer	20
Assamese	20
Muhafiz	25
Treasurer's Mohurer	12
Contingencies	5
Duftry	5
2 Chaprasies @ 6	12
1 Dak Mohurer	5
1 English Writer	5
1 Govt. Vakeel	10
	174

There were two panchayat courts, viz., senior and junior panchayat with an estimated expenditure of Rs. 275 and Rs. 191 respectively.

CENTRAL ASSAM

FAUJDARI ESTABLISHMENT

Designation of Officers	Salary/Expenditure in Rs.
Sheristadar	60
Roobkari Novis	30
Mahafiz	25
2 Mohurers @ 20	40
2 Mohurers @ 15	30
2 Mohurers @ 12	24
Persian Mohurer	25
English Writers	40
Nazir & Jail Darogah	35
Nazir's Mohurer	10

contd.

CENTRAL ASSAM contd.

Designation of Officers	Salary/Expenditure in Rs.
Treasurer's Muhorir	15
Duftery	4
Koranee	5
Gangajollia	5
Jamadar	10
4 Borkandozes @ 5	20
4 Chaprasies @ 6	24
10 Teckelas @ 2/8	25
Contingencies	16
	443

JAIL ESTABLISHMENT

Jamadar	10
2 Duffadars @ 6	12
30 Barkandozes @ 4	120
Native Doctor	25
	167

CENTRAL ASSAM (DARRANG)

Roobkari Navis	30
Mahafiz	25
Persian	25
Mohurer	20
2 Mohurers @ 15	30
4 Chaprasies @ 6	24
Contingencies	12
Sadar Ameen	100
Sadar Munsif	60
Munsif	40
Munsif	30
3 Mohurer @ 12	36
	432

NOWGONG

Designation of Officers	Salary/Expenditure in Rs.
Munsif	30
2 Mohurer @ 10	20
Burra	4
6 Teckelas @ 2/8	15
Contingencies	8
	77

ESTABLISHMENT FOR THE SIX-PARAGANAS OF LOWER ASSAM

DEWANI ESTABLISHMENT

2 Mohurers @ 15	30
2 Chaprasies @ 5	10
Sarjamnee	5
1 Munsif	50
1 Head Mohurer	20
1 Under Mohurer	10
Sarjamnee	5
1 Chaprasie	5
	135

FAUJDARI ESTABLISHMENT

Peshkar	30
Mohurer	30
Sarjamnee	5
	65

Growth and Development of the Administration of Justice 115

ESTABLISHMENT PROPOSED FOR THE OFFICE OF THE
LOCAL SUPERINTENDENT AND POLITICAL AGENT
STATIONED AT BISWANATH

JUDICIAL DEPARTMENT

Designation of Officers	Salary/Expenditure in Rs.
1 Peshkar	50
2 Muharer @ 25	50
1 Record Keeper	30
1 Interpreter	10
1 Parwana Novis	10
2 Chaprasies @ 6	12
1 Duftery	5
1 Bhaugratee	6
1 Koranree	6
Contingencies & Stationery	10
Jail Establishment	57
Sadar Police	119
2 Out Chowkies	50
Munsif with establishment	75
	490

REVENUE DEPARTMENT

1 Parwana Novis	20
1 Record Keeper	15
1 Juma Novis	20
1 Sadar Novis	15
1 Duftery	5
Stationery	10
2 Chaprasies @Rs. 3	6
	91

contd.

GENERAL DEPARTMENT

Designation of Officers	Salary/Expenditure in Rs.
1 Sheristadar	100
2 English Writer @ Rs.50	100
1 Treasurer	40
1 Mohurer's Treasurer	12
1 Pedea	10
1 English office Duftery	5
1 Jamadar	8
6 Chaprasies @ 6	36
1 Burmese Interpreter	8
1 Shan Interpreter	8
Intelligence Department	150
Gun Boat Establishment	276
	753
Extra Allowance to Surgeon of the Assam Light Infantry for attending jail	100
Total Sicca Rupees	1,434

Source: TP (Revenue), 12 August 1833, no. 2. Also see FPP, 30 May 1833, no. 94.

CHAPTER 4

Judicial Administration from the Promulgation of the Assam Code till the End of the East India Company's Rule

PREPARATION OF A CODE

Prior to 1837, Assam did not have any code of civil and criminal laws nor was there any law of limitation and penal code. By and large, the laws administered by the courts of Assam up to 1837 were same as those in force in Bengal and most of them were issued during the time of David Scott in the form of circulars and orders. Later, Commissioner Robertson prepared a very brief code for the administration of civil justice. This code, though a great improvement over the previous one, was found to be quite inadequate to meet the growing needs of the time. The mixed system of Regulation laws and *lex-loci* created much confusion, especially amongst the native judges. No one was clear as to which Regulations or which parts of the Regulations were in force in Assam. The decisions of the court were not regulated by a uniform method of dispensing justice based on a properly written law, civil or criminal, and as such the verdicts varied depending upon the individual interpretation of rules and regulations by the men who composed the court. There was also no well-defined procedure for filing a suit, or for the conduct of proceedings after it had been filed.

Under the circumstances a set of definite civil and criminal laws and procedures was found to be most essential for the efficient administration of justice. Otherwise, there would be unnecessary expenses, delays and uncertain application of laws and as a result, the administration of justice would be worthless and ineffective. With this aim in view, the Government of Bengal directed the local authorities in Assam to prepare a simple but comprehensive code of civil and criminal laws and procedure. Accordingly, local authorities prepared a draft of this code with great labour and pain, which was approved by the government and introduced in the province in May 1837. It was known as Rules for the Administration of Civil and Criminal Justice, commonly called the Assam Code.[1] This code had been compiled from the rules already in force in Assam, collated with those observed in other provinces to which the ordinary Regulations had not yet been extended.[2]

After the introduction of the code, the civil and criminal courts of Assam were bound to administer justice in accordance with its provisions; but in laws not provided in the code, they were required to conform, as nearly as the circumstances of the province would permit, to the provisions of the Regulation in force elsewhere in the Presidency of Fort William.[3] It included rules of procedure, both civil and criminal, a short penal code, rules relating to mortgage, registry of deed, employment and remuneration of vakeels, *nazirs* and their peons.

ADMINISTRATION OF CIVIL JUSTICE

In the administration of civil justice, the object of the local government was to avoid technicality and circumlocution and to simplify and abridge every rule and procedure. It was believed that by doing so substantial justice could be extended to the people, who were unused to the intricacies of legal proceedings.

Procedural Law

The process to be followed in the trial of suits was prescribed by definite rules. First, if the suit was for land, house, money due on a bond, agreement, or commercial transaction, the petition of the complainant was to be filed and numbered according to its place in the yearly list. Second, 15 were allowed to the defendant for giving an answer. In the event of the reply not being filed within that period, a proclamation was to be affixed, if possible, to the abode of the defendant, and a copy of it to be affixed in the courtroom, calling upon the defendant to file a reply within 15 days from its date. On the expiry of the second period, if no reply were submitted, the case would be tried *ex-parte*. Third, on a reply being filed within the prescribed period, the plaintiff was to be asked if he wished to rejoin. If the plaintiff wishes to do so, ten days time was to be allowed for that purpose and a further period of five days for a replication, in the event of the defendant wishing to file one.[4]

On the pleadings being completed in the manner above prescribed, the parties were to produce their proofs. The parties were to be allowed an option of bringing up their own witnesses or of having subpoenas served upon them by *peadas*. When the witnesses were be in attendance, their depositions were to be taken in writing in the Bengali language, in the presence of the assistant in-charge of the district. The assistant, however, was allowed to delegate this duty to a junior assistant, or to the head ministerial officers of his court in the event of his other avocations rendering it impossible for him to attend to this duty. On all evidences, documentary and parole, being filed, the assistant was to proceed to pass judgement in open court, recording the substance of his decision immediately, in a book to be kept by him for that purpose, and attesting the entry therein with his signature before leaving the court.[5]

The assistants were authorized not to admit any petition of a plaint in an original suit if it appeared to be *prima facie* inadmissible. The assistants were to make a summary enquiry into the merits of each petition before bringing it to their regular file. If the suit appeared to be frivolous or vexatious, they were at liberty to reject the same without calling upon the defendant for a reply. The parties discontented with such order of rejection could appeal to the commissioner, who might, after calling for the original petition and proceedings held upon it, direct the assistant to admit and proceed upon the same as a regular suit.[6]

It was not to be incumbent on the assistant to bring any petition of a plaint relating to a question of caste or marriage on his file of regular suit. But he might summarily dispose of it recording the result briefly on the back of the petition. The commissioner, however, could direct that the case be tried as a regular suit.[7]

The assistant could insist on the attendance, in person, both of the plaintiff and the defendant in any original suit and examine them on oath before bringing the suit on his file. In all cases in which the meeting of the parties could be affected, their depositions had to be recorded and taken to be the plaint and reply in the suit. But any party feeling aggrieved by such a requisition, might appeal to the commissioner and the execution of the order could be stayed pending the appeal.[8]

Vakeels or Pleaders

There were no regular vakeels or pleaders attached to any of the courts in Assam. It was an important feature of the system of civil procedure to bring the litigants face to face with the courts. However, if any party wished to appoint a vakeel, they could employ any person to act in that capacity. The remuneration of the vakeel was settled by mutual agreement. The commissioner was empowered to dismiss any vakeel in any court if he found him to be incompetent. The individual affected by such a decision could make an appeal to the Sadar Dewany Adalat, which could revise the decision of the commissioner. The courts of the province were also competent, after recording reasons, to reject any individual whom a party might wish to employ as vakeel in any particular suit. But the superior court might cancel such an order allowing the person affected by it to act as vakeel for the party wishing to employ him.[9]

The parties appointing vakeels had to deposit in the court the usual fee of 5 per cent of the value of the property litigated. The vakeel could recover any further sum, to which he might be entitled under the agreement concluded between him and his employer.

Execution of Decrees

The petitioner praying for a warrant to enforce a decree, whether given in the court of the commissioner, the assistant, the Sadar Ameen, munsif or other European functionaries was to present his petition to the commissioner or the principal assistant. Petition for the enforcement of decrees had to be presented within one year from the date on which such decree was passed. The commissioner, however, was empowered to relax the above provision if good and sufficient reasons were shown for the delay in submitting the petition.[10]

The execution of a decree passed by an Assistant Sadar Ameen or munsif could not be stayed except in case of appeal. But the appellant had to give security for the due fulfilment of the decree. If the appellant failed to furnish security, the respondent was at liberty to cause the decree to be carried into execution on giving security for performing the final order to be passed by the higher court.

The superior court in which an appeal was admitted was competent to stay the execution of decree, pending trial of such appeal, even without exacting security from the appellant. In case of decrees not appealed against, *dustak* was to be issued for the arrest of the party cast. Should the party absent himself or fail to pay, the *peadas*, entrusted with the enforcement of the process were to attach all his movable property. The property so attached had to be disposed of by the *nazir* after getting order from the court of the assistant. The amount of proceeds arising from the sale was to be paid over to decree holder. Otherwise the proceeds had to be deposited in the court of the assistant. A deduction of 5 per cent was to be made from the proceeds to cover the expenses of sale.[11]

If the amount realized from the sale of the movable property did not satisfy the decree, all the immovable and landed property of the party, against whom a decree had been passed (debtor), was to be attached by the *nazir* in the presence of some of debtor's neighbours. All landed property had to be attached by the collector of the district, which was to be sold on the expiry of the period to be fixed by the commissioner, after receiving details of such properties from the assistant. The collector in whose presence the property was to be sold had to remit the proceeds of the sale to the assistant to satisfy the balance of the decree.

If the proceeds arising from the sale of a debtor's movable and immovable property did not satisfy the amount of the decree, the claimant could file a petition for the arrest of the debtor. But in that case, he was required to deposit money for the subsistence of the debtor, who might then be placed in jail.[12]

The party applying for the arrest of another for the amount of a decree was required to lodge with the *nazir* fund for the subsistence of the detainee for two months. At the expiration of the first month, the claimant was to be called on to lodge funds for two more months' subsistence. If he failed to lodge the amount before the expiration of the first month, the *nazir* was to report it to the assistant who would then release the debtor. No debtor so released was to be liable to any further process of arrest on the same ground or at the instance of the same party except on proof of dishonest conduct.

The rates for the subsistence of the debtor could not exceed 3 *annas* and could not be lower than 1 *anna* per *diem*. The actual rate was to be fixed by the assistant based on the social status of the debtor.[13]

The fraudulent concealment of property with a view to evading the execution of decrees, or of obtaining permission to sue as a pauper, and also any act of violent resistance to the enforcement of a decree or order of a civil court was to be accounted as a misdemeanour punishable by a fine or imprisonment with or without labour.

The court enforcing a decree might order the release of the debtors in confinement upon their surrendering their property in satisfaction of the judgement passed.

Should a claimant discover more of a debtor's property after his release the same might be attached and disposed of by the assistant to satisfy the balance of the decree.[14]

REGISTRATION

The code provided that an office for the registry of deeds had to be established in the districts of Assam, under the immediate charge of the junior or the sub-assistant, as the Commissioner might determine. A single book made of English paper would be used as register. The pages of this book were to be numbered and each leaf was to be signed by the senior assistant in-charge of the district.

He was to certify at the end of the book the number of pages affixing his signature at full length along with the date. A fee of Re. 1 was to be paid on the registry of any deed, and a fee of 8 *annas* on a copy being taken from the book. The fees were to be the perquisite of the junior or sub-assistant having charge of the books, who was to defray the expense attending their purchase and preservation. The registry of deeds, however, was not compulsory. In 1844, the junior or sub-assistant detached to the interior of the district allowed a office of the registry of deeds other than the district Registration Office.[15]

MORTGAGES

It was enacted that if the property mortgaged had been held from the date of the mortgage by the mortgagees, the party who had mortgaged the same was entitled to recover possession on the expiration of the term of mortgage by tendering the amount due on the said deed.

Wherever it might appear that the profits accruing from the usufruct of the property ought, under the conditions of the transaction, to be received in lieu of interest, the payment, tender, or deposit of the principal of the sum borrowed should be sufficient to entitle the mortgager to recover possession of the property mortgaged.

In the event of any mortgagee refusing to receive the sum due to him, according to the conditions of the transaction, the mortgager might deposit the sum in the court. The officer presiding over the court should then issue a notification to the mortgagee, calling upon him within a given time to receive the money. After the expiration of the period specified in the notification, the assistant in-charge of the district might either proceed to conduct further enquiry himself, or might prefer the case for trial to the Sadar Ameen. If it was satisfactorily established that the transaction was a bonafide one and the party applying to the court had deposited the full amount due to the mortgagee, the complainant might, forthwith and without further suit, be replaced with possession of the property mortgaged.[16]

Any person holding a deed of mortgage could foreclose the same after the expiration of the period specified in the deed. In that case the person or his representative had to petition the court with the original deed of mortgage praying that the opposite party might be called upon to pay the amount that might be due thereon. The officer presiding over the court would serve a notice to the mortgagor calling upon him to pay the stipulated amount into the court within the term of one year from the date on which such notice might be served. In the event of the mortgagor not being found, a proclamation was to be issued. In case the mortgagor failed to attend and pay on the expiration of the terms prescribed, the mortgage would be held to have foreclosed.[17]

In every case of mortgage, the court before which it might be tried had to enquire into the amount that might have accrued to the mortgagee from the proceeds of the estate and had to make a corresponding deduction from the sum that must be paid in order to procure the redemption of the same. If it should appear that the sum originally lent with legal interest had been realized out of the profits derived from the possession of the property, then the mortgage should be held to have been from that date redeemed. The mortgagee was to be held liable to the mortgagor for any surplus that he might thus have appropriated.[18]

In cases, where no term was specified in the deed, the parties concerned could, at any period, take advantage of the provisions of this rule, to either redeem or foreclose the mortgage. Such cases were common in Assam.

To prevent the ill-effects of a mortgage, in which money was lent upon the implied security of persons not actually parties to the transaction, it was held that a decree was never to be passed or enforced against any individual not actually or and severally indicated by name in the petition of a plaint.

Many transactions partaking of nature of a mortgage had been concluded in Assam on the basis of verbal agreement. It was enacted that the conditions of all existing contracts of that description were to be enforced as far as possible in conformity with the provisions of this Assam code. But no mortgage not supported by a written deed was, henceforth, to be taken cognizance of by any civil court in the province.[19]

Summary Suit Court

The assistant in-charge of a district had to hold the summary suit court in his capacity as collector. A junior or sub-assistant could also hold such court with the sanction of the commissioner. The assistant might employ one of the *munsifs* of his division to sit and act with him as an assessor in the Summary Suit Court.[20]

All the complaints related to arrears or undue exaction of rent, or disputed revenue accounts, were to be received by the assistant in his capacity as collector, and be heard and decided in the Summary Suit Court. No suit for arrears, exactions of rent, or the adjustment of revenue accounts, could be received in the Summary Suit Court, unless it was preferred within one month from the close of the year to which they were related.

Parties convicted of unduly exacting or attempting to exact money on the plea of revenue were declared liable to be fined or committed to civil jail. A portion of the fine, which could not exceed four times the value of the amount extorted or wrongfully demanded, might be awarded as compensation to the party aggrieved. The persons discontented with the decision of the Summary Suit Court might appeal to the commissioner, provided their petition of appeal be presented within six weeks from the date of the order complained of. The commissioner had the right to reject or admit the appeal. He could also amend, cancel or confirm the decision of the Summary Suit Court and refer the party complaining to a regular suit for redress. The parties, preferring that course, might, in the first instance, seek redress in matters connected with arrears, or undue exaction, or settlement of revenue accounts, by a regular suit in the civil court. But such court could not take cognizance of the case unless the plaint was accompanied by the order of the commissioner by which the party was referred to a regular suit. A special appeal, if presented within three months from the date of the final order of the commissioner on the case, might be received by the Sadar Board of Revenue.[21]

Claims instituted by the collector against any individual denominated as *bhakats (bhugguts)* or descendants of persons attached in former times to any religious institution for revenue alleged to be due from them to the government, could be cognizable in the

Summary Suit Court. This court was considered competent to take decision on the matter as it deemed fit and proper.[22]

APPEAL TO COURTS

The parties discontented with the decision of a *munsif* or *sadar ameen* might, within one month from the date thereof, submit a petition of appeal to the assistant, who was in-charge of the district. The Assistant might refer for trial to a *sadar ameen* appeals from the decisions of a *munsif*.[23]

The parties discontented with the decision of an assistant in any suit tried in the first instance before him, might within a period of two months from the date of such decision, present a petition of appeal to the Commissioner of Assam. They could also present the same to the assistant himself, whose duty it would then be to forward, with the least possible loss of time, the said petition, with a copy of the decision appealed from, to the commissioner.

A special appeal might be received within three months by the assistant from the judgement of a *sadar ameen* on an appeal from that of a *munsif*, and by the commissioner from the judgement of an Assistant on an appeal from the award of a *munsif* or *sadar ameen*, if it might appear necessary for ends of justice, in consequence of a decision being at variance with some existing law or established custom of the country or for any other good and sufficient reasons. Such an appeal could also be submitted to the Sadar Dewani Adalat from the decision of the commissioner. No second appeal was to be received on any but special grounds mentioned above, whether the previous decisions of the two subordinate courts might have been concurrent or not. When, however, it should appear that the judgement against which the appeal was preferred was clearly in opposition to, or inconsistent with, another decree of the same court or of another court having jurisdiction in the same suit, or in a suit founded on a similar cause of action, a second or special appeal could in all cases be admitted.[24]

Thus, it was found under Section III of the Rules for the Administration of Civil Justice in Assam that in a case tried by the principal assistant, regardless of its value or amount involved, there should be an appeal to the commissioner and a special appeal to the Sadar Dewani Adalat. This law admitted of easy practical application to all cases below Rs. 10,000, but difficulties arose when the value of the suit was above that amount. Under the existing rules, appeals to Sadar Dewani Adalat could be made only on special grounds, even if the value of a suit was Rs. 10,000 and upwards. On the other hand, the existing law allowed an appeal on merit to the Privy Council in every case decided by the court of Sadar Dewani, in which the value of the property might be Rs. 10,000 and above.[25] Therefore, it became necessary to amend the provisions made in Clause 3 of Section III of the Assam Code.[26] The amended provision of the section provided that parties discontented with the decision of an assistant in any suit of the value of Rs. 10,000 and upwards, tried in the first instance before him, might, within the period of three months from the date of such decision, present a petition of appeal to the Sadar Dewany Adalat. The such party or parties might submit the same to the assistant, if they prefer it, whose duty it would be to forward the petition, with the least possible loss of time, in the usual manner to the Sadar Dewani Adalat. The system prevailing at present of appeals against the decision of the assistant in trials below Rs. 10,000, could, as heretofore, be tried by the commissioner.[27] This rule was inserted in the revised code made effective from the year 1847.

With the appointment of deputy commissioner having powers of Civil and Session Judge, supplementary rules were passed for the administration of civil justice of the province. The supplementary rules provided that all regular and special appeals from the judgement of the deputy commissioner were to be referred to the Court of the Sadar Dewani Adalat. The commissioner, however, was declared competent to call for proceedings in any case, original or appealed, decided by the deputy commissioner but not appealed to the Sadar Dewani Adalat and to recommend to the deputy commissioner a review of that officer's judgement should he see good and sufficient cause for so doing.[28] Appeals against the orders of the deputy commissioner, passed in miscellaneous cases were to be referred to the commissioner of Assam, whose judgement thereon was to be final.

By a resolution dated 20 May 1846, passed by the Sadar Dewani

Adalat, it was decided that all applications for the admission of special appeal had to be referred to the court of Sadar Dewany under the provisions of Act III of 1843. In 1844 this provision was inserted as clause 5, Section III of the Administration of Civil Justice in Assam.[29]

The assistant or the commissioner on appeals being referred to them, were not required to summon the respondent in the first instance, but merely to call for the original records of the proceedings of the case. If after the perusal of the same in the presence of the appellant or his agent, the commissioner or the assistant, as the case might be, sees no reason to alter the decision appealed against, he should be competent to confirm the same, communicating the order of confirmation through the court against whose judgement the appeal was made to the respondent, with a view to enabling him to take measures for carrying the decision in his favour into execution.

Should an appeal be admitted, a notice had to be issued to the respondent. At the expiration of the term assigned, the *sadar ameen*, assistant or commissioner, as the case might be, should, after receiving the respondent's reply to the petition of appeal, would proceed to try and decide the merits of the appeal and should pass a decision confirming, modifying or reversing the decision of the *munsif, sadar ameen* or assistant. If the respondent failed to attend within the period fixed in the notice, the appeal was to be tried exparte.

The Sadar Dewani Adalat, commissioner, assistant, or *sadar ameen*, as the case might be, were empowered to call for further evidence in a case appealed, or to refer the case back to the concerned courts for re-investigation, if it appeared to have been imperfectly enquired into or 'to re-examine the witnesses examined by the lower court'.[30]

The appellate court might admit appeals after the expiration of the term fixed for their presentation on sufficient cause for the delay being shown.

Security for the costs of an appeal which was obligatory in case of regular appeal was later made discretionary of the appellate court in the revised code of 1847.

In the year 1845 principal *sadar ameen* was appointed to render substantial relief to the work of principal assistant of the district in civil cases. Appeal from the decision of principal *sadar ameen* for suits below Rs. 1,000 was to be preferred to the principal assistant of the district, and all suits above Rs. 1,000 to 10,000 were to be preferred to the court of the deputy commissioner,[31] and all cases above Rs. 10,000 to the Sadar Dewany Adalat.[32]

ARBITRATION OR COMPROMISE

Clause 6 of Section II of the Administration of Civil Justice provided that the

Assistant may insist on the attendance, in person, both of the plaintiff and defendant in any original suit; and he is strongly enjoined, in all cases in which it shall be practicable, so to confront them as at once to elicit the truth, and abridge the necessity of further legal proceedings; and he may take their examination on oath, if he judges it necessary previously to bringing the suit on his regular file; and in all cases in which such meeting of the parties can be effected, their depositions shall be recorded and taken to be the plaint and reply in the suit. But any party feeling aggrieved by such a requisition, may appeal to the Commissioner, who is hereby empowered to cause it to be withdrawn recording his reasons for doing so at length in his proceedings. It is also to be understood that the filing of a petition of appeal by a plaintiff against such a requisition shall bar its enforcement pending reference to the Commissioner.[33]

This rule did not bring the desired results. Most of the assistants neglected this rule and in course of time, it became dead letter. Almost all the cases in the provinces were now tried by the inferior courts, and the principal or senior assistant seldom or never tried any original suit. The mofussil courts were, however, not empowered under this rule to confront the parties to a suit. On the other hand, the assistant had little time to take up these cases himself. Moreover, there was much opposition from the influential section of the natives from personally appearing in public tribunals. The respectable and influential section of the people always preferred to refer their complaints and lodge defence through their agents and attorneys lest their dishonesty and falsehood were publicly exposed. It would, however, be a boon to the honest section of the natives, who for their 'simple and honest habits, would be led at once to elicit the facts of a case when they were personally examined in a public tribunal'.[34] This rule, however, would have affected hardly the interest of the cunning and dishonest agents, attorneys and *mukhtears*.

Capt. Agnew who took charge as the principal assistant of Goalpara on 29 December 1854[35] beneficially used the rules provided in Clause 6, Section II of the civil rules. He caused the attendance in person of the parties to every suit where the litigants resided at or near the Sadar station for the purpose of confronting them, and settling, if possible, their disputes without further proceedings being taken. The result achieved was very encouraging. Out of 126 cases in which the parties were confronted 76 settled without further proceadings being taken.[36]

In some of these cases, the parties agreed to abide by the evidence of a certain witness or witnesses, in some by the account books of the plaintiff, in some by the oath of one or other of themselves, or by assistant's decision, and a *quabalah jowab*, or *razenamah* as the case might be, was then filed.

The deduction that had been drawn from the experience in confronting the parties was incalculable to the people and Capt. Agnew suggested to authorize all officers for the summary decision of civil suits below a certain amount. He remarked, 'for the sake of the people that I could proceed to the trial of every petty civil suits that comes before me, as quickly as the parties, their witnesses and documentary proofs could be got together'.[37] He also received cordial assistance from the vakeels in his endeavour to curtail litigation.

In 1852, out of 342 cases in which the parties were confronted in Goalpara, 249 were settled without the necessity of further proceedings being taken and 11 were referred to arbitrators. The time in all other cases was shortened by 25 days for a reply and rejoinder.[38]

The Sadar court in its resolution dated 5 July 1855 observed 'great success which has crowned Agnew's efforts and hoped this example may be followed by other officers of the district other than Goalpara'.[39] It was not aware of any reason which could prevent the introduction of this practice of confronting the parties in the subordinate courts. And on the receipt of this resolution the deputy commissioner issued instructions for the first time for the introduction of the system throughout the province.

Further, it was enacted in Section II, Clause 10 of the Assam Civil Rules that the

> several courts in Assam are hereby authorized to use every proper means for inducing the parties in suits to refer their disputes to arbitration, either with a view of settling some particular issue; or of obtaining a complete and final adjustment of their differences. An agreement shall, in such cases, be taken from the parties, in which it shall be distinctly stated whether the award is to be partial, that is, confined to a particular issue; or final, as embracing the whole merits of the case. In the former case, the Court will take the finding of the arbitrators as conclusive upon the particular point referred to them; in the latter case, the award of the arbitrators shall, if open to no just cause of impeachment on the score of flagrant and palpable partiality, be confirmed by the courts, and held of the same force and validity as a regular judgment.[40]

However, this excellent and noble rule had fallen into disuse and this provision had not been carried out by the assistants in charge of the district. An inquiry into the records of the courts would clearly prove that in not one in a hundred cases did the courts even consult the wishes of the parties to adjust their disputes by any of the above means, much less induce them.[41]

SUIT IN FORMA PAUPERIS

Any party desirous of instituting an original suit as a pauper could do so under Clause XI of Section II. He had to appear in person before the assistant in-charge of the district. His petition was to include a general statement of the nature and grounds of the demand, the value of the object claimed, the name of the person or persons to be sued, and a schedule of the whole real and personal property belonging to the petitioner, with the estimated value of such property. In special cases, the assistant could receive such petitions through an authorized agent or *mukhtear*. On receipt of such a petition, the assistant had to institute a summary enquiry with a view to ascertaining the accuracy of the petitioner's allegations regarding his own circumstances. If the assistant was satisfied, he was to admit the petitioner to sue as a pauper. Otherwise he would at once refuse to admit his suit in that form, and would refer him to the general rules in force. All orders passed by an assistant under the provisions mentioned above were open to revision by the commissioner, if appealed within the term of three months from the date on which the order were passed.

The statement in Table 4.1 shows the number of petitions in *forma pauperis* presented in the courts, of different districts during the five years from 1833 to 1838 and the result of the petitions including appeals.[42]

The provisions of Clause XI of Section 2 extended considerable benefits to the poor and needy who could not afford to file a suit in a court of law due to his miserable economic condition.

ADMINISTRATION OF CRIMINAL JUSTICE

Rules of Procedure

The assistant in-charge of a district could ask the sub-assistant and *sadar ameen* to refer a case to them, to make preliminary magisterial proceedings, if on the face of the police report or complaint, he found it advisable to do so. Again, under circumstances if he found it unadvisable to refer the preliminary enquiry to a subordinate, he could take down the reply of the party accused in the event of his wishing to confess. He could also record the substance of the evidence with a view to facilitate the proceedings on the trial and to fix an earliest possible date for trial.[43]

Confession

Confessions in heinous cases had to always to be made before the senior, the junior, or the sub-assistant attested by two or more competent witnesses. All such confessions had to be superscribed as follows by the officer before whom it was made:

TABLE 4.1: NUMBER OF PETITIONS FOR BEING DECLARED AS PAUPER

District	No. of petition presented	Admitted	No. of pauper cases decreed in favour of plaintiff	No. of cases decreed in favour of defendant
Kamrup	21	20	2	18 (* Off the 18 cases 8 struck off—5 in default of attendance and 3 in consequence of the causes of action having originated upwards of 12 years antecedent to their institution)
Darrang	16	9*	1	4* (*of remaining 4, 2 struck off the file and 2 under trial)
Nowgong	12	11	3	8

Source: BJP (Civil), 2 October 1838, no. 6.

I, A.B. Senior Assistant (Junior or Sub-Assistant, as the case might be) hereby certify that this confession of . . . was made by the said—and taken down in writing and attested by the subscribing witnesses, before me, and in my presence, on the . . . between the hours of . . . that, to the best of my belief, the confession was voluntary, and that no interference, directly or indirectly, on the part of any person likely to influence or intimidate per prisoner, was permitted.[44]

Upon the date being fixed for the trial, the assistant in-charge of the district was to empanel a jury to consist of not less than three members, before whom he would proceed to record the evidence for the prosecution and defence. At the close of the examination, which had to all be taken down in writing, he would call upon the jury, after allowing them sufficient time to deliberate, to return a verdict which had to be taken down in writing in open court. The verdict had to be attested by the signature of each member of the jury.

In the event of an acquittal, the assistant, if he concurred with the jury, might direct the immediate release of the prisoner. But in the event of the verdict being for conviction, or if the assistants disapproved the verdict of acquittal, he had to submit the case to the commissioner, who would either pass sentence or refer it to the Nizamat Adalat.

In all petty criminal cases (viz. misdemeanors, theft to the amount of Rs. 50, and offences for which the magistrates in the Regulation provinces were empowered to pass sentence of imprisonment not exceeding six months) evidences might be taken *viva voce*, and the substance merely be recorded, either in English or Bengali language, as the commissioner might direct.[45]

A register of all trials held before the assistant and his subordinates, was tobe kept in the prescribed form as directed by the Nizamat Adalat. Monthly returns of trials referred to the commissioner and disposed of by him, were also be made to the Nizamat Adalat in a prescribed form. An annual report on the administration of criminal justice, showing the aggregate number of trials held and prisoners punished in each division, and such other particulars as the court might require, were also to be made to the Nizamat Adalat.

Attendance of Witness

It was enacted since Robertson's code that the parties to a suit were allowed to bring up, if they preferred, their own witnesses. Should they require *peadas* for this purpose, the usual summons were to be served; should a witness not attend upon this process, a proclamation to the effect was to be issued allowing them 15 days time; in case of default their property was to be attached and sold. By Section III, Clause 6 of the Assam Code (Civil) it was provided that if the witnesses failed to appear upon serving process to the proclamation made, a fine was to be imposed, to be levied by the attachment and sale of their property. It was further provided that parties applying for a process to enforce attendance were to clarify that they were ready to indemnify the said witnesses for any necessary expenses to be incurred by them in attending the court. The court passing final decision had to include whatever sum not exceeding the rate of 3 *annas* per diem which would be paid to the witnesses.

The rule for attendance of witnesses was later modified by Deputy Commissioner Vetch and it was made compulsory that all witnesses be summoned through the court at whatever distance they resided. Minor changes were also made in the provision for payment of subsistence money to the witnesses. The whole object of this provision was to prevent vexation and exaggerated complaints, but it hit hard on the poor and downtrodden. It had nearly closed the courts to the poor classes of complainants, who could never afford to deposit Rs. 6 or 4 in a petty criminal case.

In view of the linguistic deficiency, the judges were authorized to employ the assistance of any of their native officers in taking down the deposition of witnesses. The general practice, however, was to have them examined by native officers even when the judge (being with other business) was physically present in the same room. Act XIX of 1853, for the first time, abolished this practice and required that the evidence of the attending witness be taken in the presence and under the personal superintendence of the judges.

Penal Code[46]

The Penal Code of Assam was based upon the Regulations of Bengal. The spirit of the Bengal code was retained but modifications were made to suit local requirements.

Offences were divided mainly into three classes: (i) General offences such as burglary, theft unattended with aggravating circumstances; (ii) Miscellaneous offences, and (iii) Heinous offences.

The gradations of punishment with reference to certain commonly prevalent crimes are listed below.

Burglary or Theft

In cases of burglary or theft, unattended with aggravated personal violence, in which the property stolen might not exceed in value the sum of Rs. 300, the offender might be awarded sentence of imprisonment with labour for two years, and of imprisonment with labour for the additional term of one year in lieu of corporal punishment.

Assault and Affrays

In all cases of assault and affrays unattended with serious wounding or loss of life, the punishment would be fine not exceeding Rs. 200, commutable to one year imprisonment or one year imprisonment alone.

Perjury

In cases of unaggravated perjury, the offender might receive sentence of imprisonment with labour for two years, and of imprisonment with labour for another one year in lieu of corporal punishment.

Receiving Stolen Property

In cases of receivers of stolen property the offender might be punished with imprisonment for six months.

Prostitution

The punishment for enticing away females for prostitution would be six months imprisonment.

House Breaking

In all cases of house-breaking with intent to steal, the offender might be punished with sentence of imprisonment for six months.

Recovering of Debt without Authority

The punishment for recovering of debt without proper authority would be a fine of Rs. 200, in default civil imprisonment up to six months extendable to a fine of Rs. 1,000 or a sentence of one year imprisonment.

Retaining or Recovering the Possession of Land

The punishment for this fault was same as that for recovering of debt without authority.

Contempt of Court

In all cases of an act of open contempt of court including a refusal to attend and to give evidence when summoned either before the senior assistant or any of the inferior tribunals in the district, the offender would be sentenced to a fine of Rs. 200 commutable to imprisonment not exceeding one year, or of imprisonment alone for that period.

Neglect of Duty

For gross neglect of duty by the *barkandoz* or *teckelas* the offender might be punished with imprisonment for two years with or without labour and of another one year in lieu of corporal punishment. The same punishment might be awarded to police officers for the same offence.

Bribery or Extortion

In cases of bribery and extortion on the part of any native officer in the pay of government in which the sum demanded or received might not exceed the amount of Rs. 300, the offender would be punished with imprisonment with labour for the additional term of one year in lieu of corporal punishment.

Resistance to Process

The punishment for resistance of process was fine of Rs. 200 commutable to imprisonment for one year.

Forcible Release of Duty Attached Property

In all cases of forcible release of duly attached property, the offender might be punished with a sentence of imprisonment not exceeding Rs. 200, commutable to imprisonment for not exceeding one year or of imprisonment alone.

Neglect or Ill-treatment of Wife

The punishment for neglect or ill-treating his wife the offender would be awarded one month imprisonment and fine along with maintenance money.

Desertion by Workmen

The punishment for desertion by workmen could be one month's imprisonment.

Murder

The punishment for wilful murder could be death or imprisonment and transportation for life. For culpable homicide not amounting to wilful murder, the punishment would be imprisonment up to seven years.

For murders committed in prosecution of robbery, burglary or theft the punishment might be death penalty.

In all cases of manslaughter, the offender might be punished with a sentence of fine not exceeding Rs. 500, or of imprisonment with or without labour, for a term not exceeding seven years.

Robbery

Robbers (including those aiding and abetting) wounding, maiming or torturing a person or burning not occasioning homicide would be punished with imprisonment and transportation for life.

Persons going forth with a gang of robbers for the purpose of committing robbery, but apprehended before they could commit such an act would be punished with imprisonment with hard labour for a period not exceeding seven years.

Wounding

The person guilty of wounding with the intent of committing murder might be punished with imprisonment with labour in banishment for a term not exceeding fourteen years.

Affrays attended with Homicide

In all cases of affrays attended with homicide the offenders might be punished with a sentence of fine not exceeding Rs. 500, or imprisonment with or without labour, for a term not exceeding seven years.

Wilful Perjury or Forgery

In cases of willful perjury or forgery the punishment would be imprisonment not exceeding seven years.

Theft, Burglary and Decoity

Offenders convicted of theft, burglary and decoity unattended with murder might be punished with an imprisonment for a term not exceeding fourteen years.

Corporal Punishment

The British rulers in case of petty crimes practised corporal punishments. The magistrates were authorized to try offences, such as petty thefts when not attended with any aggravating circumstances or committed by persons of notorious character. In such cases there would be corporal punishment not exceeding 13 *rattans* or imprisonment not exceeding one month. There was, however, a growing feeling of revulsion against corporal punishment as it failed to prevent crime.

Accordingly, Regulation II of 1834 abolished corporal punishment. But the system was continued by Commissioner Jenkins in his capacity as the head of non-Regulation Assam.

In Regulation provinces, corporal punishment was substituted by fine or extended terms of imprisonment. But in Assam the commissioner found that the people were unable to pay fine due to poverty. Regarding extended imprisonment he observed it would be, 'attended with great deprivation of families in the loss of the labour of perhaps the only person of a family capable of labouring for the subsistence of the other members of it, who must thus necessarily be driven to distress and perhaps crime'.[47]

In 1844 moderate whipping was again sanctioned by way of school discipline in case of juvenile offenders. It was practised even after the Code of Civil and Criminal Procedure was adopted.

THE *VIVA VOCE* EXAMINATION

Clause 6, Section II of the Administration of Criminal Justice in Assam provided that in all petty criminal cases (viz., misdemeanors, theft to the amount of Rs. 50, and offences for which magistrates in the Regulation provinces were empowered to pass sentence of imprisonment not exceeding six months) evidence might be taken *viva voce*, and the substance merely be recorded, either in English or Bengali, as the commissioner might direct.[48] But this provision of deciding petty criminal cases had been greatly neglected and had fallen into disuse. In most of the districts, the mode of conducting and recording petty criminal trials as practiced in Regulation provinces had been generally adopted.[49]

Judicial Administration from the Promulgation 141

The object of this section was to expedite proceedings in petty cases as to render the intervention of native ministerial officers unnecessary in taking down the evidence. It was found that even a very petty case contained voluminous record of written evidence, which must have taken much time in transcribing. However, it was the discretion of the assistant in-charge of the districts to adopt the provision of this section or not, and to 'those who do not approve of it, it may become a dead letter'. Deputy Commissioner Capt. Matthie who always conformed to Regulation laws in criminal trials did not encourage the assistants to use this noble law disregarding the peculiar circumstances of the province. But things began to change with the departure of Capt. Matthie.

The new Deputy Commissioner Capt. Vetch after taking charge issued a circular on 18 May 1852 (No. 182) to all magistrates in charge of districts, requiring them to adopt the *viva voce* system in the trial of petty criminal cases as per the provisions of Clause B, Section II of criminal rules.[50] Vetch urged the magistrates that the rule quoted be acted on as far as possible and that the intervention of *mohurers* in recording the evidence in such cases be discontinued. Magistrates, joint magistrates and assistants could draw up the final *roobkari* (vernacular summary) from the substance of the proof adduced in their English casebooks and attached to the original plaint as the native record of the case. The examination was to be recorded in English by the European and in Bengali by the native judges. A translation of the magistrate's decision in the vernacular of the country was affixed to the prosecutor's original plaint for the satisfaction of the parties and use of the native office.

The procedure of submitting a complaint was simple. The person aggrieved could put up a petition stating his case. He was then examined on oath as to its bonafide. The court might require the attendance of the prosecutor's witnesses or examine them *ex-parte* with a view to elucidate the truth of the complainant before summoning the accused. The court, on being satisfied that it was a proper case deserving enquiry, would issue summons to bring up the parties, as soon as the prosecutor had lodged the expenses. If the prosecutor was too poor to do so, summon might be served through the police free of charge. The parties were also allowed to present their own witnesses without the intervention of a summon if they wished to do so. On the arrival of witnesses of the parties, i.e. of the plaintiff and the defendant, the trial was taken up at the earliest.[51]

By his further letter dated 12 August 1853, to all magistrates in the province of Assam, Deputy Commissioner Vetch asked the principal *sadar ameens* to keep up case books in all criminal trials and also in all *viva voce* examinations. His order stated that:

in such cases as the proceedings have heretofore been recorded in the form of a separate *nuthee*, the record should be made over at once in the case book and when the investigation have been held viva voce, the number of the case, the name of the parties, the crime, as well as, the name of every witnesses adduced either for the pro-secution or defence should be recorded.[52]

A very concise but sufficient history of the case as put forward by the prosecutor and the defendants' plea were to be noted. In addition, the substance and the hearing of the evidence of the witnesses were recorded. Where the evidence of witnesses was corroborant of the foregoing it would not be necessary to do more than noting the points of difference. The substance of the defence was also to be prepared in a concise form so as to enable proper dealing of the case in appeal. Where the witnesses were named but not examined, the reasons for their non-examination was to be noted.

This instruction was also to be followed by the magistrate and his assistants in their casebooks, where no Bengali record of the case was kept.

Capt. Vetch urged that the rule for *viva voce* examination be kept absolute as it would not only improve and expedite decision-making but remove the frequent complaint that the *omlah* distorted the evidence while taking it down. Moreover, it would make young officers trust in their own persons and their own notebook instead of the native records. This would also give general satisfaction to all but those who worked for obstructing or delaying justice. In respect of cases sent up through the agency of the police, the same system would be pursued in all cases of petty thefts. As all the witnesses would be in attendance at the same time, the viva voce investigation would not take a quarter of the time taken to note down the evidence.[53]

The operation of the *viva voce* system had entirely met the expectations. Justice being greatly expedited, the influence of the native officers in the court was checked, the swarms of petty attorneys who made a livelihood by fomenting litigation nearly lost their occupation and false and frivolous complaints deceased; whilst to the people the change proved most beneficial and popular as it saved them time, energy and money.[54] The quiet discharge of witnesses and the speedy decision of suits were the favourable results of the *viva voce* system. The people began to hold the Company's court in high esteem. 'Even a favourable decision', remarked Capt. Agnew, Assistant-in-charge of Goalpara, 'loses half its value when obtained after the party has been kept in weary suspense till he has become sick of the whole thing, and the detention of witnesses, for any length of time, from their hoes and household duties is a grievous hardship felt with an acuteness few of us are sensible of.'[55]

The *viva voce* investigation was introduced in the districts of Kamrup, Darrang, Sibsagar and Lakhimpur only in October 1852 and the result was highly favourable everywhere.[56] Capt. Vetch reported that when the practice would be fully introduced it would enable the courts to dispense with the portion of their (judicial) establishment.[57]

RESUMPTION OF UPPER ASSAM

Since 1833, Purandar Singha ruled Upper Assam smoothly. Although there was a little fall in revenue, he cleared off his tribute in full and collected in addition a fairly good amount on account of the outstanding arrears when the territory was under British occupation. Early in 1834 Robertson observed:

I am happy to be able to speak well of the Raja Purandar Singh. Though many of the higher order of the Assamese were discontented with his rule, yet we were sure to receive the most favourable accounts of his actions and all agree in admitting, that he has, hitherto, proved to the bulk of the people a mild and beneficent master, and this is confirmed by the fact of no emigration having as yet taken place into our territory nor as far as we can learn into those of the Barsenapati and other independent chiefs in the remote parts of Upper Assam.[58]

Purandar Singha also tried to win the confidence of the Political Agent by apprehending Dhanjay and Harakanta, the leaders of the resistance movement, whose heads carried a reward of Rs. 500 each. In view of the changed circumstances and the peaceful nature of the country the vice-president-in-council condoned their guilt and they were accordingly released.

Despite his sincere efforts to give the people an orderly administration, the situation in Upper Assam became increasingly embarrassing for Purandar as his own officials became inimical to him. They could not compromise with the *raja*, who in his bid to meet the demand of the Company government in Bengal left his own officers unpaid and ignored their interests, traditional rights and immunities.

The short-sighted and ambitious nobles, thinking that the removal of Purander would put an end to their difficulties, began to lodge complaints to Major Jenkins, the Commissioner of Assam, against their own king. As a result, the British got the opportunity they had been looking for to annex Upper Assam with its vast potentialities of tea, coal and petroleum to the British Indian empire.[59] In October 1838, Upper Assam was permanently annexed to the Company's territories. For a period of one year, the two districts of Upper Assam-Sibsagar and Lakhimpur were governed by the political department. From 1 August 1839, they were placed under the Government of Bengal to be governed by the Commissioner of Assam as per government's laws and regulations[60] (Appendices 4.1 & 4.2). Brodie and Capt. Vetch became the principal Assistants of Sibsagar and Lakhimpur respectively.

ANNEXATION OF MATAK TERRITORY

David Scott made an agreement with the Barsenapati of the Matakas in May 1826, by which the latter agreed to give the British the service of an armed contingent of 300 soldiers (*paiks*) and to supply provisions to any British expedition passing through his territory.

So long the British authority in Upper Assam was not consolidated, the British followed a conciliatory policy towards the Matakas. All the time, however, the Matak territory had been attracting their attention as the best tea growing area in Upper Assam.

In January 1839, the Barsenapati died. He was succeeded by his second son Maju Gohain. A few days before his assassination by the Khamtis, Captain White visited the Matak kingdom and tried to revise the settlement with a view to increasing the tribute to Rs. 10,000 and getting the wastelands in the territory for tea cultivation.[61] The Barsenapati agreed to the second proposal but not to the first which he resisted. Meanwhile, internal feud developed between the Marans and the rest of the Matak population, taking advantage of which the British annexed the kingdom in December 1840.

The territory was placed under Capt. Vetch, Political Agent, and Upper Assam to be administered under the political department. From 1 September 1842, the territory, like Upper Assam, was brought under the operation of government laws and regulations[62] (Appendix 4.3).

Historians have, with remarkable unanimity, condemned the resumption of Upper Assam. Commissioner Jenkins was of the opinion that maladministration was the main reason for annexation of Upper Assam, but, in fact, the English were themselves responsible for maladministration. It was a fact that Purandar was only a *de jure* ruler of Upper Assam, the English being the de facto masters. The fundamental point that the harsh clauses of the treaty between Purandar and the British were greatly instrumental for misrule of the former's territory had been ignored. As de facto rulers, it was the duty of the Company to help reform the administration, but they did not do so. Actually, they never had an intention of effecting any reforms in the administration of Upper Assam. Instead, they only wanted to make the maladministration and ill-governance a pretext for grabbing the region.

Commissioner Jenkins skilfully planned the annexation. He sent his officers and he himself investigated the charges of misrule in Upper Assam, wrote lengthy reports about the rottenness of Purandar's administration and won over the Supreme government to his view point. Even Lord Auckland admitted that no grave crime was laid to his charge. There were charges of corruption and oppression no doubt, but these were not of such a flagrant nature as would have called for such a drastic step. In reality, it was the immense potentiality of Upper Assam which excited Jenkin's greed and aroused his imperial interest.

Likewise, the annexation of Matak territory was not justified. There was no charge of misgovernment, exactions or incapacity against the Barsenapati and his family; rather their liberal and efficient administration bestowed peace and prosperity on the people. It was not the trifling amount of tribute that sealed the fate of the Matak kingdom, but the growing demand for tea as the Matak country contained the best tea producing areas.

ANNEXATION OF SADIYA

The territories of the Singphos and the Khamtis situated between the British and the Burmese territories were looked upon with concern by the British. In the middle of 1838, a European officer was stationed at Sadiya with the authority to exercise judicial powers. The inhabitants of the area grew apprehensive of the real motives of the British, yet they failed to organize a united resistance because of a quarrel between the Sadiyakhowa Gohain, the chief of the Khamtis, and the Barsenapati, the chief of the Mataks, over their claims to Saikhowa. Lt. Charlton, who was stationed at Sadiya, directed the Sadiyakhowa Gohain to refer the dispute for arbitration to the Political Agent. But the Khamti chief not only defied the direction but also took forcible possession of the land under dispute. The matter was referred to the Commissioner, Mr. Jenkins, who first suspended the Khamti chief and finally removed him from office and brought the whole tract under the Company's possession.

ANNEXATION OF CACHAR

While the British were implementing measures for consolidating their rule in Upper Assam, they also, in pursuance of the policy of territorial expansion, turned their attention to the hills of North Cachar ruled by a Kachari chief named Tularam. The struggle between Kachari king Gobinda Chandra and Tularam over the sovereignty of Cachar gave the British an opportunity to interfere in its affairs. Gobinda Chandra sought British assistance to suppress Tularam. But David Scott, the Agent to the Governor-General, North-East Frontier was reluctant to resort to arms against Tularam, who had already allied himself with the Burmese. He, therefore, brought about a compromise between Gobinda Chandra and Tularam. Accordingly an agreement was arrived at by which Gobinda Chandra would acknowledge the latter as his Senapati or General with the formal charge of the areas under his jurisdiction then.

But trouble again broke out when Gobinda Chandra was murdered in April 1830. There were several claimants to the throne of Cachar. The Company's government in Assam, however, wanted to annex it and sought the opinions of Commissioner Jenkins and Captain Pemberton, who had recently visited this region. Jenkins suggested annexation, which was immediately carried into effect in August 1832.

The annexation of Cachar enraged Tularam, who soon afterwards in September 1832, invaded Dharampur, then under the management of a local officer of the Company government, burnt about five villages and carried away several individuals. This was considered a grave offence by the government which issued orders for the apprehension of Tularam. Accordingly, Tularam was arrested by Captain Fisher on 3 October 1832 and sent to the magistrate of Sylhet for trial. He was, however, set at liberty and a fresh treaty was concluded between the Company and Tularam.

Meanwhile, Tularam, worn out by age and internecine strife, had been facing fresh troubles in the form of frequent inroads made to his territory by the Angami Nagas. Tularam died in 1850 and Captain Butler, who was in-charge of Cachar, advised the resumption of this territory on the ground that the arrangement made with Tularam was a life tenure only. A.J. Moffatt Mill, the judge of the Sadar Court, who was then visiting the districts of Assam, was directed to make a report regarding the affairs of North Cachar.

His recommendation ultimately led to the occupation of Tularam's territory by the Company government in 1854. This territory was merged with the Nowgong districts of Assam and administered under the direct control of principal assistant, Nowgong.

ANNEXATION OF JAYANTIA

After the conclusion of the Yandabo Treaty, Raja Ram Singh began his reign in a cordial atmosphere. This atmosphere continued till 1831 when a conflict between the Company and the *raja* arose on the issue of the seizure of two British subjects. The Company government pressed the *raja* to surrender the culprits responsible for the incident. When negotiations were going on Raja Ram Singh died and was succeeded by his grand-nephew Rajendra Singh. The relation between the Company and the Jayantia *raja*, however, did not improve in spite of the change of rulers in the Jayantia hills; rather the relations deteriorated on the issue of the amount of tribute to be paid by the *raja* to the Company. On 15 March 1835 the Jayantia kingdom was annexed by the Company government. The plains of the kingdom in the south including Jayantipur was joined to Sylhet, Gova in the north to Nowgong district while the hilly tracts were added to the Khasi Hills.

GREAT NATIONAL UPSURGE AND THE ADMINISTRATION OF JUSTICE

The most important event in the history of nineteenth-century India was the Revolt of 1857, which is generally accepted as the First War of Indian Independence. The great revolt rocked almost the entire country and threw the mighty British power into a whirlwind of confusion and insecurity. In the wake of the great revolt, the nobles in Assam led by Maniram Dutta Barbhandar Baruah Dewan (popularly Maniram Dewan) planned to reinstate the Saring Raja, Kandarpeswar Singha, grandson of Purandar Singha as the king of Assam. The Saring Raja, dissatisfied with the British failure to relieve him of poverty and distress, joined his Dewan Maniram Dutta. When the mutiny broke out in northern India,

Judicial Administration from the Promulgation 149

Maniram was in Calcutta to submit petitions and memorials to the government on behalf of Kandarpeswar Singha. Through his several letters, Maniram urged the Saring Raja to raise the standard of revolt, with the help of local regiments, his friends and nobles. Peali Baruah, Lukee Senchoa Barua, Kamala Saringia Baruah, Ugrasen Gohain, Saru Gohain, Balram Neog Phukan, Maju Aideo besides many others of rank and influence responded to the call from Maniram. They had frequent meetings with the Saring Raja at his residence at Jorhat which were attended by almost all dispossessed officers of the Ahom government and the *mouzadars*.

A good deal of alarm had been felt throughout Assam owing to the defection of the three regiments at Danapur and the revolt of Konwar Singh, from whose estates many of the Hindustani Sepoys of the local regiments in Assam came.[63] An officer of the 1st Assam Light Infantry, viz., Noor Muhammad called on the Saring Raja and offered him the assistance of men to place him on the throne. The sepoys were persuaded to believe that the British rule had actually come to an end and Emperor Bahadur Shah regained his throne. The rebels were ignorant of the resources and real strength of the English; they were confident that they would be able to drive away the British. As the martial laws were withdrawn in Assam and there was not a single European regiment, the rebels thought that their success would be easy. The lead was taken by Peali alias Mohesh Chandra Baruah, who along with three others visited Golaghat and met Shaikh Bhikan, the *subedar* of a military detachment stationed there. Bhokool a *mahaut*, who accompanied Peali to Golaghat reported:

I went in *Ahar* (June-July) to Golaghat with Peali, Mouzadar, . . . the day previous I went with Peali in the evening to the Raja's place who gave him (Peali) a letter, which had been written by Kinaram Pandit to take to Golaghat, Peali left the Rajah to go to his own house about 10 o'clock at night. The next morning we left for Golaghat, which we reached by evening, on reaching the station he got off the elephant . . . went to the Sepoy lines . . . he remained there about a couple of hours.[64]

The letter sent by the Saring Raja is said to have contained tempting baits: 'The Rajah would double the pay of the Sepoys and give the native officers pay like Jongie Paltan, if all the Sepoys would join and get him the Country'.[65] Similar negotiations were carried on with the sepoys at Sibsagar, Dibrugarh and Saikhowa. Charles Holroyd, the principal assistant, Sibsagar reported:

> In the month of *Sawan* (July-August) Roostam Singh Jamadar, and two sepoys went to Jorhat, and having visited the Saring Raja by night conferred with him regarding the arrangement made with Peali at Golaghat. In the month of Bhadra Debiduta Sarma Mouzadar (Brother of Luckiedutta) received gold from the Rajah for the collection of russud for the troops; for a similar purpose gold was also distributed to the other parties.[66]

The evening before the *rajah* was arrested, he sent Kamala Saringia Baruah to Saikhowa to meet Neog Phukan Darogah. 'He (Rajah) told Kamala Saringia Baruah to go to Panee Phukan and tell him of all the arrangements and consultations, with him to go to the darogah at Saikhowa and get him to come down here.'[67]

An uneasy feeling began to display itself amongst the men of the 1st Assam Light Infantry at Dibrugarh and military detachment at Golaghat and other places. The sepoys were evidently spurred on to activity by the intrigues at Jorhat, where the Saring Raja Kandarpeswar was forging plans to drive the British out of the province. The guiding spirit of the whole plot was, of course, Maniram Dewan, then residing in Calcutta. Capt. Holroyd reported that two or three native officers of the 1st Assam Light Infantry had interviews with the Saring Raja and offered him the assistance of the men to reinstate him on his throne and that the young *rajah* has been instigated to the line of conduct he seems inclined to adopt by letters from Maniram Dewan who is believed to be in Calcutta.[68]

Through his numerous letters, the Dewan goaded the young prince to plunge head-long into the daring project with the aid of the local Regiment; and through his friends, mainly Madhu Mallick, a Bengali *mukhtear*, he prepared the ground for the insurrection. Holroyd, however, was able to gather intelligence about the designs of Maniram and the Saring Raja Kandarpeswar Singha. In early September 1857, he succeeded in intercepting a bundle of letters concealed inside a stick believed to have been written by

Judicial Administration from the Promulgation 151

Maniram or under his direction, which proved the complicity of the *raja* and the *dewan* in a plot against the British, Holroyd in his letter of 6 September 1857 to Jenkins, commissioner of Assam, reported.

One of these letters was addressed to the Pandits (Teachers) of the government school at this place (Sibsagar). I (Holroyd) believed it to be written by Maniram himself though in a disguised hand and it is signed in cipher, the key to which is given in verse. This letter is in Sanskrit and is dated the 14 August bearing the Calcutta postmark of the 16 August. The other letter has no signature or date and is not written by Maniram, though evidently by the context dictated by him and intended for the Saring Rajah.[69]

The mischievous and inflammatory letters caused a great deal of restlessness and alarm throughout Assam. Holroyd, meanwhile, obtained permission to apprehend the Saring Raja who had been corresponding with some of the disaffected sepoys of the 1st Assam Light Infantry and endeavouring to take possession of Assam.[70] Captain Holroyd sought assistance from Col. Hanny, Commandant of the Assam Light Infantry to secure the person of the Saring Raja, as this step had become necessary from the situation prevailing in the district. Accordingly Saring Raja along with his *mukhtear* were arrested on 9 September 1857[71] (Appendix 4.4).

The residence of the Saring Raja was thoroughly searched by Capt. Holroyd assisted by Capt. Lowther to find out objectionable or inflammatory paper, which might be used as documentary evidence against the *raja*. A similar operation was also conducted in Mukhtear Madhu Mallick's place, who resided in a rented house of the dewan. A large number of papers were said to have been found but Holroyd believed the most important document had been destroyed.[72] The entire operation was done with maximum secrecy and without the slightest information being leaked. The *raja* was sent to Dacca through Tezpore and Goalpara without delay and kept there temporarily. On 30 September 1858, government directed the Magistrate of Dacca to send the *raja* to Alipore.[73]

The arrest of the Saring Raja was followed by that of Maniram in Calcutta and of Peali Baruah, Lockenath Sensoa Baruah, Juran Nawbaisha Phukan, the Marangikhowa Gohain, Mayaram Nazir, Dutiram Baruah, Bahadur Gaonburah, Seikh Farmud and several others—all alleged to have been involved in the conspiracy against the state. Even before the arrest of the Saring Raja and other prominent leaders, Commandant Hanny ruined the cause of the sepoys by apprehending Shaikh Bhikan, the ring leader of the sepoys.

The Commissioner of Assam then heaved a sigh of relief and on 9 October, he was to report to the Government of Bengal that 'there is no further cause for any apprehension of any out-break in Assam',[74] although panic continued and Europeans of the province felt their lives and properties still insecure. Major Hanny had in the meantime affected the arrest of the remaining mutinous sepoys of the regiment and put them before a Court Martial at Dibrugarh. Balavant Singh, Ramtahol, Kripa Ram, Seshwai Singh, Ali Khan, Seikh Oogni (Gani), Chundar Singh and Hidayat Ali were all sentenced to transportation for life.[75]

With the arrest of the Saring Raja and other leaders including the sepoys, the mutiny—rather an attempt for mutiny—met its natural death.

The trial of the persons accused of treason and complicity in the mutiny commenced in January 1858. The prime mover of the plot, Maniram Dewan was brought to Jorhat to stand trial by the steamer *Kaladyne*.[76] Initially there was some confusion regarding the place of the trial. The Government of Bengal desired to proceed with Maniram's trial at Calcutta itself soon after his arrest there. But Capt. Holroyd considered it to be convenient and in many respects preferable to have it in Assam rather than in Calcutta. He stated:

I see no reason why Maniram should not be tried in Assam and I would urge his being tried in this the Sibsagar district, the scene of his villainy. I am of opinion it would have grand moral effect on all the disaffected, and if the sentence awarded against him should be capital, I would recommend the execution of it be carried out at this place Jorhat.[77]

It was also thought that Maniram's trial at his native place would facilitate collection of evidences from witnesses, because, it was both expensive and almost impossible for them to proceed to Calcutta for that purpose.[78] Therefore, it would be more judicious to bring Maniram to Jorhat for trial instead of compelling the

Judicial Administration from the Promulgation 153

witnesses to proceed to the Presidency. Commissioner Jenkins supported the contention of Capt. Holroyd with the observation 'many who may be able and willing to give evidence at Jorhat, will be inclined to withhold what has come to their knowledge if forced to go to Calcutta'.[79] The Government of Bengal was ultimately convinced of the proposal and the Lieutenant Governor left it to the commissioner to determine the place and the manner of the trial after the arrival of the prisoner in the province.[80] Jenkins concurred with Capt. Holroyd and issued necessary orders to proceed with the trial at Jorhat, the nerve centre of the mutiny.

Meanwhile, the stage was set for beginning the trial. Capt. Holroyd had already been appointed by General Order No. 1136 of 1 August 1857[81] as the commissioner under Section VII of Act XIV of 1857 and was given full powers to try the persons accused of conspiracy against the government. He was also vested with powers to try the mutineers under Act XVII of 1857.[82]

The charge-sheet against the accused was prepared by Haranath Parbatia Baruah, the *darogah* of Jorhat, on the basis of depositions given by certain individuals. Of them, Somnath Sarmah, the *hazarie mohurer* stated:

> From the time the disturbances commenced in Hindustan, Madhu Mallick used to come to Raja and read to him the news in the *Samachar Darpan* newspaper. Sometimes Peali went there, and sometimes others attended, after this in the month of Baisack or Jeit a letter came from Maniram Dewan in Calcutta to the Raja; Madhu Mallick brought the letter, it was in the evening . . . there was a long letter about tea and indigo and miscellaneous matters, inside of this was a smaller letter Madhu Mallick read it, in the small letter Maniram wrote that in Hindustan the Badshah had taken all the country that but a little distance remained for his reaching Calcutta, that the Raja should consider and arrange matters for ascending on the Ghaddee that he (Maniram) would reach Assam shortly, that the sepoys were ready to rise to join with them. Madhu Mallick said the Rajah should see to this matter at once . . . after this Madhu Mallick, Lockee Sensoa Baruah, Peali and Kamala Saringia Baruah had continued meetings to arrange matters.[83]

Another individual Nirmal Hazarie narrated in his deposition:

It was in the month of *Sawan* (July-August) Madhu Mallick, Lockee Sensoa Baruah, Peali Mauzadar and Kamala Saringia Barua used to assemble frequently and hold secret consultations with the Raja . . . the Saring Raja gave me 4 letters to take to Golaghat one addressed to the Sadar Ameen, one to Mohesh Chandra Doolia Baruah, Mauzadar, one to Bhobol Kungia Baruah, Mauzadar and one to Mayaram Nazir. He (Raja) told me in confidence to tell Mayaram that he the Raja had received a letter from Maniram Dewan from Calcutta (which he at the time held in his hand showing it to me) that Maniram wrote that there everything was accomplished, that in 2 or 3 days Calcutta would be taken and that I was to tell Mayaram that he was to come quickly to the Raja and to send some rice and the Raja said I was not to mention the matter to anybody, when I reached Golaghat I delivered my letter and message to Mayaram he gave me a letter for the Raja in reply.[84]

Both Somnath and Nirmal contended that Peali went to Golaghat to arrange their plan with the sepoys. This was also supported by Bhekool Mahaut on whose elephant Peali rode to Golaghat.[85]

The Muslim population of Jorhat promised to give help to the *raja*. Bahadur Gaoburha, Farmud Ali, Dil, his brother Farmud, the son of Kaliman Saikia, Khersa, Hazut Bar Hathkhowa and Bapie, came to see the *raja*. The *raja* received them in the *booleni-ghur* (drawing room). Bahadur Gaon Burha said to the *rajah* that there was no cause for fear when they had 100 guns in their houses and rice and money and all were at the Raja's service.[86] In his deposition Maniram Sarmah, the Gandhia Baruah, stated:

Some 12 or 13 days before the Raja's arrest Kaliman Saikia, Bahadur Gaon Burha and Hazut Hathkhowa told the Raja that in all the mussalman's houses there were guns and if he requested their services they would bring them and be presented.[87]

Nirmal Hazarie also gave depositions explaining the role of the Muslims and their assurance to give aid to the *raja*. Maniram Gandhia Baruah stated that Bahadur Gaon Burha offered to place 80 to 100 muskets in the *raja's* possession and Bahadur Gaon Burha received 11 *tolas* of gold to make a feast for the Mussalmans at the *masjid*.[88] Bahadur Gaon Burha and Farmud had frequent conversations with the *raja* in which Madhu Mallick, Peali and many

Judicial Administration from the Promulgation 155

others participated. Furmood was the person who brought Noor Muhammad Jemadar of the 1st Assam Light Infantry of Dibrugarh to the *raja*.[89]

On the basis of statements given by different individuals and on the enquiry conducted by Haranath, the police Darogah of Jorhat, a report was prepared by Captain Holroyd, for possible legal action against the following persons accused of conspiring against the state:

1. Saring Raja Kandarpeswar Singha
2. Maniram Dutta Dewan
3. Mohesh Chandra Baruah alias Peali
4. Madhu Mallick
5. Bahadur Gaon Burha
6. Lockee Sensoa Baruah
7. Farmud Ali
8. Kamala Saringia Baruah
9. Mayaram Barborah
10. Dutiram Baruah
11. Neelakantha Choladhara Phukan
12. Morangi Khowa Gohain

Besides the above, criminal proceedings were also drawn against a number of persons for aiding or abetting the conspiracy against the state. There included Madhoram Koch, Joran Naiboisha Phukan, Ugrasen Gohain, Umakanta Sarmah Borthakur, Debi Dutta Mouzadar, Ganesh Chandra Kath Baruah, Isweshar Sarmah, Narayan Borborah and others of rank and influence, who readily responded to the call of the 'Saring Raja' and Maniram Dewan.

Two pavilions were constructed at Jorhat to hold the trial. In one of them the Court of Captain Holroyd, Commissioner under Act XIV of 1857, had its sittings; in the other, Haranath Parbotia Baruah, the Darogah of Jorhat conducted his office for the purpose of facilitating the trial and preparing evidence.

The first to stand trial in Holroyd's court was Mohesh Chandra Baruah alias Peali who was arrested by Capt. Lowther with the assistance of the Darogah (Haranath) from a residence at Choladhora Ali.[90]

In a mock trial held on 9 February 1858, Mohesh Chandra Baruah alias Peali was awarded capital punishment. The sentence passed against him reads as follows:

> Court of Commissioner Appointed under Act XIV
> of 1857 for Sibsagar in Upper Assam.
> Trial No. 3, 1858

To
The Magistrate of Sibsagar,

Whereas at a Court of the Commissioner holden (sitting) at Jorhat in the Sibsagar District under Act XIV of 1857, for the year 1858 on the 9th day of February 1858, Mohesh Chandra alias Peali, son of Ram Sarma, having been convicted for treason, be it ordered that said convict be hanged by neck until he is dead. Further it is ordered that execution of the said sentence respecting the aforesaid convict be made and done by you on or before the 26th day of the month of February, 1858, in such manner as prescribed in the regulation enacted by the Governor-General and that you do return this warrant to me with an endorsement attested by your official seal, and signature certifying that the sentence as ordered herein has been executed. Herein fail not, given under my hand, this 9th day of February in the year 1858.

C. Holroyd
Commissioner Appointed
Under Act XIV of 1857.[91]

Commissioner Holroyd himself certified the performance of the death sentence as the magistrate of Sibsagar which reads as follows:

I hereby certify that the sentence of death passed on Mohesh Chandra alias Peali, son of Ram Sarma has been duly executed at Jorhat on Friday, the 26th day of February 1858, and said Ram Sarma's son Mohesh Chandra alias Peali was hung by the neck till he was dead. I further certify that the body of Peali, son of Ram Sarma was buried. Given under my hand and official seal of the court the 27th day of February 1858.[92]

C. Holroyd

Meanwhile, the steamer *Koladyne* with Maniram on board left Calcutta on 31 December 1857.[93] Maniram reached Jorhat on

22 February to stand trial. On the very next day, he was directly brought to Holroyd's court although he should have first been produced in the Darogah's court.[94] Maniram was charged with waging war against the government and Holroyd had gathered enough material to prove the charge. In a single-day trial on 23 February, he was found guilty of conspiracy and was sentenced to death.[95] The judgement given by Commissioner Holroyd read as follows:

> Court of Commissioner Appointed under Act XIV
> of 1857 for Sibsagar in Upper Assam,
> Trial No. 4, 1858.

To
The Magistrate of Sibsagar,

Whereas at a Court Holden (sitting) at Jorhat in the Sibsagar district under Act XIV of 1857 for the year 1858 on the 23rd day of February, 1858, Maniram, son of Ramdutt having convicted of treason and sentenced to suffer death by being hanged by the neck until he is dead. It is, hereby ordered that execution of the said sentence be made and done on or before the 26th of the month of February 1858 and that you do return this warrant to me with an endorsement attested by your official seal and signature, certifying the manner in which the sentence has been executed as commanded by the regulation enacted by the Governor-General-in-Council and now in force. Herein fail not, given under my hand, this twenty third day of February in the year 1858.

> C. Holroyd
> Commissioner Appointed Under
> Act XIV of 1857.[96]

Maniram was publicly hanged on 26 February 1858 along with Peali at Jorhat. Holroyd certified the performance of the death sentence as follows:

I hereby certify that the sentence of death passed on Maniram, son of Ramdutt has been duly executed and that the said Maniram son of Ramdutt was accordingly hung by the neck until he was dead at the town of Jorhat on Friday, the 26th day of February 1858.

I further certify that the body of the said Maniram, son of Ramdutt was afterwards buried.[97]

Given under my hand and official seal of this Court, the 27th day of February, 1858.

C. Holroyd
Magistrate

The manner in which the trial of Maniram was conducted has been inviting severe criticism ever since. Since both the Saring Raja and Maniram were lodged in Alipore Jail at that time, it would have been fair and easy to establish the alleged intriguing correspondences between the two, had the trial held at Calcutta. In fact, the Government of Bengal was interested in proceeding with the trial of Maniram in Calcutta itself immediately after his arrest. But due to strong opposition from Capt. Holroyd supported by Commissioner Jenkins such a judicious decision could not be taken. Capt. Holroyd was determined to try Maniram at Jorhat and interestingly by himself, who had personal enmity with the latter. For, Maniram submitted two memorandums to Mills during the latter's visit to Assam in 1853, without getting them forwarded by Holroyd. In one of these, he prayed for some favours from the government in recognition of his past services to it and in the other, the more significant one, he pleaded for the restoration of the Ahom monarchy in the person of Ghanakanta Singha, son of Chandrakanta Singha. This he did because he believed that Kandarpeswar's nomination to the throne, as the grandson of Purandar Singha, whom the Company had deposed earlier, would not be acceptable to the Company.

Maniram's second memorandum was a 'balance sheet of the administration of the East India Company for over a quarter of a century'.[98] In it, the emphasis was laid mainly upon the grievances of the people, the higher classes in particular. To quote his words:

> By the stoppage of such cruel practices as extracting the eyes, cutting off noses and ears, and the forcible abduction of virgins from their homes and by the removal of all wayside transit duties . . . the British Government has earned for itself inestimable praise and renown; but the introduction into the province

of new customs, innumerable courts, an unjust system of taxation, an objectionable treatment of the hill tribes . . . neither the British Government nor their subjects have gained any benefit.[99]

Maniram also complained against the appointment of men of Marwar and the Bengalis of Sylhet as *mouzadars*, when several respectable Assamese were out of employment.[100] He expressed his great discontent with the British rule in the following words:

We are just now as it were in the belly of a tiger and if our misfortunes yielded any advantage to the Government, we should be content, but the fact is, there is neither gain to the people nor to the Government, and so long as the present state of things continue, we see no prospect of improvement in future.[101]

Much of the ill-conceived measures Maniram attributed to the inexperience and indiscretion of the district officials whom he considered as wholly unfit to discharge the responsible duties entrusted to them. 'The bad temper of the young military officials', he alleged, 'is a source of much tribulations ... their youth and indiscretion prevent their discriminating between good and evil or regarding with any consideration the manners and customs of the people.'[102]

Maniram was particularly annoyed with the arrogant and injudicious attitude of Capt. Holroyd. Holroyd's style of functioning was criticized by the inhavitants of the district. In one of the petitions submitted to the Lieutenant Governor the people complained that:

Although the Principal Assistant Commissioner Captain Holroyd visits all the mofussil villages under his magistracy according to the orders of the Government, yet the result of it becomes quite contrary to the said orders, (that is) the orders are to the Magistrates to visit the mofussil villages for the only purpose to hear personally the every grievances from the mouth of each of the tenants. Whenever this officer attends tour of inspection, instead of hearing anything from any one, rather forbids the tenants to enter in his tent, eve, there are also kept some Barkandozes to the door for the prohibition of the entrance into it.[103]

Serious charges of misusing his authority and power were also brought against him. It was stated:

That Holroyd in collaboration with one Mr. Tud opened tea cultivation in fictitious name in village Shingee Boolia Kutchary (?) by destroying many crops. When people complained, Holroyd never heard their prayers but later under compelling circumstances paid Rs. 20 per family whose houses were destroyed by the action of Tud . . . Mr. Tud who served Assam Tea Company for 2 months and was discharged for his own fault declared that he was a nephew of Holroyd. In rainy season lot of timbers came floating on the Dikhow River. The ryots used to catch them in which operation; many of them lost their lives annually. Holroyd with his darogah forcibly took possession of such timbers and prepared boxes for tea. The poor ryots could not complain against such injudicious actions of the Principal Assistant.[104]

Besides the charges mentioned above, other complaints of extensive cultivation in government lands with the labour of the jail convicts were also brought against him. Holroyd denied all the charges as baseless and malicious. Since these charges were brought by the natives, he became a staunch enemy of the Assamese people and particularly of Maniram whom be considered to be an instigator. His hatred towards the natives was reflected in the irregular and high-handed proceedings against the rebels.

Holroyd, it seems, was determined to award Maniram capital punishment. The trial was therefore prejudiced and biased. The Europeans and the missionaries of the province were also aware of the fate of Maniram even before the actual trial took place. Whiting, an American Baptist, writing about the mutiny on 20 February 1858 stated that Maniram, the chief instigator, who was at Calcutta, was being tried at Jorhat and it is said that he will be executed.[105]

The materials to prove the charges against Maniram remained legally untested, as he was not in a position to be cross-examined or to defend himself, nor was he provided with any legal aid. Saring Raja Kandarpeswar Singha offered to swear to the signature of Maniram and the Government of Bengal desired to send him to Assam for that purpose. But Holroyd strongly objected to that move and stated:

With regards to the offer made by the Saring Raja to swear to the signature of Maniram, I look on it merely as an excuse to get back to this country; for he is, I imagine, perfectly acquainted with the fact that, Maniram is in the habit of not signing his name in many letters he writes, and certainly to none of a seditious nature but the Raja's affidavit on this point is quite unnecessary.[106]

Therefore, the decision against Maniram was arbitrary and solely on the unexamined evidence of prosecution. The manner in which Maniram was brought to a hasty trial and the way the depositions were recorded leaves no doubt that the whole trial was a farce. There is hardly any instance in any contemporary civilized society anywhere in the world in which a death sentence had been passed after a single day's trial. It is shocking to note that the English who claimed to have civilized the backward people of the east could deal with law in such an uncivilized manner.

The trial of the other convicts followed soon. Marangikhowa Gohain was tried on 12 March, and was sentenced to transportation for life to the Andaman island.[107] Ganesh Chandra Kathbaruah, son of Adiram, and Umakanta Sarma alias Umai Muktear, son of Saruman Sarma, were also tried on the same day along with Narayan of Bhatia Barbaurah's family. They were sentenced to three years rigorous imprisonment each.[108]

Mayaram Barbora was tried on 18 March by Capt. Holroyd. Mayaram was charged with two offences:

First, 'for having during the months of Jeit, Ahar, Sawan and Bhadra 1779 Assam Suk (May-June, July and August 1857) read out to the sepoys on the Golaghat command, the newspaper with a view to excite them to rise in rebellion against the Government and having himself promised assistance, and endeavoured to excite discontent by seditious talking', and second; 'For having held seditious communications with the Saring Raja'.[109]

Mayaram was sentenced to fourteen years imprisonment in banishment with hard labour in irons in any jail in the Bengal Presidency that the government might be pleased to direct. It was also ordered that all his property and effects of every description was to be forfeited to the government.[110]

On the same day, i.e. 18 March 1858 Neelakanta Choladhara Phukan, Kamala Charingia Baruah and Luki Senchowa Barua were tried and each of them was sentenced fourteen years deportation to the Andaman Island.[111]

This was followed by the trial of Madhu Mallick by Capt. Holroyd at Jorhat on the 26 March, for the offence of 'having during the months of Jeit, Ahar, Sawan and Bhadro, 1779 Assam Suk (May, June, July and August 1857), conspired with the Saring Raja of Jorhat to rebel and wage war against the Government, and having sided and abetted the said Raja by advice and counsel to rise in rebellion against the state'.[112] He was sentenced to transportation for life. The sentence passed against him reads as follows:

The evidence adduced in this case against the prisoner Madha Mallick is conclusive, and the fact of the Prisoner having been the direct agent of Maniram in his intrigues with the Saring Raja is fully established. That Maniram sent letters to the Raja under cover to the Prisoner as stated by the witnesses on oath is fully proved by the fact of documents having been found so addressed among the attached papers. The Prisoner's knowledge and complicity in the Act is established beyond doubt, I fully convict the Prisoner on the charge preferred against him. The Prisoner from his position as the accredited Agent of Maniram was in a position to influence the Saring Raja to persuade him to carry out the dictates of his employer in Calcutta, and that he did so to influence the too willing Raja, and encourage and exhort him to rebel against the Government is proved. Taking these facts into consideration, and the leading part taken by the Prisoner in the conspiracy, I sentence him to be transported as a felon beyond sea for the term of his natural life.[113]

In May 1858, Dutiram Baruah, *sheristadar* of the Fauzdari Court in the district of Sibsagar was brought to trial on the following charges:

First instance accessory before and after the fact in the late conspiracy against the Government.

Second Exerting himself both before and after the capture of the Saring Raja to screen from justice, those concerned in the Conspiracy against Government.

Third Privy to the rebellious acts stated in the first instance of the charge and willfully guilty of gross neglect of duty in not reporting the same to the proper authorities.[114]

Captain Holroyd found the prisoner guilty of all these charges 'after much anxious deliberations in this case'.[115] Having found the prisoner guilty to the extent afore stated, he sentenced him to

Judicial Administration from the Promulgation 163

be banished from the province of Assam, and to be detained in such safe custody as the government might direct.[116] His property and effects of every description were forfeited to the state. Dutiram was at first lodged in Alipore Jail. Later on 2 September 1858 he was carried to Andaman Island on board the *Boanerges*, where he was eventually disembarked.

Bahadur Gaonburha, and Farmud Ali were charged of fomenting sedition among the Muslims of Jorhat and other areas and tried on 19 August 1858.[117] They were awarded the same punishment as Mayaram Borborah and Dutiram Baruah.

Over and above the persons already mentioned, there was a host of others who directly or indirectly took part in the mutiny or the national upsurge. They suffered from various kinds of punishments and humiliation at the hands of the British officer. Among them the names of the some significant ones are given in Table 4.2.[118]

The Saring Raja Kandarpeswar Singha was not brought to trial but lodged in Alipore after his arrival at Calcutta in October 1857. On 15 October 1857 a warrant was issued by the Government of Bengal to the Superintendent, Alipore Jail detaining him as a state prisoner, which reads as follows:

Where the Lt. Governor of Bengal for good and sufficient reasons has been fit to determine that the Saring Raja, Kandarpeswar Singha, shall be placed under personal restraint at the Alipore jail, you are hereby required and commanded, in pursuance of that determination, to receive the person above named into your custody, and to deal with him in conformity to the orders of the Lt. Governor of Bengal and provisions of Regulation III of 1818.[119]

In Calcutta, the Saring Raja made a petition to the Lt. Governor of Bengal and challenged his detention as illegal and unjustified. By his petition dated 21 November 1857, he solicited permission to defend himself through Mr. Fagan a member of the Bar of the Supreme Court. In the said petition, the Saring Raja stated:

Your petitioner is most anxious to place before your Honour the grounds on which he bases his assertion of his own innocence and as a means to this humbly entices of your Honour to allow him to have an interview with Mr. Fagan a member of the Bar of the Supreme Court to whom he desires to give further instructions than he can at present give with a view to the presentation of a further petition to your Honour for the final release of your Petitioner.[120]

TABLE 4.2: SOME SIGNIFICANT PERSONS WHO SUFFERED UNFAIR PUNISHMENT AT THE HANDS OF THE BRITISH

Name	Reason for Conviction	Punishment
Krishna Chandra Majumdar	For reading Newspaper in the Military detachment at Golaghat	Banishment from, Assam
Bisweshawar Chandrakanta Dubey	For revolting at Negeriting T.E.	Eight years imprisonment
Khogeswar Thakur	For refusing to be witness	Suspension from employment
Shashadhar Sarmah Darogah	Neglect of duty	Suspension
Laxman Singh Barkandoze	”	”
Lambai Aidew Mohesh Baruah	” ”	Loss of Mouzadari
Mihiram Gogoi	”	”
Jogeswar	Not helping the Govt.	Suspended from employment for six months
Sashadhar Mohori	”	”
Purnananda Mohori	”	”
Devidutt Baruah	Not informing Govt. about Mutiny	Loss of Mouzadari
Isehwar Sarma	”	”
Shaikh Bhikan	For taking part in revolt	Life imprisonment
Noor Muhmood	”	”
Roostum Singh	”	Seven years imprisonment

Source: Benudhar Sarmah and Mani Ram Dewan, pp. 221-2. See also K.N. Dutta, *Landmarks of the Freedom Struggle in Assam*, pp. 136-8.

The Government of Bengal granted the interview vide Secretary Young's letter to Fergusson, Barrister-at-Law No. 2783 dated 26 November 1857 on the condition that the Superintendent of the Alipore Jail would be present at the time of interview.[121]

Meanwhile Capt. Holroyd took up the case of the Saring Raja in his absence and forwarded his finding to the Government of Bengal on 28 June 1858.[122] Condemning the high-handed action of Cap. Holroyd, Kandarpeswar Singha in a petition to government stated:

Your Petitioner was suspected without grounds, of instigating mutiny in Assam, and in consequence of which was arrested and sent up to Alipore jail by order of the Principal Assistant Commissioner of Sibsagar, that notwithstanding the common right and privileges enjoyed by every subject under British rule, of being allowed to bring in his defence when a charge is brought against him, your Petitioner's case was taken up by Principal Assistant Commissioner during his absence, without giving him any notice of the same, and allowing him the opportunity of vindicating his character.[123]

Kandarpeswar Singha submitted 'a memorial' on 11 August 1858 praying for a re-hearing of his case either by Jenkins, Agent to the Governor-General or by some other competent tribunal and appointed G.H. Fagan, the Counsel to plead in his favour. He stated:

That during his apprehension and the investigation into the inner part of the royal house, made by the Principal Assistant Commissioner, no tokens whatever of ammunition or warlike preparation, were found there. The suspicion of the mutiny, with which he has been charged was not proved at all; but the charge brought against him was fabricated by the Principal Assistant Commissioner and the Police darogah through an enmity against him, and established by the deposition of a set of mercenary perjurers.[124]

On 22 November 1858, the Lieutenant Governor issued an order pardoning the Saring Raja, but directed him nevertheless to remain out of his native country, and to take up residence either at Midnapore, Bhagalpore or Burdwan.[125] The Raja preferred to stay in Burdwan. He, however, renewed his prayer to the government to allow him to return to Assam. On 11 July 1860, he was allowed to stay at Goalpara which he refused as 'it is the frontier of Assam, about more than 300 miles distant from Jorhat my nativity and secluded from all social communities necessary on several occasions'.[126] He wished to return to Jorhat; if, however, the government did not permit this he might be allowed to stay at Guwahati. His persistent efforts ultimately softened the attitude of the Government of Bengal and in December 1860, the Lieutenant Governor issued an order allowing him to move to Guwahati.[127] Accordingly the Saring Raja returned to Guwahati in 1862.

Kandarpeswar Singha suffered all sorts of humiliation and indignities during the period of his detention. Capt. Holroyd went to extremes in his vendetta against the Saring Raja. He auctioned the Raja's valuable moveable properties in spite of the government's clear instruction to restore all such properties to him.

His landed properties were, however, saved due to the timely intervention of the Government of Bengal. In a communication to the Agent to the Governor-General, Young, Secretary of the Government of Bengal warned the local authorities and observed, 'the Raja has not been tried and convicted of the offence with which he was charged, there is no judicial sentence against him, by virtue of which he can be held to have forfeited his property. The Government has therefore, no authority to sell his land,'[128] The sale proceeds of his movable properties that had been disposed of in auction were remitted to him after satisfying a decree and other maintenance expenses.

Kandarpeswar's prayer for pension to meet his livelihood was approved by the Governor-General-in-Council in February 1863 after his return to Guwahati. Living in a state of destitution and impoverishment Kandarpeswar Singha died in 1880 at Guwahati.

The other convicts also did not receive due attention from the government in spite of the Queen's Proclamation for General Amnesty in 1858. Among others Bahadur Gaon Burha was released from Andaman on 27 April 1862[129] while Dutiram Baruah was released in August 1862.[130] Seikh Furmood Ali was released by order of Lieutenant Governor dated 2 January 1863[131] and Mayaram Borbaruah on 20 May 1863.[132] Dutiram Baruah, was, however, not allowed to return to his native place Sibsagar. He died on 6 July 1872 at the age of sixty-six years and six months at Guwahati.

Marangikhowa Gohain was said to have died far away from his home, while Kamala Senchowa Baruah died in prison. Nothing definite was known about Madhu Mallick.

It is believed, as appears in many writings that the attitude of Capt. Holroyd was even criticized by the British government itself and later his commission was withdrawn. This is, however, not true. In fact, Holroyd was promoted to the rank of Major and in March 1863 his service was placed under the military department.

NOTES

1. Bengal Judicial Proceeding (Civil), 6 July 1837, no. 2.
2. Bengal Judicial Proceedings, December 1870, no. 2.
3. Ibid.
4. Bengal Judicial Proceedings (Civil), 6 July 1837, no. 2, see Assam Code.
5. Ibid.
6. Ibid.
7. Ibid.
8. Ibid.
9. Ibid.
10. Ibid.
11. Ibid.
12. Ibid.
13. Ibid.
14. Ibid.
15. Bengal Judicial Proceedings, 23 June 1847, no. 151; Matthie to Jenkins, 23 June 1847.
16. Bengal Judicial Proceedings (Civil), 6 July 1837, no. 2.
17. Ibid.
18. Ibid.
19. Ibid.
20. Ibid.
21. Ibid.
22. Ibid.

23. Ibid.
24. Ibid.
25. Bengal Judicial Proceedings (Civil), 26 September 1842, no. 39, Hawkins to Halliday, 5 August 1842.
26. Bengal Judicial Proceedings, 26 September 1846, no. 160, Hawkins to Government of Bengal, 4 October 1844.
27. Bengal Judicial Proceedings (Civil), 5 December 1842, no. 27, Hawkins to Halliday, 18 November 1842.
28. Bengal Judicial Proceedings (Criminal), 7 November 1842, no. 39.
29. Bengal Judicial Proceedings, 23 September 1846, no. 160, also see BJP; December 1870, no. 13, Appendix A, revised code for civil justice, section III, clause 5.
30. Ibid. See Section III, Clause 7.
31. Bengal Judicial Proceedings, 23 September 1846, no. 167, Matthis to Jenkins, 11 August 1846.
32. Ibid., no. 162.
33. Bengal Judicial Proceedings (Civil), 6 July 1837, no. 2.
34. Report on the Province of Assam, p. 121, Appendix J.
35. Bengal Judicial Proceedings, 9 September 1852, no. 100.
36. Bengal Judicial Proceedings, 27 January 1859, no. 309.
37. Ibid.
38. Ibid.
39. Ibid.
40. Bengal Judicial Proceedings (Civil), 6 July 1837, no. 2, see Assam Civil Code.
41. Report on the Province of Assam, p. 122 (Appendix J).
42. Bengal Judicial Proceedings (Civil), 2 October 1838, no. 6.
43. Bengal Judicial Proceedings (Civil), 6 July 1837, no. 2, see Rules for the Administration of Criminal Justice.
44. Ibid.
45. Ibid.
46. For penal code see Bengal Judicial Proceedings (Civil), 6 July 1837, no. 2, (Rules for the Administration of Criminal Justice in Assam, also see M.N. Gupta's *Analytical Survey of Bengal Regulations*).
47. Bengal Judicial Proceedings (Civil), 25 August 1836, no. 23, Jenkins to Mongles, 10 May 1835.
48. Bengal Judicial Proceedings (Civil), 6 July 1837, no. 2, see Rules for the Administration of Criminal Justice.
49. Bengal Judicial Proceedings, 4 June 1857, no. 174.
50. Bengal Judicial Proceedings, 6 July 1854, no. 140.

Judicial Administration from the Promulgation 169

51. Bengal Judicial Proceedings, 4 June 1857, no. 174.
52. Ibid.
53. Bengal Judicial Proceedings, 6 July 1854, no. 140.
54. Bengal Judicial Proceedings, 4 June 1857, no. 174.
55. Bengal Judicial Proceedings, 27 January 1859, no. 309, Agnew to Dy. Com., 14 July 1858.
56. Ibid., also see Bengal Judicial Proceedings, 4 June 1857, no. 174.
57. Ibid.
58. Bengal Political Consultations, 25 March 1834, no. 38, quoted in *Assam in the Days of Company*, p. 120.
59. *A Comprehensive History of Assam*, p. 474.
60. Bengal Judicial Proceedings (Criminal), 15 August 1839, no. 28.
61. *A Comprehensive History of Assam*, p. 477.
62. Bengal Judicial Proceedings (Criminal), 30 August 1842, no. 3.
63. Bengal Judicial Proceedings, 1857; 10 September, no. 482.
64. Bengal Judicial Proceedings, 24 December 1857, no. 211, see deposition of Bhokool Mahout. In his deposition Kinaram Choudhury, the school Pandit corroborated the evidence given by Bhokool Mahout, see deposition of Kinaram Choudhury.
65. Bengal Judicial Proceedings, 14 January 1858, no. 155, see deposition of Trilochan quoted in *Assam in the Days of Company*, p. 184.
66. Bengal Judicial Proceedings, 29 July 1958, no. 115, Holroyd to Young, 28 June, quoted, in *Assam in the Days of the Company*, p. 185.
67. Bengal Judicial Proceedings, 14 January 1858, no. 156, see deposition of Maniram Sarmah Gandhia Baruah, 30 October 1857.
68. Bengal Judicial Proceedings, 10 September 1857, no. 482, Agent Jenkins to Secretary, Government of Bengal, 29 August 1857.
69. Bengal Judicial Proceedings, 29 October 1857, no. 331, Holroyd to Jenkins, 6 September 1857.
70. Bengal Judicial Proceedings, 22 October 1857, no. 276, Jenkins to Secretary Bengal, 17 September 1857.
71. Bengal Judicial Proceedings, 22 October 1857, no. 276, Holroyd to Jenkins, 12 September 1857.
72. Ibid.
73. Bengal Judicial Proceedings, 22 October 1857, nos. 279 & 280; Secretary, to Magistrate of Dacca, 30 January 1857.
74. Bengal Judicial Proceedings, 29 October 1857, no. 329, quoted in *Assam in the Days of the Company*, p. 192.
75. Bengal Judicial Proceedings, 14 January 1858, no. 159, A quoted in *Assam in the Days of the Company*, p. 194.

76. Bengal Judicial Proceedings, 14 January 1858, no. 170.
77. Bengal Judicial Proceedings, 14 January 1858, no. 154, qouted in A.K. Dutta's *Maniram Dewan and Contemporary Assamese Society*, p. 176.
78. Ibid.
79. Bengal Judicial Proceedings, 14 January 1858, no. 155, Agent to the Governor-General to Lieutent Governor, 28 November 1857.
80. Bengal Judicial Proceedings, 14 January 1858, no. 170.
81. Bengal Judicial Proceedings (Mutiny), 14 January 1858, no. 155, Agent to the Governor-General to Holroyd, 1 December 1857.
82. Bengal Judicial Proceedings (Mutiny), 10 August 1858, nos. 836-8, Secretary to Commissioner of Assam, 11 July 1857.
83. Bengal Judicial Proceedings (Mutiny), 24 December 1857, no. 211, Commissioner to Government of Bengal, 14 December 1857, see deposition of Somnath Sarmah, 21 November 1857.
84. Bengal Judicial Proceedings (Mutiny), 24 December 1857, no. 211, see deposition of Nirmal Sarmah Hazarie, 31 October 1857.
85. Ibid., deposition of Bhokool Mahaut taken on 3 November 1857.
86. Ibid., no. 211, deposition Somnath Sarmah.
87. BJP (Mutiny), 14 January 1858, no. 156, see deposition Maniram Sarmah Gandhia Baruah, 30 October 1857.
88. Ibid.
89. Bengal Judicial Proceedings, 24 December 1857, no. 211.
90. Amulya Chandra Sarmah, *Satawan Sal Aru Piyali Baruah*, p. 42.
91. Benudhar Sarmah, 'The Rebellion of 1857, *vis-a-vis* Assam', quoted in B. Hazarika, *Political Life in Assam During the Nineteenth Century*, pp. 65-6.
92. A.C. Sarmah, *Stwan sal aru Piyali Baruah*, p. 46.
93. Bengal Judicial Proceedings (Mutiny), 14 January 1858, nos. 171-2.
94. Dutta, op. cit., p. 177.
95. Bengal Judicial Proceedings, 24 June 1858, no. 619, quoted in *Assam in the Days of the Company*, p. 195.
96. Benudhar Sarmah, *Maniram Dewan*, p. 187.
97. Ibid., Ajit Kumar Dutta, *Maniram Dewan and Conyemporary Assamese Society*, p. 179, published by Anupama Dutta, Neemati, Jorhat, 1990.
98. H.K. Barpujari, General Editor, *Political History of Assam*, vol. I, p. 67.
99. Report on the Province of Assam, Appendix K.B, p. 607.
100. Ibid.
101. Ibid., p. 605.

102. Barpujari, *Assam in the Days of the Company*, p. 177.
103. Bengal Judicial Proceedings, 2 July 1857, no. 758; see petition of Bogoodas Bairagi, 2 March 1857.
104. Ibid.
105. American Baptist Foreign Misson Society, 1858, Whiting to Peck, Sibsagar 20 February, quoted in AIDC, p. 195, see fns.
106. Bengal Judicial Proceedings (Mutiny) 1858, no. 158, Holroyd to Jenkins, 28 November 1857.
107. B.B. Hazarika, *Political Life in Assam During the 19th Century*, p. 369.
108. Ibid.
109. Surya Kumar Bhuyan, *Studies in the History of Assam*, p. 165.
110. Ibid., pp.165-6.
111. Hazarika, op. cit., p. 370.
112. Bhuyan, op. cit., p. 171.
113. Ibid.
114. Bengal Judicial Proceedings, October 1860, no. 127; J. Nemarch Esq. Barrister-at-Law to the Secy. Government of India, Home Department 13 September 1860.
115. Ibid.
116. Ibid.
117. A. Sattar, *Bahadur Gaon Burha*, p. 19.
118. Benudhar Sarmah, *Maniram Dewan*, pp. 2213-22. K.N. Dutta, *Landmarks of the Freedom Struggle in Assam*, pp.136-8
119. Bengal Judicial Proceedings, 3 February 1859, no. 98, Young to Superintendent Alipore Jail, 15 October 1857.
120. Bengal Judicial Proceedings (Mutiny), 3 December 1857, no. 204 see petition of Kandarpeswar Singha, 21 November 1857.
121. Ibid.
122. Bengal Judicial Proceedings, May 1860, no. 497, see petition of Kandarpeswar Singh.
123. Ibid.
124 Ibid.
125. Ibid.
126. Bengal Judicial Proceedings, November 1860, no. 222, Kandarpeswar Singha to Commissioner of Burdwan, 30 October 1860.
127. Bengal Judicial Proceedings, December 1860, no. 344, Bell under Seceretary, Bengal to Commissioner of Burdwan, 27 December 1860.
128. Bengal Judicial Proceedings, 19 May 1859, no. 169, Young to Agent to the Governor-General, 19 May 1859.

129. Bengal Judicial Proceedings, September 1862, no. 159.
130. Ibid., no. 163.
131. Bengal Judicial Proceedings, January 1863, nos. 1-4.
132. Bengal Judicial Proceedings, June 1863, no. 70.

APPENDIX 4.1

PROCLAMATION FOR RESUMPTION OF UPPER ASSAM

No. 28
15 August 1839

CRIMINAL

Read a letter from the Agent to the Governor-General North-East Frontier dated 27 June, suggesting the propriety of bringing the two Zillahs of Jorhat and Luckimpore under the operations of Government Laws and Regulations in like manner with the three Zillahs of Lower Assam.

Order: Order that the following proclamation be issued for the purpose of annexing the districts of Upper Assam to Bengal and transferring the administration to the Deputy Governor in order that the Laws and Regulations applicable to Lower Assam may be applied and executed thereto as recommended in the above letter.

PROCLAMATION

The territory of Upper Assam which in 1833 was placed by the British Government under the administration of Rajah Poorunder Singh, has, in consequence of the failure of that chief to provide adequately for the protection and well being of the country and its inhabitants, and inconsequence also of his neglect to defray the tribute reserved to the British Government, been resumed and taken into direct management of the British Officers. The administration of this territory has hitherto been conducted by officers of the province, who have received their instruction through the Commissioner of Assam from the Government of India in the political department, and the territory has been formed into two districts divided by the Brahmaputra River and designated North and South Upper Assam. The Head Station of the former has been fixed at Luckimpore and Captain Vetch has been vested with the civil charge and Lt. Brodie has been appointed to administer the southern district and Seebsagar near Rangpur has been fixed for the headquarter station.

The President-in-Council deeming it no longer necessary for the government of India to retain its own direct management, the civil administration of the two districts of Upper Assam above described, has resolved that they shall be annexed to Bengal from the 1st proximo, to be administered after that date in the same manner as the districts of Lower Assam now under the Commissioner of that province and his several Assistants and from the date mentioned the offices employed in the said two districts of Upper Assam will be placed under the authority of the Board of Revenue in revenue matters and of the Sadar Dewanee Adawlut, and Sadar Nizamut Adalat, in matters connected with the administration of civil and criminal justice, as provided by Act No. 11 of 1835 accordingly as may be ordered by the Deputy Governor of Bengal in the Revenue and Judicial Department.

31 July 1839

By order
Sd./H.J. Prinsep
Sect. to the Govt. of India

Source: BJP (Criminal), 15 August 1839, no. 28.

APPENDIX 4.2

ORDER OF INSTRUCTION FROM THE SECRETARY TO THE GOVERNOR OF BENGAL TO THE COMMISSIONER OF ASSAM TO GOVERN THE PROVINCE IN CONFORMITY WITH THE TERM OF THE PROCLAMATION

No. 765
15 August 1839

CRIMINAL

To,
Captain F. Jenkins
Commissioner of Assam

Sir,

I am directed by the Hon'ble the Deputy Governor of Bengal to call your attention to the proclamation issued from the political department under the date 31st ultimo (Published in the Government gazette of date the 3rd instant page 620 by which the two Districts designated North and South Upper Assam formerly under the administration of Rajah Poorunder Singh have, in all revenue and judicial matters been placed under the Government of Bengal. From the 1st instant you will therefore be pleased to act in conformity with the tenor of that proclamation.

Fort William   F.A. Haliday
The 15th August 1839   Secy. to the Govt. of Bengal

Source: BJP (Criminal), 15 August 1839, no. 29.

APPENDIX 4.3

Proceeding No. 3					30 August 1842

CRIMINAL

Proclamation
Fort William,
Political Department,
The 17th August 1842

The Hon'ble the President-in-Council is pleased to direct and notify that the districts of the North East Frontier of Upper Assam, now under the management of Capt. Vetch in Political Department commonly called the Sadiya and Matak District, and the tracts which may hereafter be annexed to the same superintendence, shall be administered from the 1st proximo in all matters of Revenue and judicial administration under the government of Bengal in those Departments. The offices employed in that country are accordingly placed under the authority of the Suddor Board of Revenue in revenue matters and of the Suddar Dewany Adalat and Nizamat Adalat in matters connected with the administration of civil and criminal justice in the manner provided by Act No. 11 of 1835, as may be ordered by the Government of Bengal in the Revenue and Political Department. The local officers corresponding with and subject to the intermediate control of the Commissioner of Assam, as in the District of Upper Assam similarly transferred from the Political Department to the Revenue and Judicial Department of the Government of Bengal by a resolution dated the 31 July 1839, which was published in the Calcutta Gazette of the 3rd of August following.

By order					G.A. Busby
17th August (Instant)			Off. Secy. to the Govt. of India
1842

Source: BJP (Criminal), 30 August 1842, no. 3.

APPENDIX 4.4

CAPT. HOLROYD'S LETTER REGARDING THE ARREST OF THE SARING RAJA

From Capt. Holroyd, P.A. at Sibsagar
To, Col. Jenkins, Commissioner of Assam,

Dated Sibsagar 12 September 1857

Sir,

I have the honour to report my return last evening to Sibsagar after having effected the arrest of the Saring Raja.

At midnight of Monday the 7th September, I left Sibsagar by a boat proceeding down the river without any one being aware of my departure having left secret instructions with Mr. Master how to act during my absence. A party of twenty picked men had left that evening by boat under orders to relieve the Golaghat detachment. This Party I overtook at Dikhowmokh and detained with me for the work for which they were engaged at Dikhowmokh. I awaited the arrival of Capt. Lowther with his detachment from Dibrugarh. They joined me between 5 and 6 o'clock p.m. and after his men had cooked and fed we proceeded down in a body to Mohgur (present Kokilamukh) which place we reached at midnight. We marched from the ghant at 1 o'clock and the men were conveyed across the swamps by my elephant which I had sent down overnight through the jungles. We reached Jorhat about one hour before day light when the houses of Saring Rajah were surrounded without the least alarm being given and his arrest quickly effected, at the same time a party was detached to surround the house of the Bangali Muktear situated in the Bazar, this was likewise done without waiting.

After securing the person of the Saring Rajah I awaited till day break (the house being surrounded by sentries) to search for papers, the destruction of which I carefully ascertained could not effected by the inmates, I was employed in this duty assisted by Capt. Lowther both at the Raja and Muktear's house till a late hour in the afternoon a large number of papers were found but whether any of importance it is impossible to say until the whole have been properly examined this day I am now employed on but I much fear, the most important document have been destroyed.

C. Holroyd

Source: BJP, 22 October 1857, no. 276, Holroyd to Jenkins, 12 September 1857.

CHAPTER 5

Administration of Justice under the Crown till 1874

EXTENSION OF CODES OF CIVIL AND
CRIMINAL PROCEDURE

Following the disastrous events of 1857, the East India Company was dissolved and the government of the country was directly assumed by the Crown in 1858. The Queen's Proclamation contained a promise to abolish all racial discrimination from the administration of justice. The existence of two separate superior courts—one for the rulers and the other for the ruled—had been discontinued. The Indian High Courts Act was passed on 6 August 1861 by the British Parliament with the object of amalgamating the two rival judicial systems—the Crown's Court and the Company's courts—and bringing uniformity in the laws to be administered.

By the time the High Courts Act was passed, the judicial administration in Assam had undergone important changes. Act VIII of 1859, known as Civil Procedure Code was extended to the province on 26 April 1860 in supersession of the Rules for the Administration of Civil Justice.[1] But the promulgation of that Code in the province had been deferred to 1 July 1860 in order to enable the vakeels and officers of the courts in Assam to procure copies of the Act.[2]

The Indian Penal Code Act XLV of 1860, which was passed in 1860 on the basis of the draft of the First Law Commission, was also extended to the province.[3] The Indian Penal Code was followed by the Criminal Procedure Code (Act XXV of 1861).[4] Both these Acts came into force from 1 January 1862.

The process to assimilate the judicial administration of Assam with that of the other parts of the country began with the extension of these codes. No major changes in the structure of the judiciary was, however, made immediately after the extension of the civil and criminal codes. The civil powers exercised by the junior or sub-assistants were continued as usual. The powers of sadar *ameens* and *munsifs* were also not disturbed.

In 1861 the designations of officers functioning in Assam were changed. The office of the deputy commissioner was converted into judicial commissioner with almost all the functions of a civil and session judge of Bengal. The designations of principal assistant, junior assistant and sub-assistant were changed to deputy commissioner, assistant commissioner and extra-assistant commissioner respectively.[5]

The new codes introduced the system of examination in the recruitment of assistants which was prevailing in the Regulation provinces. Under the new rules, an assistant commissioner was to receive a salary of Rs. 400 on his first appointment. In the administration of criminal justice, he was to exercise the powers of a subordinate magistrate of second grade. After passing the first or lower standard of examination, they would be eligible for the power of subordinate magistrate of the first grade with a salary of Rs. 450 per month. On passing the second or higher standard and if by the time they acquired sufficient experience, they would be eligible for the full powers of a magistrate with a salary fixed for an assistant commissioner, viz., Rs. 500 per month.[6] Hitherto an assistant with the lowest class of powers (subordinate magistrate of second grade) and an assistant with special powers (subordinate magistrate of the first grade) received equal amount of salary, notwithstanding that the duties and responsibilities of one class were much greater than those of the other. Under the new rules made effective from 1 March 1862, an intermediate grade of Rs. 450 was created consisting of officers who had passed the first standard and were exercising the powers of a subordinate magistrate of first grade, corresponding with what were formerly called special powers. The arrangement sought to derive two-fold advantage—first, officers would be induced to pass the first standard more rapidly, and second, the inconsistency of paying equally for the performance of functions of very different degrees of importance, would be avoided.[7]

The magistrate of a district was authorized by the Criminal Procedure Code to invest any officer in the district with the powers under Section 66B to take up cases on the complaint made to them, or on the report of a police officer. But such power was not to be delegated to other officers in the Sadar Station except in the absence of the magistrate for tour or any other purpose.

The pressure of work on the Magistrate increased with the extension of the Code of Criminal Procedure. By Section CCLXXVI of this Code, in every case where the presumption was that the accused, if guilty, would have to be committed and in cases which were beyond his jurisdiction, a subordinate magistrate must forward the parties to the magistrate, who must himself record the evidence *de novo*.[8] As there were few officers in a vast province like Assam to exercise full powers of a magistrate, the greater part of work fell heavily on the single magistrate of a particular district. It was also a great hardship for the witnesses and parties themselves in such cases, who were required to come, sometimes traversing a distance of 60 to 70 miles to the Sadar Station, not only to attend the session trial but also for the preliminary enquiry before the magistrate and, as a result, the benefit to be had in creating sub-divisions were in a great measure nullified.[9]

To put to rest all the anomalies described above, the Lieutenant Governor empowered all officers-in-charge of a sub-division to make preliminary enquiry into cases that could be tried by the Court of Session, or by any Supreme Court of Judicature under Section XXXVIII of the Code of Criminal Procedure.[10]

In the administration of civil justice, all assistant commissioners and extra assistant commissioners were vested with the powers of *munsif* on passing first level examination and powers of *sadar ameen* on passing the second level examination.[11] However, on special grounds, the powers of *munsif* might be given to assistants and extra assistant commissioners who had not passed the first level examination, and powers of *sadar ameen* to those who had passed first level examination. In the same manner, the power of principal *sadar ameen* might be given to the assistant commissioners and extra-assistant commissioners who had passed the second level examination.

Under the Assam Code, the officer in charge of a district exercised the powers of civil judge and appeals against the decisions of assistant commissioners (formerly junior assistants) and *munsifs* were also to be heard by him. But after the extension of the new code such power was taken away from him in 1864. Henceforth, it was provided that all appeals would have to be lodged in the judicial commissioner's court.[12] This led to delay in dispensing with cases, involving more expenses and inconvenience to suitors coming from great distances.

In 1872, the Bengal Civil Court Act (Act VI of 1871) was extended to Assam and, consequently, the system of judicial administration of Assam was brought in line with that of Bengal and other provinces of the country. Under Section 10 of that Act, the officers of the province who were given civil court power is given in Table 5.1.[13]

Appeals against the decisions of *munsifs* of the district of Kamrup, Nowgong, Darrang, Sibsagar and Lakhimpur were to be preferred to the court of the deputy commissioner of each of these districts respectively in their capacity as subordinate judge. However, appeals from the extra assistant commissioner and *munsifs* of Barpeta,

TABLE 5.1: OFFICERS WITH CIVIL COURT POWERS

Officer	Powers to be exercised
Judicial Commissioner	Powers of district judge
Deputy Commissioner of Kamrup, Durrong, Nowgong, Sibsagar, Lakhimpur	Powers of subordinate judge[14]
Assistant Commissioner of Barpeta, North Lakhimpur, Jorhat, Mangaldoi	Power of subordinate judge
All EAC's and Assistant Commissioners of Kamrup, Darrang, Nowgong, Golaghat, Sibsagar and Khasia and Jayantia Hills	Power of *munsif*

Source: BJP, February 1872, no. 173, notification, 28 February 1872.

Mangloyde, Jorhat and North Lakhimpur were to be preferred to the assistant commissioner's court of these subdivisions in their capacity as subordinate judge.[15]

With the abolishment of the *munsif* court in 1872 the power of the *munsif* was distributed amongst different officers. All first grade *munsifs* were made fifth grade extra assistant commissioners on a salary of Rs. 400 and all second grade *munsifs* were made sixth grade extra assistant commissioners on a salary of Rs. 300 per month.[16] These officers continued to exercise the powers of the *munsif* under Section 10 of Act VI of 1871 (Bengal Civil Court Act).

PEASANT UPRISING

The history of our country is replete with anti-colonial uprisings and Nowgong, in Assam, occupies a distinct place in the history of anti-colonial struggle. It was the centre of a great peasant revolt in 1861, which shook the very foundation of the British rule in the district. Even in 1836-7 the people of Nowgong showed their defiance when capitation tax was substituted by garden tax and it almost led to an open insurrection.[17] The prompt action by the assistant in-charge of the district, however, quelled the disturbance.

Peasant uprisings in this district occurred mostly due to the economic policies of the British rulers and the various measures that led to the destruction of traditional ways of livelihood. The exploitation in the form of revenue collection angered the *ryots* and they rose up to challenge their rulers whenever they were able to assemble in large numbers. In fact, the agrarian unrest in Nowgong was the result of untold hardship the people had to face after the introduction of British rule. High revenue assessment in different kinds of taxation created general discontentment amongst the poor peasants. The resentment was ubiquitous. In 1834-5 the land tax and plough tax were further enhanced, and later, assessment on the garden land was also taxed. When Mills, a judge of Sadar Court visited Assam for enquiring into the affairs of the province, he received numerous petitions expressing the dissatisfaction by the peasants. Further, the taxation of the gardens caused great resentment and the peasants openly opposed it. Apart from the rate of assessment and the kind of taxes, the system or machinery of collecting taxes was also oppressive. The district officials engaged hosts of revenue collectors to collect revenue without any supervision. They, 'collected where and from they could, paying what they pleased of their collections to the Government'.

There were occasional demonstrations against the oppressive taxation policies. The government, however, controlled these disturbances by carrot and the stick policy.

The miserable state of things went on for a number of years. The government called upon the officers in Assam to report on the feasibility of a tax on betel nut and *pan* cultivation. When this news reached the masses already facing the burden of excessive taxing, it led to an agitation in Nowgong because the district extensively cultivated *pan*. The people of the district were already hit hard by the stoppage of opium cultivation in 1860 as many peasants survived on the income derived from opium trade, which was widely used by the common people. Further, Nowgong was the largest producer of opium at that time.

The *ryots* about 1,500 of Kaliabor, a *pargana* of Nowgong, first showed signs of dissatisfaction with the measure of taxation which they believed to be impending over them. On 17 September 1861, the *ryots* assembled in a considerable number and tumultuous manner, around the deputy commissioner's office. The deputy commissioner addressed them, and promised attention to their grievances provided they were embodied in a petition to be presented in a proper and a respectful way. Notwithstanding this assurance, about a score of them forced open the closed door of a room in which Deputy Commissioner Lieutenant Herbert Sconce was transacting business. It was found necessary to convey the unruly *ryots* to the *thana*, where they were confined until evening when one Dheer Singh, an influential native merchant of Nowgong, obtained their release from the deputy commissioner.[18] A few days after 17 September some *gaon burhas* and *ryots* submitted a petition to the deputy commissioner, Nowgong, stating that they had suffered hardship from the stoppage of poppy cultivation. On Wednesday, 9 October, there was another gathering of *ryot*, who presented a petition to the deputy commissioner, in which, after a reference to the hurt done to them by the prohibition of opium cultivation, they made an earnest remonstrance against any impost on their house, or on *baree* and *pan* cultivation. They were heard with attention. The deputy commissioner drew a carefully worded order in which the real scope and intent of the Act for the levy of duty on trades was explained to them. They were also informed that, the deputy commissioner had only received instructions to ascertain the conditions under which *pan* cultivation was carried on.[19]

The feeling of the people was also profoundly stirred by the introduction of Income Tax Act 1861. The income tax payees were very much hostile to the government. With the idea of procuring a repeal of the obnoxious impost, they spared no opportunity of fomenting general discontentment. Meanwhile, the government passed another Act for imposing a duty on 'Arts, Trades and Dealings'. Based on the Act district officers were asked to make a survey on *pan* cultivation. The peasants were given a questionnaire, which, it would seem, tended to confirm to the people that the tax on *pan* would be a matter of time. Deputy Commissioner Lieutenant Herbert Sconce believed that the cause of the uprising was 'remotely the interference with the cultivation of the Poppy and dread of further taxation and directly, it was attributed to an anticipated tax on *pan*'. Commenting on the introduction of income tax and feeling of the people Hopkinson said, the amount levied from the people under income tax hardly disturbed them, nor so much the manner in which it had been collected; but it was the principle on which, in their understanding, it is based that had so greatly alarmed them: they regard it as an assumption of the right by the dominant power to make inquisition into, and take as much or as little as it likes of every men's property—4 per cent now, 40 per cent, hereafter perhaps; and they conclude that our exactions, henceforward, will be likely to know no other measure than their endurance. In a word, the measure has alienated their confidence, and there is nothing too outrageous for their belief of what we may do next. Hopkinson further observed that he inferred them what he heard and saw around him, and from the concurrent testimony of those

Europeans, whether officials and non-officials, who had the best opportunities, and were most capable of ascertaining native opinion. On 15 October 1861, the deputy commissioner of Nowgong, Lieutenant Herbert Sconce received information that a large number of peasants had assembled in a place called Phoologooree and he asked his sadar *daroga*, Hollodhur Baruah to reach there, as Baruah had adequate knowledge of Assamese character. The sadar *daroga*, reached Phoologooree in the early hours of 16 October and observed nothing unusual occurred. However, by evening around 600 people gathered in an open field. Barua, the sadar *daroga*, reported that the mob became too large and it would be unwise on his part to arrest the ringleaders. The *daroga* sent police Mohurer Anadur to meet the people and to ask them not to make any disturbance. The peasants was aggressive and some of them were armed with clubs and bamboo sticks. He thought it prudent to observe their behaviour and report the matter to the deputy commissioner. In the night the people dispersed quietly and nothing happened.

On 17 October people began to collect again and by 2 p.m. there were around 3,000 to 3,500 people, of whom 500 had sticks. Hollodhur appealed to the people to not create any disturbance. He also asked them to submit their representation to the district officer, even to the commissioner if they had any grievances. The people again dispersed peaceful in the night.

On 18 October, Friday, Lt. Singer, third class deputy commissioner arrived at Phoologooree at about 10.30 a.m. along with the jail *daroga*. Lt. Singer approached the people and asked them why they had met. They answered that formerly they had been lightly taxed, now taxation was becoming very heavy, and new tax was going to be introduced (besides which poppy cultivation had been stopped); how were they to pay? They said they had met to consult upon these matters. One Jatee Kalita was their spokesman. Lt. Singer then enquired why they came with sticks if they only met for discussion. Scuffles broke out between the peasants and the police and Lt. Singer himself tried to disarm the people. While he was snatching a stick from one Mr. Moira Singh, Damoo, Thoolobh, Asyootanonda and Jatee Kolita cried out, '*Dhuro*! (capture) *dhuro*!

Maro (hit)! *maro*'. In the midst of this, a man struck Lieutenant Singer from behind. This man was recognized as Bahoo of Kaibatya caste, and belonged to Kahighar mouza. Others were Moni Kooch, Kolian Kooch Koli Deka, Thomba, Dhoolarai, Bhogpoor, Thadhi, Kola, Jobo and Katia—all belonging to Lalung (Tiwa) caste. Lieutenant Singer fell on his back and he was continuously bleeding. The police team sent by sadar *daroga* to assist Singer had been chased away by the crowd. Lt. Singer lost his life without getting any support at the hour of his worst peril. His body was recovered from the Kallong river by the *daroga* of Jagge *thana*, a place about half-way between Guwahati and Nowgong, on 24 October. The uprising then spread to Joomonamukh or Dharampoor and Dantipoor or Jynteeahpoor in the same district.

The news of Lt. Singer's death reached the deputy commissioner that evening. It was also informed that the peasants might advance to the Sadar Station. The deputy commissioner immediately detached a police force, confining himself to Nowgong to protect the Sadar Station. The force had to return as the peasants did not allow them to advance to the spot. The force fired upon the people who were still holding the *mel* and 'good many *ryots* (Peasants) were killed or wounded'. As per government records most of the peasants who died (six to nine) in that clash belonged to the Kaibatya caste. However, many Lalungs (Tiwa) were also killed. On 21 October, an expedition was carried out under the command of Captain Campbell and it too received stiff opposition from the peasants and had to return to the Sadar Station. On 22 October, a large force proceeded along with the deputy commissioner, Lt. Sconce. Lt. Sconce stationed himself at Phoologoore for a few days. The incident triggered a brutal retaliation by the Raj. Altogether 41 persons were arrested as per government estimate, including Bahoo, the alleged principal killer. They were tried at Nowgong and even at Calcutta. Many of them were awarded death sentence or life imprisonment.

The simmering discontent burst out into a violent storm in 1861 which shook the British rule in Assam. Whatever might have been its original objective, it became a symbol of challenge to the mighty British power in the province and projected the anti-colonial character of the Assamese people. It forced the local government of Assam to defer the decision in imposing License Tax. The situation was very alarming for the authorities as there was no regiment at Nowgong and only 50 sepoys were at Tezpur. The situation fortunately turned in favour of the British rulers due to the presence of commissioner Hopkinson in Tezpur. In fact, on 18 October the commissioner was in a steamer called *Lucknow*, for his annual tour to Dibrugarh. He received news of the revolt while anchoring at Tezpur on 19 October. Major Campbell, commandant of the 2nd Assam Light Infantry and Lt. Johnstone of the 46th Regiment were passengers of that steamer. The commissioner had the opportunity to utilize the services these two military commanders. They were asked to rush to the aid of the deputy commissioner at Nowgong Lieutenant Sconce; Commissioner himself proceeded to Guwahati in the same steamer. On 21 October, the commissioner returned along with Captain Chambers of 2nd Assam Light Infantry with 80 soldiers. They reached Nowgong on 23 October via Tezpur. The presence of large number of troops ultimately turned the situation in British favour. The gravity of the situation can easily be inferred from what Lt. Hopkinson, Commissioner of Assam, remarked, 'My arrival in the steamer Lucknow at Tezpore was therefore most opportune, for, in the ordinary course of communication, ten days would have elapsed before I could have put a man down in Nowgong, and in ten days we might have had a province to reconquer'.[20] This saga of popular resistance of the peasants against the taxation policy of the Raj is still fresh in the collective memory of the people of Assam as the *Phulaguri Dhawa*. Whatever might have been its original objective, it became a symbol of challenge to the mighty British power in the province and projected the anti-colonial character of the Assamese people. It forced the local government of Assam to withdraw the imposition of License Tax.

RAIJ MEL AT GOBINDAPUR

In the year 1869 large number of *ryots* gathered at Gobindapur in the Kamrup district to protest against the manifold increase of land revenue. The rate of land revenue was doubled in 1869 on both *rupit* and *non-rupit* lands. The abrupt increase of land revenue by 20-5 per cent was a matter of grave injustice to the people of the province. The people of Gobindapur assembled in a *namghur* to oppose the new rate of assessment introduced in the province. A.L. Campbell, assistant commissioner of Barpeta, received information from the head constable of Bajali *thana* about 3000-4000 men had gathered at Gobindapur on 24 January 1869, in a temple within the sight of the *thana* and they were discussing the new rate of assessment.[21] Those assembled there were determined not to pay the new rate of assessment. The assistant commissioner feared that such large numbers of people might create law and order problem and asked the Police Inspector of Barpeta *thana* to enquire into the matter and also to apprehend the ring leaders. Although the inspector of Barpeta could not collect the information properly, the assembly dispersed without creating any trouble.

ACT XIII OF 1859 (WORKMEN BREACH OF CONTRACT ACT, 1859)

Act XIII of 1859 was entitled 'Act to Provide for the Punishment of Breaches of Contract by Artificers, Workmen and Labours in Certain Cases Extended to Lakhimpur and Sibsagar in 1863'.[22] Workman's Breach of Contract Act, 1859, treated such relations as a form of general law dealing with contractual obligations. The Company needed labour to work in the tea plantations as the local people were apathetic to and also not suitable to work in plantations. In 1863 by Act III of 1863 the duty of recruiting labours was assigned to license contractors. However, the system of recruitment by non-license holders was not stopped. In 1870 the job of recruiting labour from outside was given to Sardars. The Sardars used to send people to various places of Chotanagpur, Bihar, Orissa, etc., to allure poor inhabitants to come to Assam for a comfortable life. Labour depots were established in the riverside of Bengal to send the designated labours by steamers and country boats. Many designated labours lost their lives in the hazardous journey and due to unhealthy conditions.

Administration of Justice under the Crown till 1874

The notification provided that the power vested by the Act in a magistrate or police were to be exercised in the district to which it had been extended. The officer having full powers of a magistrate could be authorized to take action under this act. The commissioner, at the same time, requested to point out to the magistrate that in administering the law, there were to look closely at the terms of every contracts and to see whether it was a bonafide one. If the contract was verbal, the officer had to satisfy himself of a clear understanding and freedom of action on both sides when the contract was made. The officers were also informed that the extension of the act to Assam was partial and would depend on its working.[23] Table 5.2 exhibits the number of cases tried under this act till 1864 and the sentences awarded.

TABLE 5.2: CASES TRIED UNDER WORKMAN'S BREACH OF CONTRACT ACT, 1859

Year of introduction	District	No. of Cases	Decision
1863	Lakhimpur	114	11 imprisoned
1863	Sibsagar	434	122 imprisoned
1864	Darrang	9	×
1864	Nowgong	37	×
1864	Kamrup	17	×

Source: BJP, August 1865, no. 34.

Almost the cases were concerning contracts made with the labour brought from outside the state to work on tea plantations. In course of time Workman's Breach of Contract Act became a most essential instrument for the owners of tea plantations to enforce unjust and deceivable verbal contracts.

ACT VI OF 1864 (WHIPPING ACT)

An Act to authorize punishment by whipping in certain cases was passed in February 1864.

The following crimes were included in the list of cases where whipping could be inflicted on the criminal:

1. Theft as defined in Section 378 in the Indian Penal Code (IPC).
2. Theft in a building, tent or vessel as defined in Section 380 of the IPC.
3. Theft by a clerk or servant as defined in Section 381 of the IPC.
4. Theft after preparation for causing death or hurt, as defined in Section 382 of the IPC.
5. Extortion by threat as defined in the Section 388 of the IPC.
6. Putting a person in fear of accusation in order to commit extortion, as defined in Section 389 of the IPC.
7. Dishonestly receiving stolen property, as defined in Section 411 of the IPC.
8. Robbery and dacoity as defined in Sections 390 and 391 of the IPC.
9. Attempting to commit robbery as defined in Section 393 of the IPC.
10. Voluntarily causing hurt in committing robbery, as defined in Section 394 of the IPC.
11. Habitually receiving and dealing in stolen property, as defined in Section 413 of the IPC.
12. Forgery, as defined in Section 463 of the IPC.
13. Forgery of a document as defined in Section 466 of the IPC.
14. Forgery as defined in Section 467 of the IPC.
15. Forgery for the purpose of cheating as defined in Section 468 of the IPC.
16. Forgery for the purpose of harming the reputation of any person as defined in Section 469 of the IPC.
17. Lurking, house-trespass or house-breaking as defined in Sections 443 and 445 of the IPC.
18. Lurking, house-trespass by night or house breaking by night as defined in Sections 444 and 446 of IPC in order to the committing of any offence punishable with whipping under this section.

It was directed that the rattan that would be used in the infliction of punishment was not to exceed half an inch in diameter and a medical officer was to be present at the time of the execution of the provisions of the Act.[24]

BENGAL ACT VI OF 1868

This Act was introduced in Guwahati in the year of its enactment. Under its provisions, town committees were formed in each town to which this act was extended. The committee was empowered to take necessary steps for the conservancy and improvement of the town. Accordingly, a Town Committee was formed in Guwahati in 1869 with the following members:[25]

1. Deputy Commissioner (Ex. Officio)
2. Executive Engineer (Ex. Officio)
3. Civil Surgeon (Ex. Officio)
4. District Superintendent of Police (Ex. Officio)
5. Col. R. Campbell, Resident
6. R. Bainbridge, Tea Planter
7. Baboo Sashi Bhuson Dutt, Deputy Inspector of Schools
8. Gopal Ch. Banerjee, Merchant
9. Lakhi Narayan Das, M.A. Headmaster, Guwahati Collegiate School
10. Boloram Phukon, Resident
11. Munshi Shekant Hussain, Government Pensioner
12. Gangoram Baruah, Pensioner, North Guwahati

Act XXI of 1856 (Abkari Law), Act III of 1857 (Cattle Trespass Act), The Indian Succession Act (Act X of 1865), The Indian Registration Act (Act XX of 1860), and Income Tax Act 1860 were extended to Assam in the years of their enactment.

NOTES

1. Bengal Judicial Proceedings, April 1860, no. 337, notification of Lieutenant Governor, 26 April 1860.
2. Bengal Judicial Proceedings, June 1860, no. 288, also see August 1861, no. 86.
3. Bengal Judicial Proceedings, November 1861, no. 165.
4. Bengal Judicial Proceedins, November 1861, no. 167, notification 16 November 1861.
5. Bengal Judicial Proceedings, May 1861, no. 177, Government Notification, no. 886B, 30 April 1861, also see January 1862, no. 265.

6. Bengal Judicial Proceedings, January 1862, no. 359.
7. Ibid.
8. Bengal Judicial Proceedings, January 1862, no. 300.
9. Ibid.
10. Ibid., notification of Lt. Gov., 25 January 1862.
11. Bengal Judicial Proceedings, June 1865, no. 217.
12. Bengal Judicial Proceedings, August 1872, no. 30, see also Calcutta Gazette, 1 June 1864, p. 1133.
13. Bengal Judicial Proceedings, February 1872, no. 173, notification, 28 February 1872.
14. Empowered to decide civil suits to an unlimited amount and to receive appeals from E.A.C.'s and Munisf. See Begal Judicial Proceedings, February 1872, no. 173 and August 1872, no. 30.
15. Bengal Judicial Proceedings, August 1872, no. 30.
16. Ibid., no. 117, Resolution, 30 March 1872.
17. Bengal Judicial Proceedings, December 1861, no. 115. See also RPA, p. 450.
18. Ibid., no. 194, Major Henry Hopkinson Agent to the Governor-General, North-East Frontier, to the Secretary to the Government of Bengal, 30 November 1861.
19. Ibid.
20. Ibid.
21. Bengal Judicial Proceedings, no. 133; March 1869, A.C. Campbell, Assistant Commissioner, Barpeta to Major Sherer, Deputy Commissioner, Kamrup, no. 120, 10 February 1869.
22. Bengal Judicial Proceedings, no. 33, May 1864, notification 2 January 1863, and Nowgong, Kamrup and Darrang in 1864, BJP; no. 34; August 1865.
23. Bengal Judicial Proceedings, no. 34, August 1865.
24. Bengal Judicial Proceedings, nos. 146-7, March 1864.
25. Bengal Judicial Proceedings, nos. 46 & 47, February 1869.

CHAPTER 6

Judicial Agencies

EUROPEAN FUNCTIONARIES COMMISSIONER

Reference has already been made to the powers and position of the commissioner as the head of a Non-Regulation province. This position remained unchanged even after the promulgation of the Assam Code and he continued to be the head of all the branches of administration, including the police and judiciary.

In the administration of civil justice, the commissioner exercised unlimited powers and heard appeals against the decrees and orders of the subordinate courts. He was competent to remove to his own court any case that might be pending in a lower court. He was also empowered to direct that any case summarily disposed of should be brought on the file and tried as a regular suit. He had the authority to admit any appeal after the expiry of the term fixed for its presentation. The Commissioner had the following establishments for his office:[1]

TABLE 6.1: ESTABLISHMENT OF COMMISSIONER'S OFFICE

Name	Country	Designation of Office	Salary	Total of Each Depatment
		ENGLISH DEPARTMENT		
A.J. Vincent		Head Writer	150	
C. More		Second Writer	100	
		Third Writer	30	
		Interpreter or Translator	100	
		Duftry	9	389

contd.

TABLE 6.1: contd.

Name	Country	Designation of Office	Salary	Total of Each Depatment
NATIVE DEPARTMENT DEWANI					
Jogobandhu	Bengali	Moonshree	50	
Krisnaram	Assamese	Mohafiz	40	
Ramsundur	Bengali	Mohurer	20	
Ramsaran Gupta	Bengali	Mohurer	15	
Punandar Kakoti	Assamese	Navis	8	
		Duftry	6	139
FAUJDARI COURT					
Ramakanta	Assamese	Moonshree	40	
Neelmadhav	Bengali	Mohurer	20	
Shambhunath	Bengali	Mohurer	15	
Rabi Chandar	Assamese	Navi Mahafiz	10	
		Duftry	6	91
REVENUE					
Sarbanand	Bengali	Moonshree	50	
Sheebnarain	Bengali	Mohurer	30	
Joy Ch. Roy	Bengali	Mohurer	25	
Nibekar (?)	Assamese	Mohurer	15	
Gouri Krishan	Bengali	Naib Mohafiz	10	
		Duftry	6	136
		1 Jamadar	8	
		5 Chaprasis @ 6	30	
		1 Gangajolli	6	
		1 Koranee	6	
		1 Bhistee	3	
		1 Methor	3	56
		Contingencies		50
		Office Boat		75
		Govt. Pleader		20
		Total Sicca Rupees		956

Source: BJP (Civil), 3 November 1834, no. 11. Jenkins to Macsween, 8 October 1834.

The commissioner was also the legislative head, making rules for the administration of the province subject to the approval of the Government of Bengal and Sadar Dewany and Nizamat Adalats. He received a salary of Rs. 2,000 per month and other allowances. The commissioner had the sole responsibility to send all monthly returns, extracts and reports to the Government of Bengal or to the Government of India. He was to submit the monthly return of prisoners tried and convicted by him.

DEPUTY COMMISSIONER[2]

The post of deputy commissioner was created in the year 1839. Captain James Matthie was appointed deputy commissioner with the powers of civil and session judge on 1 April 1839.[3]

The deputy commissioner was vested as many powers of the Commissioner as the government might direct.[4] The deputy commissioner received a salary of Rs. 1,500 per month besides traveling and deputation allowances.

THE PRINCIPAL ASSISTANTS

Below the court of commissioner and deputy commissioner, were the courts of the principal assistants at the headquarter stations of each of the four districts into which Assam was then divided. With the extension of British laws and regulations to Upper Assam, principal assistants were also appointed in the districts of Sibsagar and Lakhimpur. A large tract of country was under one principal assistant, who united all the powers of the different departments and the executive was managed by him. In addition to his duties of collector, civil judge and police, he had the functions of an executive engineer, education officer and post master. These appointments were chiefly held by military men.

The onerous and responsible duties of a military officer in civil employ in Assam can scarcely be imagined; he was expected to do everything. For six months of the year, he was constantly travelling about the country, inspecting roads, causing them to be repaired, opening new ones, instituting local fiscal enquiries in villages. His duties involved enduring great fatigue and being exposed to perils of climate, wild beasts and demi-savages in the hills.[5]

The principal assistants had to proceed to the spot to conduct police enquiries in case of disturbance in the district. Further, they were expected to visit the neighbouring hills occasionally either on peaceful missions or warlike expeditions. The frequent transfers and their liability to be recalled to the regiment at any time deprived the principal assistants of the opportunity of gathering useful local knowledge and experience so indispensably necessary for a civil officer.

In the administration of civil justice, the principal assistants were authorized to decide suits for moveable or immoveable property of a value exceeding Rs. 1,000, as well as suits for land claimed as *lakhiraj*. All petitions of plaint were in the first instance to be presented to them. The principal assistants were to refer suits to the *munsifs* and *sadar ameen* to be decided in their courts. The principal assistant had the authority to remove to his own court or any other court any case that might be pending in a lower court. Appeal against a decision of a principal assistant lay to the commissioner and after 1839 to the deputy commissioner. The principal assistant would in general hold the Summary Suit Court in his capacity as collector.

In the administration of criminal justice, the principal assistant was vested with the charge of the police and the trial in the first instance of all persons charged with offences. He was empowered to pass sentence of imprisonment with labour for two years, and of imprisonment with labour for an additional term of one year in lieu of corporal punishment. In all cases demanding more severe sentence, he was to send up his proceedings, with his opinion recorded thereon, to the commissioner. He was also the head of the police in his jurisdiction.

The principal assistants drew a salary of Rs. 1,000 besides other allowances. In spite of the incessant and arduous nature of their duties, their emoluments rarely increases. On the other hand, there was little or no prospect of promotion. This had produced a feeling of dissatisfaction affecting to a great extent the efficiency in service.[6]

With the introduction of the Police Act of 1861 into the province in 1862, the police duties of the principal assistants were somewhat lightened.

Junior Assistant

This post was created in 1832, when Capt. Archibald Bogle of the 2nd Regiment Native Infantry was appointed junior assistant to the Commissioner of Assam.[7] He assisted the commissioner and his assistants in the discharge of their duties in the absence of any properly demarcated power and authority. Neither the Rules of Practice issued by Scott nor Robertson's code gave them any power in the administration of civil and criminal justice. It was only after the introduction of Assam Code in 1837 that they were allowed to exercise specific duties as junior assistant in civil cases and joint magistrate in criminal matters. Even the Assam Civil Code empowered them initially to try certain civil cases referred to them by the assistant which otherwise should have been tried by the *sadar ameens* or *munsifs*. In 1939 a supplementary clause was added in Section I of Assam Code in the Rules for Civil Justice.[8] This amendment gave them authority to decide original civil suits for movable or immovable property not exceeding Rs. 1,000 in value. Further the commissioner was competent to invest them with the powers conferred on the principal assistant of the district whenever state of business might deem such a measure expedient.

In the administration of criminal justice, the junior assistants were competent to award sentence of imprisonment not exceeding one year and a fine of Rs. 100. The commissioner was empowered to invest any experienced junior assistant with the powers conferred on the assistant. The junior assistants normally discharged the duties of the principal assistants in case of the latter's absence from the Sadar Station.

The junior assistant received a salary of Rs. 500 per month with other allowances. The salary was so meagre for a respectable living that even the officers of the army expressed their unwillingness to accept such assignments. Jenkins observed, 'the salary of a Junior Assistant is the least for which officers of some standing could not be induced to take civil employ and it is not more than sufficient for a respectable maintenance'.[9] On the recommendation of Commissioner Jenkins, an intermediate cadre of second class principal assistant was introduced by the government on a salary of Rs. 750. The senior and experienced junior assistants were added to this cadre with a prospect of promotion to the higher cadre of the first class principal assistant. The addition of Rs. 250 was regarded to be a very considerable increase, as it was believed that 'any longer continuation on one rate of salary has the effect of producing a feeling of dissatisfaction'.[10]

SUBORDINATE ASSISTANT

The lowest classes of European functionaries were the sub-assistants on a salary of Rs. 250 per month. The Assam Code gave them limited powers in the administration of civil justice. In 1839, they were vested with more enlarged judicial powers under the supplementary clause that was added to Section I of the Rules for the Administration of Civil Justice. They could now decide original cases for movable and immovable property not exceeding in value the amount of Rs. 1,000. The commissioner was also competent to invest in them the powers of principal assistant, whenever he might deem such measure expedient based on the state of business in the district.

In criminal matters, sub-assistants were competent to pass sentence of imprisonment with or without labour, for six months and fine not exceeding Rs. 50. In all cases calling for a severe sentence, they were to send up their proceedings to the principal assistant of the district.

POWERS AND DUTIES OF SUB-ASSISTANTS
IN-CHARGE OF SUB-DIVISIONS

In the sub-divisions the sub-assistants enjoyed independent powers. As deputy magistrate, they were to hear and pass orders on all reports which might be submitted by the police, receiving petitions from the inhabitants within their jurisdiction and deciding or committing all cases brought before them.[11] On the occurrence of any heinous offence, they were to report the circumstances to the magistrate and to keep that officer informed about the progress and result of their proceedings for the apprehension and conviction of the parties concerned. All criminals and others convicted by the sub-assistant were to remain in custody in the place set apart at the headquarter of the sub-division. The prisoners whose sentence might exceed one month, together with all prisoners sentenced to hard labour, and prisoners committed to the sessions, should be forwarded to the Sadar Station under a guard of Barkandozes, as often as might be practicable. The warrants and the calendars of commitment, together with such other papers as might be necessary were also to be forwarded by the sub-assistants. The sub-assistants were to forward to the Magistrate's office the records of cases finally disposed of by him. In cases of felony misdemeanor, and of simple theft the sub-assistants had to proceed to take evidence, even though the case might be beyond their competence to decide. Where the sub-assistants might consider the charges not proved, they would dismiss the parties, with the exception of defendants, whom they would retain on bail, until the receipt of the magistrate's order for the discharge of the defendant or for their transmission to be tried before him.

The sub-assistants were to dispatch monthly statements of work discharged by them on or before the fifth day of each month and the yearly statements not later than 10 January. They were to remit all sums they might receive on account of fines to the magistrate. All refunds of fines were to be made from the magistrate's treasury, on receipt of a *roobkari* from the sub-assistant. They were prohibited from making any refund themselves without the magistrate's sanction or that of other superior authorities. The sub-assistants were to keep in their office at all times ready for the magistrate's inspection, the books and registers, the headings of which would be furnished to them from the magistrate's office. This included book of daily receipts and disbursement, book of prisoner's ration, register of *hajjut* (prisoners) and bail cases pending, register of parties who had eluded the pursuit of justice, register of prisoners who had broken jail, register of petitions, etc.

The sub-assistant was to supervise the functions of police in the sub division. He was particularly directed to visit the *thanas* under him, investigating serious offences on the spot where they occurred. He was to acquire every possible information from every available source as to the character of the police officers and other subordinates. Further, he was to take such measures as might appear most advisable for suppression of crime and maintenance of peace and order.

The posts of commissioner, deputy commissioner, principal assistant and junior assistant had been a monopoly of the European officials, both civil and military. No native of this province held even the office of an un-covenanted sub-assistant until the close of 1850 when, Anandaram Dehekial Phukan, son of Haliram Phukan, a young Assamese of excellent abilities was made the sub-assistant of Nowgong on a salary of Rs. 250.[12] In 1859 another Assamese, Gunaviram Baruah, a cousin of Anandaram, was appointed as sub-assistant.[13] The junior and sub-assistants had to pass an examination conducted by the principal assistant in order to make themselves qualified for appointment to senior cadre: They were to Take the following oath before entering into their duties.[14]

I,— solemnly swear that I will faithfully and diligently discharge the duties of the said office of—That I will duly account to Govern-ment for all presents or *Nuzzurs* in money or effects of any kind which I may receive from any native, whosoever—that I will not engage in any commercial concern, that I will not have any pecuniary dealing whatsoever with any native states, princes or chieftains, their ministers, officers, or dependants except in the course of my public duty that I will not permit any persons whatsoever to extract or receive any emoluments or advantage (other than their authorised salaries of allowances) on account of any matter or from any consideration connected with my official status and that I will not derive directly or indirectly any emoluments or advantages, from my office, but such as the orders of the Governor-General-in-Council do or authorise me to receive.

OFFICER

NATIVE JUDGES

Munsif

The native judicial agency in Assam in the initial stages of the British rule consisted of the *munsif* and *sadar ameen*. Only qualified Assamese were appointed as Munsifs, who could rise to the position of *sadar ameen* if they showed efficiency in the job. In the beginning, there were no specific rules for the appointment of *munsifs*. Any respectable native having adequate local knowledge could be recruited to the post (Appendix 6.1). The rules for the administration of civil justice promulgated in 1837, popularly known as the Assam Code, laid down specific rules and procedure for the appointment of *munsifs*.[15] Under the provisions of this code, a *munsif* should be selected by the commissioner out of a panel of three names submitted by the assistant-in-charge of the district. Later it was found that under this system, there was little chance for the native employees, either of the deputy commissioner or of the commissioner's court, for promotion to native judgeship, because their nomination could not be recommended by the assistant, they having been working not under him but under the deputy commissioner or the commissioner. To remove such anomalies in the mode of selection for munsifship, a system of examination was first introduced in the year 1842. This examination offered diplomas to the successful candidates and all future selections to the post had to be made from them. The method of examination was in line with the rules of 1840 promulgated for the Bengal Presidency.[16] But in view of the difficulties of the Assamese to go to Bengal to appear in the examination, the Sadar Dewany Adalat provided for holding that examination, in Assam itself. Under the new provision, munsifship examinations, were to be held twice a year at some central places in Assam. Candidates appearing for this examination were required to produce besides a certificate of their intelligence, responsibility and character, proof of a certain number of years' actual residence in the place where they were supposed to sit for the examination.[17] Every future vacancy had to be filled up by a candidate who had passed the examination, in order of seniority in past service. Till the arrangement for examination was made, the commissioner was empowered under the modified rules to select any person he found to be fit and qualified for the post of *munsif*, from any part of the province.

The preparation of a code of rules for the examination of the candidates for based on the local situation and the condition of the province was for the first time, taken up by Major Matthie, the then deputy commissioner of Assam. Major Matthie had long correspondence with the Sadar Dewani Adalat regarding the rules, as well as about the subjects for the examination.

Under the new rules made effective in 1851, every applicant was to be of such respectability, situation and circumstances in life and good character as was calculated to do honour to the office of the *munsif*. He had to obtain a certificate ordinarily from the assistant in-charge of the district to which he belonged or resided in or from the commissioner, if he was an employee of his office, to that effect[18] (Appendix 6.2).

The applicant had be of Assamese parentage. If Bengali or Hindustanee, he must have served in the province in public office for ten years, at least three of which must have been in the capacity of a permanent *sheristadar* or *peshkar*. Any Assamese, Bengali or Hindustanee, who had attended the government school in Assam, or Goalpara, for at least seven years and obtained, from the Inspector of Schools a certificate that he attained high proficiency in Bengali, Urdu and Persian and possessed all other qualifications enumerated above were deemed to be entitled to appear in the examination.[19]

Applications from candidates for examination, and certificate from the commissioner, the assistant in charge of the district, and the Inspector of Schools, were to be drawn up in a particular form, and were to be written both in English and Bengali.

Applicants generally could not be under the age of twenty. However, downward relaxation could be made by three years in case of one who possessed extraordinary qualifications and had certificates to that effect.[20] But on no account whatsoever could applicants under the age of seventeen years be admitted to the examination.

All application forms were to be submitted to the assistant-in-charge of the district where the candidate resided at least three months before the examination, who would then forward a copy of the application to the Commissioner by the first day of every November.

The commissioner would form a committee to scrutinize the applications. There would be two such committees, one for Upper and the other for Lower Assam.[21] The committee would consist ordinarily of (1) the principal assistant or junior assistant with special powers, (2) junior assistant or sub-assistant with special powers, (3) sub-assistant, (4) principal *sadar ameen* or *sadar ameen*.

The examination, as stated earlier, consisted of two parts-written and viva voce. The questions were to be set by the committee meant for each division as per the regulations, and rules of practice for the guidance of the courts of civil justice. Diplomas to the successful candidates were to be awarded by the committees (Appendix 6.3).

The *munsifs* were to be appointed by the commissioner but he was to report all appointments to the Sadar Dewany Adalat. On a vacancy occurring in a Munsifship, a panel of three names from the concerned district who had obtained diplomas was prepared by the assistant-in-charge of the district. He would then forward the names to the commissioner, who would select one of them at his discretion and grant that person commission or *sunnud* from his office.

This appointment of a *munsif* from the locality of the district was later criticized by all because it was believed to be biased, local connections and associations influencing the selection of candidates.[22] To meet this objection, Commissioner Jenkins provided that a general register of the diploma holders of all the districts should be prepared and the deputy commissioner should be empowered to select one from the general register for any vacancy occurring in any district. With reference to a vacancy in the nomination roll of the particular district from which the individual might be taken, the principal assistant should then be called upon to add third name to his district roll, so that all the nominations would still be with the principal assistant. The commissioner thus was not to be confined in his selection to the nomination roll of the district only and was free to select any qualified person from any other district within the province of Assam.

The post of *munsif* appointed under the new provisions were made transferable and no one of them would be allowed to remain longer than two years in any district.[23]

In 1860, the Government of Bengal issued a specific order to subject all judicial covenanted and un-covenanted officers employed in the civil administration of the province to an examination, which similar classes of officers were required to pass in the Regulation provinces.[24] But this was not given effect until 1869. With the equalization of salaries of the native judges with their counterparts in Bengal their appointment also was directed to be conducted under the same rules as in the Regulation provinces.[25] It was further provided that future vacancies in Assam would be filled from the general service, the officers from Assam also having claim to promotion and vacancies in Bengal.

However, the method of examination and the procedure of appointment for the post of un-covenanted native judges at par with the Regulation districts created lot of inconveniences to the people of Assam. The rule in the Regulation provinces was that 'no one is appointed to be a Munsif who is not qualified to be a pleader of the highest grade'.[26] It would be out of capabilities for the applicants of this province to fulfill this requirement of a pleader under Clauses 1 and 2, Section 9 of Act XX of 1865. To sit in the examination, a candidate was required to hold a certificate of having passed the entrance examination of the universities of Calcutta, Madras or Bombay. He was also to hold a certificate of having regularly attended a full course of lectures in law at one of the colleges affiliated to the Calcutta University. Further, he must be between the ages of twenty to forty years.

In September 1867, a native gentleman, an aspirant for the post of *munsif*, submitted a petition and urged the Government of Bengal to relax the rules considering the backwardness of the province. Acting on this petition, the local authorities convinced the Lieutenant Governor about the necessity to depart from the strict rules and to relax the qualifying norms for appearing in the examination. It was stated in the petition that for the Assam candidates the major obstacles were the age bar and language. Further, it was extremely difficult for a candidate from Assam to attend a full course of law in a college in Bengal, especially for those who were in government employment.

Considering their genuine grievances, the Lieutenant Governor issued a notification in March 1868 by which he relaxed the Clauses 1 and 2 of Section 9 of the rules passed by the Calcutta High Court for the candidates of Assam.[27] It was ordered that such relaxation would not be valid after 1869.[28]

The *munsif* as an independent court was, however, abolished in 1972 when all the *munsifs* of the first grade were made extra assistant commissioners of fifth grade and all those of second grade were made extra assistant commissioners of the sixth grade.[29] The *munsifs* were given pension when they became old and unable to work (Appendix 6.4).

SADAR AMEEN

Bengal Regulation XLIX created the post of *sadar ameen* in the year 1803. In Assam this post was first created in the 1835. *Sadar ameens* were selected from persons of good character, known ability, education and past services. Juggoram Kharkharia Phukon, *sheristadar* of the revenue court and head *mohurer* of the Dewani court, was first appointed as the *sadar ameen* of Kamrup. Juggoram served the East India Company in various capacities before being appointed as *sadar ameen*. He was the Superintendent of Police in Upper Assam, head of a panchayat and the President of the Bar Panchayat in Upper Assam. Commissioner Jenkins had a high opinion about Juggoram's qualification. In 1837, specific rules were framed in the Assam Code for the appointment of *sadar ameen*. Under Clause 1 of Section I of the rules for the administration of civil justice, *sadar ameens* were to be appointed by the commissioner, subject to confirmation by the Governor of Bengal.[30] They would be chosen from the best-qualified *munsifs* in the district or province, except in special cases that were to be fully reported.

This rule was continued for a long time. However, variations or departures from this rule were noticed when political expediency superseded the strict rules of the code. In June 1844 Maju Gohain in place of Bhogirath Barsenapati, son of the last Matak chief Matibar was appointed *sadar ameen* at Dibrugarh with a salary of Rs. 100 and an establishment allowance of Rs. 55.[31]

In 1847 Indoo Gohain, Sooroo Mallia Raja, an uncle of Purandar Singha, was appointed *sadar ameen* of Sibsagar departing from the usual rule. Recommending his name for the office, Jenkins, the Commissioner of Assam, observed, 'there is little in the circumstances of the Sibsagar district which seems to call for a departure from the usual rule of preferring a Munsif to the vacant appointment, and yet there are so many of the royal and noble families of Assam unconnected with office that it may be considered still expedient to depart from the strict rules in their favour'.[32] The government at the time of taking over the management of Upper Assam suggested such appointments from the noble and respectable families of the region. Sorro Mallia Raja was acquainted with

Bengal and the Company's courts as he was connected by marriage with the Raja of Tippera (Tripura) with whom he had frequently resided.[33]

In August 1847, another such appointment was made in Dibrugarh. Kamal alias Nalliah Gohain, son of Sarbananda Barsenapati was appointed *sadar ameen*, in place of Bhogeroth who died in February 1847.

Under the revised rules of 1851 *sadar ameen* were to be appointed by the Commissioner from the best qualified *munsifs* having diplomas subject to the approval and confirmation of the Government of Bengal and Sadar Dewany Adalat, except in special cases, to be fully reported for approval from the Government of Bengal.[34]

There was one *sadar ameen* in each district by the year 1840 with a salary of Rs. 150 and 80 as allowance for the establishment. These officers were trying civil suits from Rs. 300 to 1,000. They were also authorized to try and dispose of all criminal cases in which punishment longer than six months, imprisonment or a fine of Rs. 50 was not necessary. The *sadar ameen* also had to prepare preliminary proceedings of other important civil and criminal case for the assistant in-charge of the district.[35]

PRINCIPAL *SADAR AMEEN*

The post of principal *sadar ameen* was created in Assam in the year 1845. This post was originally created in Bengal by Lord William Bentick by Regulation V of 1831. On 23 July 1845, Chunder Sein Bhandari Kakoti, *sadar ameen* of Darrang was appointed as the first Principal Sadar Ameen at Kamrup with a salary of Rs. 250 per month.[36]

The Principal *sadar ameen* could exercise the same powers in civil cases as were vested in the principal assistant as regards the trial of original suits, and disposing cases in appeal from the courts of the *munsifs* and the *sadar ameens*. He was the first native judge having wide powers in civil suits. Since he could dispense with all suits of the value of Rs. 1,000, this provision gave considerable relief to the litigants as they could now settle their minor disputes within their own districts. Previously appeals to all suits for whatever amount it might have been could be made to the court of the Deputy Commissioner of Assam only, whose occasional and prolonged absence from Guwahati caused serious inconvenience and heavy expenses to the appellants. The principal *sadar ameen* was denominated subordinate judge in 1866.

POWERS AND POSITION OF THE NATIVE JUDGES

The powers and position of native judges were not at par with their counterparts in the Regulation Provinces. Initially *munsifs* of Assam enjoyed far less powers than the same class of officers in Bengal. In 1835, the powers were made equal under the provisions of the Regulation V of 1831.[37] But this equalization did not continue for long as their powers were reduced to the original position in 1837 after the introduction of Assam Code. However, there was regular correspondence between the local authorities and the government at Fort William regarding the expediency of equalizing the *munsifs* of Assam with those of Bengal. Although Regulations could not be applied to a Non-Regulation province, yet the local authorities realized the urgent necessity of enhancing the powers of native functionaries in order to give essential relief to the European officers to devote their time to other important departments, specially revenue. The Government of Bengal, after careful scrutiny approved the measure proposed by the local authorities, and accordingly from May 1839 the native judges in Assam were invested with the same powers as their counterparts in the Regulation provinces.[38] The institution of suits in the *munsif's* court was, however, not accorded for a long time in spite of such provisions in Regulation V of 1831 promulgated by Lord William Bentinck. The rules framed by Commissioner Robertson for the administration of civil justice in Lower Assam provided that except in such cases as could be investigated in the *munsif's* own court, all petitions of plaint as well as of appeal, including special appeal, were to be presented to the assistant in-charge of the district.[39] This position was later changed during the Commissionership of Jenkins, who in his instruction to Captain Bogle, Principal Assistant at Kamrup stated that all suits should be instituted at the first instance at the assistant's court instead of *munsif*'s court.[40] The Assam Code also laid the same condition.

The measure led to much delay in disposing of the cases and made the procedure of lodging complaints complex and cumbersome.[41] Consequently in 1842, the rules were modified and the power of the *munsif* when stationed in the interior of the district was enhanced. Under the provision of this rule, he might be, at the Commissioner's discretion, invested with the powers of a *sadar ameen* in the Regulation provinces under Regulation V of 1831 and all subsequent regulations. As a result, the *munsifs* stationed in the interior were authorized to receive plaints[42] and to execute their own decrees.[43] Further, they could also investigate such summary suits of their respective sub-divisions as the assistant in-charge of the district might in his capacity as collector deemed it advisable to refer to them.[44] Such *munsifs* were also allowed to have *nazirs* in their courts.

In 1846 *munsifs* of the detached stations like Barpeta, Mangaldoi, Lakhimpur and Golaghat were also vested with the powers of *sadar ameen* in order to enable them to try larger number of civil suits and petty criminal cases.[45] This measure saved the people of those localities from incurring additional expenses in going to Sadar stations. The junior and sub-assistants of the detached stations were constantly employed in the interiors of their respective circles of jurisdiction to look after public roads, schools, markets, holding mofussil enquiries and inspecting the *mahals* composing their sub-division. During the period of their absence from the headquarters, the whole of the criminal and much of the civil business were postponed. Under the circumstances, the *munsifs* exercising the powers of *sadar ameen* maintained regularity in trying petty criminal and much of the civil suits, easing the work pressure off the superior officers of the administration and also saving the litigants time and money.

Not only were the powers unequal but even the allowances of the native judges were not at par with those prevailing in the Regulation provinces. By government order of 1 November 1831, the monthly salary of the *munsif* was fixed at Rs. 100 and that of *sadar ameen* at Rs. 250 in the Regulation provinces.[46] This order was modified in 1837 and the personal allowance of one-fourth of

Judicial Agencies

the existing *munsifs* was raised from Rs. 100 to 150.[47] But in Assam, a *munsif* received a salary of only Rs. 40, and a *sadar ameen* much less than their counterparts in Bengal and that too varied from person to person. It was only in 1839 that the salaries of the native judges were enhanced for the first time (Table 6.1).[48]

Deputy Commissioner Matthie, however, increased the salaries of three *munsifs* from Rs. 80 to 100 as a reward for their meritorious service. Such a decision was strongly objected by the government of Bengal, as the supreme government fixed the salaries of *munsif* of Assam at Rs. 80 only.[49] Later when the proposal for increase of salary of another *munsif* came up, the government not only turned down the proposal but asked the local authorities to reduce the salaries to those who were allowed to draw more than what was prescribed by the supreme government.[50]

TABLE 6.1: SALARY INCREASE OF NATIVE JUDGES

District	Name of the Person	Amount of salary upto 1 July 1839	Amount of augmented salary from 1 July 1839
Goalpara	Kazee Nurudin Ahmed, Sadar Munsif	150	150
	Kazee Aslamuddin	73.2.5	80
	Golam Hukary	52.4.1	80
	Gauri Prasad Sadar Ameen	146.4.9	150
Kamrup	Preonath Parbatia Phukan	40	100
	Lukhee Dutta Kotoky	40	100
	Digombor Deka Baruah	40	100
	Madheb Ram Rajkhowa	40	80
	Ganga Ram Baruah	40	80
	Debor Bordoloy Sadar Ameen	150	150
Darrang	Raja Bijoynarayan	50	80
	Mohesh Ch. Sarmah Baruah	40	80
	Chandra Sein Sadar Ameen	84	150
Nowgong	Madhab Ram Sarmah	40	80
	Som Dutta Bordoloi Sadar Ameen	70	150

Source: BJP (Civil), 22 August 1839, no. 5.

The Supreme Government fixed the salaries of the native judges in Assam as follows:

Sadar Ameen	150
Allowance for establishment and stationery	80
Total	230 per month

Munsif	80
Allowance for Establishment	40
Total	120 per month

Of course, the amount of salaries given to native judges at the time was sufficient to maintain their standard, because nearly all the Assamese ex-nobles holding the appointments were well-to-do persons. They owned large farms which they could get tilled by the slaves and could even keep an appearance of the rank of a civil judge.[51] They all resided at the Sadar Stations, the place of their court with or very near to their families. But in course of time, the condition of the province underwent radical changes. The cost of living doubled and that of labour fourfold. The abolition of slavery made matters worse for the nobility as it was on the labour of the slaves that their prosperity largely depended. Shortage of labour meant they had to reduce considerably their domestic establishment. Besides, they had been detached from their families. Accordingly, the salary which they thought at one time to be very handsome now proved so meagre that they could not even meet their daily needs out of it.[52]

By that time even the salaries of judicial officers of the lower provinces were found to be inadequate considering their duties and responsibilities. In his minute of 1 April 1854, the Marquis of Dalhousie, then Governor-General of India declared that inadequacy of salaries allotted to the native judicial officers in the lower provinces 'was an evil not to be doubted, nor could it be denied'.[53] It was impossible, he said, 'for the Government to feel that it had done all that it ought to be towards setting the native judges about the temptation of betraying their trust so long as it keeps nearly three-fifths of native judges of Bengal on a salary of no more than rupees one hundred a month'.[54] One could safely imagine the

Judicial Agencies

plight of the native judicial officers of Assam, whose salaries were much less than their counterparts in the Regulation districts. The disparity in the pay scales of the *munsifs* of Assam and Bengal between the years 1833 and 1866 is shown in Table 6.2.[55] It is to be noted that between the years 1833 to 1866, the salary of a *munsif* in Bengal was raised from Rs. 100 in 1833 to Rs. 250 in 1863 while in Assam it went up from a meagre Rs. 40 to 250. With the revision of pay scale of the *darogahs*, the position of the native judges got lowered to this officer. Thus, when a first grade *darogah* received a salary of Rs. 100 per month in 1845, a *munsif* received only Rs. 80. It was believed even by the local authorities that it was unreasonable to expect talent, rank, honesty and other essential qualifications requisite for a civil judge serving on such a fixed salary. The *munsif's* salary was raised to only Rs. 100 in 1856.[56]

The salaries of the *sadar ameen* and principal *sadar ameen* were also unequal and much lower in Assam. A *sadar ameen* did not receive the salary fixed for this class of officers in Bengal (in 1831 it was Rs. 250), until the year 1866; while in Bengal their salary was raised to Rs. 300 in 1862. On the other hand, principal *sadar ameens* in Assam received a salary of Rs. 250, while in Bengal their counterparts were receiving Rs. 600 per month for the First Grade and 400 for the second grade. This salary was further enhanced to Rs. 700 and 500 respectively in 1862. But in Assam the maximum salary fixed for a principal *sadar ameen* in 1866 was only Rs. 400 per month.

TABLE 6.2: DESPARITIES IN THE PAY OF *MUNSIF* OF ASSAM AND BENGAL (1833-66)

Assam	Bengal
Original in 1833 Rs. 40	Scale in the year 1833 Rs. 100
Revised in 1839 to Rs. 80	Revised in 1837 to
in 1956 to Rs. 100	Rs. 150 1st Grade
	Rs. 100 2nd Grade
in 1966 to Rs. 250	Rs. 250 for 1st Grade
1st Grade	in 1863
Rs. 150 2nd Grade	Rs. 200 2nd Grade

Source: BJP, March 1866, no. 69 and BJP, February 1846, no. 300.

It is strange that the local authorities while admitting the low and inadequate salaries of the native judges never advocated equalization with the corresponding class of officers in Bengal. Commissioner Jenkins observed while recommending better pay in 1846, 'the pay of these officers is comparatively small compared to that of the same class in Bengal but nevertheless I should not advocate any general increase or equalization'.[57] In a like way Major Matthie, the deputy commissioner of Assam said, 'the pay is still good, as compared with the means of living commonly engaged by the native gentry in Assam'.[58] Major Matthie, however, as stated earlier, enhanced the salaries of three *munsifs* with the approval of Sadar Dewany Adalat making them at par with their counterparts in Bengal on account of their long service and extraordinary good conduct. But the Supreme government reversed his decision. However, in 1866 the salaries of *principal sadar ameen, sadar ameen* and *munsifs* were brought at par to those of the corresponding class of officers in Bengal. Henceforth, the Assam officers could claim promotion to vacancies in Bengal.[59]

The duties performed by the native judges were not less arduous or responsible than those of their counterparts in Bengal. Matthie observed, 'in good character they stand second to none in India.[60] Almost all the principal assistants gave favourable opinions on the native judges, as evident from numerous extracts and returns in their periodical reports. Nearly all the civil suits were decided by the native judges, each of them disposing of 200-300 suits per year besides Summary Suit cases in the revenue department.[61]

HONORARY MAGISTRATE

In 1860, another class of judicial officers known as honorary magistrates was appointed in the provinces. They were empowered to receive complaints on all cases except those of heinous offences, including affrays; to issue summons, warrants and subpoena; and to record evidence. They were authorized to award punishment of 15 days imprisonment and a fine of Rs. 50. In cases of theft, they could inflict one month's further imprisonment in lieu of stripes and refer the matter to the magistrate or deputy magistrate for final orders in cases requiring a more severe measure of punishment.

Judicial Agencies 213

The honorary magistrates were also competent to take evidence in all complaints or prosecution of felony or misdemeanor, which were beyond their power to decide. Complaints of simple theft of property not exceeding Rs. 50 in value, simple burglary and like cases they had to forward the prisoner with the papers to the magistrate if the charges were proved or to release him on bail if he considered the charges were not proved.[62] In all cases of heinous nature, such as murder, decoity, aggravated burglary or serious affray occurring within the notice of the honorary magistrate, his duty was to report the same to the magistrate. The complainant in such cases was to be referred to the police. The honorary magistrate was to report any misconduct on the part of the police.

In 1873, the powers of the honorary magistrate were enhanced under the new Criminal Procedure Code (Act X of 1872). In the district of Kamrup, the honorary magistrate might be authorized to try criminal suits, sitting as a bench with the magistrate of the district, or any subordinate magistrate having second class power. The bench so constituted was vested with the power of a first class magistrate in respect of offences cognizable by a magistrate of that class.[63]

The magistrate of the district might ask the honorary magistrates to sit as a bench with any salaried subordinate magistrate exercising not less than second-class power. The bench so constituted was authorized to exercise second-class powers in respect of offences cognizable by a magistrate of that class, and powers of summary trial under Section 225 of the Code of Criminal Procedure in respect of all the offence set out in that section.

The benches constituted with the honorary magistrate were to sit and try such classes of cases, and within such limits, as the magistrate of the district might direct or such particular cases as might be referred to them by an officer empowered to refer cases.

In any town within the district where there was a municipality, any two or more honorary magistrates might sit together as a bench for the disposal of municipal and conservancy cases, without the assistance of any salaried magistrate.[64] Such a bench could exercise, in respect of all such cases which they were empowered by the magistrate of the district to take up, third-class powers. The

TABLE 6.3: SCHEDULE OF HONORARY MAGISTRATES AND THEIR POWERS[65]

Name	District	Powers
Mr. W. Beeher	Kamrup	2nd Class
Baboo Jugosen Das Choudhury	Kamrup	"
Col. Campbell	"	"
Shekait Hussain	"	"
Baboo Gopal Ch. Banerjee	"	"
Baboo Man Singh Majumdar	"	"
Baboo Gobind Ram Mazumdar	"	"
Baboo Chandaram Mazumdar	"	"
G. Leslie	Darrang	3rd Class
F. T. Severien	"	"
Raja Bolindra Narayan	"	"
Mr. J. Herriol	Nowgong	3rd Class
Mr. T. Henderson	"	"
Mr. E. Tye	"	"
Mr. H.L. Jenkins	Sibsagar	3rd Class
Mr. R. Spiers	"	"
Mr. H.E.S. Hanny	Lakhimpur	3rd Class
Rev. E.H. Higgs	"	"
Mr. W.G. Wagentrieber	"	"
Mr. H.L. Michel		

Source: BJP, January 1873, nos. 144-5.

bench was also authorized to exercise the powers of summary trial under Section 225, in respect of any offences against Municipal Acts, and the conservancy clauses of Police Acts and others specified in Section 225 of the Criminal Procedure Code. Such municipal benches were further vested with powers under Section 141, 518 and 519 of the Code.

The powers of the honorary magistrate to hear complaints and other matters were regulated by the magistrate of the district under the provisions of the Code of Criminal Procedure.[66] The honorary magistrate was to keep such registers and to make such returns as directed by the magistrate of the district. The latter was to supply the honorary magistrate with a seal and all needful official stationery and forms. The honorary magistrate in his turn was to remit to the sadar station or sub-divisional headquarters all records and all sums of money received as fines, deposits, etc., and to render such cash statements as desirable. He was also to hand over the person sentenced by him to imprisonment to the police immediately with warrants or papers in case of non-bailable offences.

The honorary magistrate was allowed an establishment allowance of 16 per month to cover the salary of a clerk and the cost of stationary.[67]

The institution of the honorary magistrate had always been a subjects of criticism. The primary motive of the British government was to enlist the support and cooperation of wealthy classes and other men of status. It also helped them in reducing the administrative cost and relieving the stipendiary magistrate for more important judicial work.

JURY TRIAL

The institution of jurors was created to guide the presiding officer or the judge in the matter of shifting evidence produced by prosecution and defence before the court during the proceedings of a trial. The introduction of trial by jury in Assam dates back to the days of Commissioner David Scott. Since the beginning of British administration in the province, trials of heinous offences in Upper Assam were held before the juries with the Barphukan as the president. The verdict was, however, subject to review by one of the commissioners who might also award punishment according to his own judgement.[68] The assistance of jurors was also obtained in Lower Assam. The assistant who performed the function of magistrate committed the offenders for trial before the panchayat to be presided over by them. Even in the administration of civil justice, the assistance of assessors was secured. The functions of assessors were identical with those of jurors, for the decision in each case rested with the presiding officer who was not bound to accept the verdict of either the assessor or the jury (Appendix 6.5 for Oath).

The jury system afforded educated members of the native community a direct interest in the good administration of justice. To the public at large, the administration of criminal justice was made more popular when the community got a voice in the matter. It was a strong check on inefficient judges and it also prevented official tyranny. The jury trial secured a more comprehensive enquiry into the merits of a case than was normally attainable. It expedited the process of deciding cases by limiting the abuses of the appeal system.[69]

The criminal trial conducted by the assistant magistrate at Guwahati in the year 1832 was entirely with the assistance of the jury. The attendance of persons to serve as jury was made obligatory and those not attending were fined Rs. 2 which would be remitted on showing good and sufficient cause for absence.[70] However, it was found that the prominent persons, whose names were in the jury list, had a strong natural declination to accept the job. It was possibly due to the reason that the jurors were not paid any remuneration for their service. It was an honour showed to a person and only one who could appreciate his own social position came out to exercise his voice. But 'a large number ignored all such ideas, and felt only the vexation and discomfort of attending a court and might regard it as time wasting'.[71] The practice of allowing the jurors subsistence money of 8 *anna* (half a rupee) for the day they attend a particular court as jury was introduced by Commissioner Crocroft in 1932. With the introduction of subsistence allowances, things began to improve and people's attachment to jury trial increased. But in 1868, the government withdrew the subsistence allowance to the jury men as there was no provision for it in the Criminal Procedure Code of 1861.

The jury trial became a statutory right under the Code of Criminal Procedure (Act XXV of 1861), which extended the system to seven Regulation provinces under the Bengal Presidency, but the trial was confined only to cases coming under chapters VIII, XI, XVI, XVII and XVIII of the Penal Code. In Assam, however, all trials in the Session Court were held by jury and no restriction was placed on the classes of cases until the year 1868. The new code which was extended to the province in 1862, however, brought a significant change as to the decision of a case by jury. Under its provision the verdict of the jury was made final and binding.

With the increasing influence of jurors in the proceedings and

Judicial Agencies

decision of a case, the respect for and confidence in jury trials got remarkably enhanced. 'It gives confidence', observed H.S. Bivar, officiating Judicial Commissioner, 'in the administration, particularly when the judge (as the practice obtained in Assam) conducts the examination of witnesses, and then sums up the evidence, in the vernacular, in Assamese himself, and as to the people I know that they like the method of trial by jury.'[72] During the nine years from 1862 to 1870, 530 session trials were decided by the verdict of jury. The judicial commissioner had occasioned to dissent only in 12 instances, and it must be admitted that such a result spoke highly in favour of the jury system.

The jury trial was, however, not free from defects. The jurors of Assam did not have the benefit of receiving assistance from learned counsels. Most of the jurors being men deficient in education, their individual independence was not to be relied on. It so happened that in some districts, a jury would convict a man charged with decoity on the basis of the slightest of evidence whereas in many places it was extremely difficult to obtain a verdict of guilty in cases of perjury and even of forgery. Caste prejudice too, at times, influenced the verdict of a jury. Commissioner Hopkinson observed,

I do not suppose that the people of Assam desire trial by jury as a safeguard of their liberties or a security for the pure and impartial administration of justice, or that the system is on any other account particularly popular with them, rather they regard it as an invention for shifting that responsibility from the judge which should be his alone, and it is in the almost unlimited right of appeal and the supervision of the High Court that their faith is placed, and as it appears to me with good reason.[73]

The jury list was also imperfect and defective. Generally the duty of compiling and preparing such list was entrusted on the magistrate's *nazir*, whose competency could not be relied on. The Assistants were frequently changing their divisions and as a result, the knowledge of a particular individual's character which long stay in a district alone could give, was not available to them. It was always desirable to complete a trial within a day. At the same time, it was not possible to adjourn a trial for further evidence because if one of the jurors were to absent himself in the interval, the trial had to be commenced *de novo*. The absence of requisite number of witnesses always created difficulties and ultimately delayed a trial. If the trial was adjourned, the jurors returned to their homes and if the person concerned was a man of wealth and influence, his conviction was hardly executed. 'It is not however to be expected,' observed a contemporary, 'that a number of persons taken promiscuously from various classes of diverse religious persuasions and diverse occupations, whose habits and vocations afford no judicial practice, should bring in to play the same careful attention to the facts elicited in the examination of witnesses, and the same careful discernment of the value of such evidence as the judge who has made a study more or less of the science of judicature and whose daily business is in the practice of it.'[74]

PROFESSIONAL PLEADERS

The pleaders or vakeels form an integral part of every judiciary. Any study of the administration of justice would therefore be incomplete without a reference to the legal profession. As the law became complex and varied, the court sought the assistance of competent legal experts for efficient administration of justice. In British legal system, the only real safeguard for the honest administration of justice lay in the high standard maintained by the legal profession. Commissioner Hopkinson observed, 'If you take care of the Bar, the Bench will take care of itself; and that the efficient administration of justice is at least as much promoted by having competent advocates as by having competent judges'.[75]

There were no regularly appointed vakeels attached to the courts of Assam. The parties in suit had the option of pleading their case in person, or appoint such vakeels for that purpose as they had thought proper. Generally these legal practitioners were either private servants or dependents of the parties in a suit or men who followed the business of being a vakeel to obtain livelihood but without any proper training. Since these persons were allowed to plead and conduct a case without any reference to their character and qualifications, it had infested the courts with the most unprincipled and ignorant men. Most of these vakeels were not ac-

Judicial Agencies 219

quainted with the constitution and procedure of the courts and were consequently exposed to the intrigues of the ministerial officers of the court. On the other hand, sometimes the parties actually lost their just claims owing to the incapacity and ignorance of their pleader or vakeels. There was a gross mistake in allowing anyone who wished to practice to be a vakeel. 'Nothing, as a general rule', Agnew to remarked, 'can possibly more disreputable than the class of men who now practice in the courts as pleader—Instead of being an assistance to Presiding Officer these men are usually speaking a hindrance, owing to their want of professional knowledge, and our courts never can be what I should wish to see them, till they are purged of such fellows.'[76] The native courts were the worst sufferers. They had no learned bar to make a learned bench. For proper administration of justice, it was therefore, necessary to have professional pleaders well versed in the British laws and regulations as well as Hindu and Muslim personal laws.

With the extension of the Civil Procedure Code, the question of examination for enrollment as pleaders attracted the attention of the government. Major Agnew, judicial commissioner of Assam strongly advocated the introduction of this system in the courts of Assam and for its implementation favoured the rules already in force in Bengal.

Under orders from the High Court, no new pleaders had been admitted to practice since October 1862. A list was prepared in that year out of the best qualified men then practising and only they were allowed to continue in their profession.

In pursuance of the provisions of Section 6, Act XX of 1865, resolutions were made by the Lieutenant Governor in 1867 for conducting the examination of applicants for admission as pleaders or *mukhtears* in the courts of Assam. Commissioner Hopkinson strongly concurred with the recommendation of Major Agnew and favoured the implementation of the Lieutenant Governor's resolution as soon as possible. 'I would at once introduce', said Hopkinson, 'the system of examination for Pleadership which obtains in Bengal, and I would also issue a notice that after a certain time none other than duty qualified Pleaders should be permitted to plead in the Judicial Commissioner's Court, and I would gradually extend this restriction to all the other courts.'[77] He also suggested examination for the enrollment of *mukhtears*.

Rules were framed in 1867 to materialize the resolution.[78] To ascertain the qualification of candidates for admission as higher-grade pleaders, the Lieutenant Governor of Bengal appointed Examiners, to be called Government Examiners of Pleaders. A local examination of candidates for the higher grade of pleaders was to be held on the last Monday of January each year. The examination would be held at the headquarters of the division before a local committee, consisting of the judicial commissioner as the president and the deputy commissioner and any other officer of the government whom the Lieutenant Governor might think of appointing as member.[79] In the absence of a judicial commissioner, the deputy commissioner of the district could preside over at the examination.

The examination was to be conducted in English. It was to consist of two parts, viz., written and viva voce. The written part consisted of three papers, one of them being on Criminal Law and Procedure. The question papers would be prepared by the government examiners. Each paper would contain 12 questions. The aggregate number of marks for full answers to all of the 12 questions would be 160. The number of marks for the viva voce examination, in which candidates would be asked at least four questions, should be fifty.

The questions in the written examination, and also those to be put in the viva voce examination, would be so framed as to test the knowledge of the candidates in the subjects mentioned in Clause 2, Section 6 of the rules passed by the High Court, for the qualification, admission, and enrollment of pleaders and *mukhtears* in mofussil courts.[80] The questions were to be so prepared that a candidate would pass only by studying the Regulations, enactments and text books mentioned in the said clause. Where two or more textbooks were mentioned in the alternatives, the questions would be framed in such a manner that they could be answered by persons who had studied any one of the two textbooks.

The papers would be examined by government officers appointed for the purpose and the vivavoce examination would be conducted by the local committee mentioned above. To pass the examination and qualify himself as a pleader of the higher grade, a candidate had to obtain not less than 100 marks in each of the three written papers, and not less than 30 marks in the vivavoce examination. A candidate securing not less than 80 marks in each of the written papers, and a minimum of 20 marks in the vivavoce examination, was considered to have qualified for the post of a pleader of the lower grade.

For the lower grade of pleaders, the candidate could take examination in English or in the vernacular of the district. The examination was to be held by the deputy commissioner and assisted, if he might think fit, by any other officer whom he might call in.[81]

The written part of the examination consisted of two papers, one on criminal law and procedure and the other on civil law and procedure. The question papers prepared by the government officials were forwarded to the deputy commissioner before the examination. There would also be a vivavoce examination conducted by the deputy commissioner.

As in the question papers meant for the higher grade pleaders, those for the lower grade had to have three papers of 12 questions each. The marks against each question had to be separately specified at the time of preparing the question papers. The aggregate marks for full answers to all the 12 questions in the examination of lower grade pleaders was to be 160. The total marks for the vivavoce examination, in which the candidates should be asked at least four questions, was 50. The written and viva-voce questions had to be so framed as to test the knowledge of the candidates in the subjects mentioned in Rule 18 of the rules passed by the High Court, for the qualification, admission and enrollment of pleaders and *mukhtears* in mofussil courts.

To pass a candidate for lower-grade pleader had to obtain 100 marks at least in each of the written papers, and 30 each in the vivavoce examination.[82]

The same procedure was adopted for the examination of the *mukhtear* under Section 34 of the rules passed by the High Court. The examination was to be conducted by the deputy commissioner and was to be held once every year, on the second Monday of February. The subjects and marks of the question papers had to be the same as those meant for the lower grade pleaders. The qualifying marks for the written and viva voce examination were also at par with the lower-grade pleaders.

The names of the successful candidates of each of the three examinations were to be published in the *Calcutta Gazette*.[83]

Under Section 9 of the rules passed by the High Court a person had to have the following qualifications to appear in the examination of pleaders and *mukhtears*: [84]

1. He must hold a certificate of having passed the entrance examination of the University of Calcutta, Madras or Bombay, or should satisfy the High Court that he had received a liberal education elsewhere in India.
2. He must hold a certificate of having regularly attended a full course of lectures in law at one of the colleges affiliated to the Calcutta University, or such law lectures elsewhere as should be deemed sufficient by the High Court.
3. He must hold a certificate of good moral character.
4. He must be between the ages of twenty and forty years. Otherwise he should have been admitted and should have practised as a pleader of the lower grade previous to his application to be admitted to the examination for the higher grade; in which case, he might be admitted to that examination if he satisfied the judge of the district of his residence up to the time of the application of the lower grade, and should produce a certificate from the judge or judges in whose court he had been so practising, that in his or their judgement, he was a proper person to be admitted to the examination for the higher grade.
5. Further, under Section 10, the person who was practising as a pleader of the lower grade on the 1 January 1966 might present himself at the first examination for a pleadership of the higher grade, which might take place after the expiry of six months from the publication of these rules.

Strict enforcement of rules passed by the High court for the appointment of pleaders and *mukhtears* created much hardship to the people of this province. It became impossible for the intending candidates for the pleadership examination to comply with the rules passed by the honourable High Court. For instance, age alone would in most cases disqualify them from the entrance examination of the Calcutta University; while those who were in government employment could not possibly get leave to attend a full course of lectures in law.[85] Further, the rules passed by the government in Assam which prescribed that the examination for the higher grade of Pleaders should be conducted in English, had prevented persons already practicing as pleaders of the lower grade before the 1 January 1866, but who did not know English from availing themselves of the benefit of Section 10 of the rules passed by the High Court which allowed such pleaders the privilege of competing at the first examination of pleadership of the higher grade without having the qualifications required under Section 9. The attention of the Supreme government was drawn by the local authorities regarding the handicaps of the Assamese aspirants for pleadership and the necessity of relaxing some of the provisions of the rules passed by the High Court.

The Lieutenant Governor of Bengal by notification dated 2 March 1868, declared that persons who, on 1 January 1866 were practising as pleaders of the lower grade should be allowed to present themselves at the examination of higher grade pleadership which would be held in January 1869, and that the examination was to be conducted in the vernacular of the district. The Lieutenant Governor also declared that Clauses 1 and 2 of Section 9 of the rules passed by the High Court would not be enforced as regards the Assamese candidate and others who had been brought up in Assam.[86] All such candidates had to produce certificate from the deputy commissioner of the district in which they lived, of their good moral character, and of their having a fair knowledge of English. Certificates given to candidates who succeeded in passing the examination to which they might have been admitted under this relaxation of rules would qualify the holders to practice in the courts of Assam only.[87] It was further declared that rules in question would be strictly enforced in all future examinations subsequent to that of 1869.

In accordance with the provisions of the regulations made pursuant to Act XX of 1865, the examination of applicants for admission as pleaders and *muktears* was conducted in 1869. The examination for junior pleadership was conducted on the 29 and 30 of March, and the one for senior pleadership on 15 and 16 April 1869.[88] Altogether five candidates appeared in the examination for senior grade and out of them Sri Ganga Gobinda Phukan was successful and, as such, he became the first senior-passed pleader in Assam.[89] The four other candidates failed to reach the standard prescribed by the rules but were entitled to get a lower-grade diploma. They were:

1. Hem Chandra Baruah
2. Benudhar Baruah
3. Permanund Dutt
4. Domboroo Dhur Barkakoti

The candidates to successfully pass the lower-grade examination were:[90]

1. Nidharm Das and
2. Baloram Chandra Das

GOVERNMENT PLEADERS

Regulation VII of 1793 provided for the appointment of government pleader in all the courts of the Government of Bengal. They were to act and appear before the judicial bodies on behalf of the government, In fact, they were the pleaders of the government in government cases. They were prohibited to advise or be concerned directly or indirectly on behalf of the opponent of the government. A pleader might, otherwise, allow doing private practice as usual. A government pleader used to prepare a number of reports and returns. He was to make drafts and plaints that were to be instituted on behalf of the government. Besides, he was to prepare written statements in suits where government was a party. His other important duty was to execute decrees in government suits. The salary of a government pleader was not proportionate to their work. As a result, competent people were not interested to take up this assignment. In Assam Goalpara district was the only one with a government pleader.[91]

NOTES

1. Benga Judicial Proceedings (Civil), 3 November 1834, no. 11, Jenkins to Macsween, 8 October 1834.
2. The designation of the European officers was changed in the year 1861 by Government Notification no. 886B dated 30 April 1861. The deputy commissioner to be styled as judicial commissioner; first class principal assistant to be deputy commissioner; 2nd class principal assistant to be deputy commissioner of the second class; junior assistant to be styled as deputy commissioner of the third class; and sub assistant to be styled as extra assistant commissioner (BJP, 30 May 1861, no. 177).

   The designation of third class deputy commissioner was changed to assistant commissioner in 1862 and both deputy commissioner of first and second class would be styled as deputy commissioner only (BJP, January 1862, no. 265).
3. BJP (Criminal), 28 May 1839, no. 34, Jenkins to Princep, 1 April 1839.
4. BJP, December 1870, no. 13, see appendix. Rules revised for administration of Civil and Criminal justice in Assam.
5. J. Butler, *Travels and Adventures in the Province of Assam*, p. 59, quoted in *Assam in the Days of the Company*, p. 207.
6. Ibid., p. 208.
7. BJP (Criminal), 14 February 1832, no. 75, extract of the proceedings of the Hon'ble Vice-President in Council in Political Department, 23 January 1932.
8. BJP (Civil), 8 January 1839, no. 20, Halliday to Hawkins, 8 January 1839.
9. BJP, 24 June 1844, no. 51, Jenkins to Davidson Off. Secy. Government of India.
10. Ibid.
11. BJP, 23 September 1846, nos. 171 & 172, Matthie to Young, Under Secy., 24 August 1846.
12. BJP, 23 October 1850, no. 102, also see Baruah Gunaviram, *Anandaram Dhekial Phukonar Jivan Charita*, p. 72.
13. BJP, 22 September 1859, no. 193.
14. FPP, 2 May 1828, no. 32.
15. BJP (Civil), 6 July 1837, no. 2, see Rules for the Administration of Civil Justice.
16. BJP (Civil), 16 April 1851, no. 22
17. BJP (Criminal), 18 March 1842, no. 20, Hawkins to Halliday, 25 February 1842.

18. BJP, 16 April 1851, no. 22.
19. Ibid.
20. Ibid.
21. Upper Assam, Sibsagar and Lakhimpur Districts Lower Assam-Goalpara, Kamrup and Darrang and Nowgong districts.
22. BJP, 11 August 1859, nos. 19 & 20, Jenkins to Young, 24 June 1859.
23. Ibid.
24. BJP, October 1860, no. 142, Jenkins to Money, Officiating Secretary, Bengal, 13 September 1860.
25. BJP, July 1866, no. 48, Eden, Secy. Bengal to Commissioner of Assam, 17 July 1866.
26. BJP, January 1868, no. 128, Agnew to Secy. Bengal, 18 September 1867.
27. BJP, March 1868, no. 3.
28. Ibid.
29. BJP, August 1872, no. 117 (Resolution 30 March 1872).
30. BJP (Civil), 6 July 1837, no. 2.
31. BJP, 17 June 1844, no. 72, Secy. Government of India to Halliday, Secy. Government of Bengal, 1 June 1844.
32. BJP, 17 March 1847, no. 135; Jenkins to Halliday, 25 February 1847.
33. Ibid.
34. BJP, 16 April 1851, no. 22.
35. BJP, 24 June 1844, no. 52.
36. BJP, 23 July 1845, no. 252; Turnbell, under Secy. Bengal to Chandra Sen, 23 July 1845.
37. BJP (Civil), 26 May 1835, no. 3.
38. BJP (Civil), 14 May 1839, no. 8.
39. BJP (Civil), 25 August 1834, no. 16, Clause IV.
40. BJP (Civil), 26 May 1835, no 3.
41. BJP (Criminal), 7 November 1842, no. 34; Matthie to Jenkins, 1 November 1841.
42. M.N. Gupta, Analytical Survey of Bengal Regulations, p. 270. See Regulation V of 1831.
43. Ibid., p. 273.
44. BJP (Criminal), 7 November 1842, no. 34.
45. BJP (Civil), 28 October 1846, no. 220, Young, Under Secretary, Bengal to Commissioner, 28 October 1846.
46. BJP (Civil), 18 February 1846, nos. 299 & 300, Jenkins to Halliday, 17 December 1845.
47. Ibid.

Judicial Agencies

48. BJP (Civil), 22 August 1839, no. 5.
49. BJP (Civil), 20 June 1842, no. 3, Halliday, Secretary, Bengal to Hawkings, Registrar, Sadar Dewany and Nizamat Adalat, 20 June 1842.
50. Ibid.
51. BJP, 18 February 1946, no. 300; Jenkins to Halliday, 17 December 1845.
52. Ibid.
53. BJP, September 1862, no. 87; Eden, Secretary, Bengal to Secretary, Government of India, 25 September 1862.
54. Ibid.
55. BJP, March 1866, no. 69 & BJP 1846, 18 February, no. 300.
56. BJP, 18 February 1846, nos. 209 & 300; Jenkins to Halliday, 17 December 1845.
57. Ibid.
58. Ibid.
59. BJP, July 1866, no. 48, Eden, Secretary, Bengal to Commissioner of Assam, 17 July 1866.
60. BJP, 18 February 1846, no. 300.
61. BJP, 24 June 1844, no. 52.
62. BJP, May 1861, no. 327.
63. BJP, January 1873, nos. 144-5, Notification of the Government of Bengal, 1 January 1873.
64. Ibid.
65. Ibid.
66. BJP, February 1873, no. 60, Resolution of the Government of Bengal; 14 February 1873.
67. BJP, November 1863, no. 299, Geophegen, Secretary, Bengal to Commissioner of Assam, 27 November 1863.
68. Foreign Political Proceedings, 19 March 1832, no. 81, Crocroft to Swinton, 21 February 1832.
69. BJP, June 1865, no. 90.
70. FPP, 19 March 1832, no. 81, Crocroft to Swinton, 21 February 1832.
71. BJP, June 1865, no. 90.
72. BJP, January 1868, no. 56, Bivar, Judicial Commissioner of Assam to Commissioner of Assam, 9 April 1867.
73. BJP, August 1868, no. 113.
74. BJP, June 1865, no. 90.
75. BJP, April 1864, no. 69, Hopkinson to Secretary, Bengal, 29 March 1864.
76. BJP, April 1860, no. 336, Agnew, Deputy Commissioner to Commissioner of Assam, 21 March 1860.
77. BJP, April 1864, no. 69.

78. BJP, January 1867, no. 117, Notification by the Lt. Government of Bengal 18 January 1867.
79. BJP, January 1867, no. 118.
80. Ibid.
81. Ibid.
82. Ibid.
83. Ibid.
84. BJP, May 1866, no. 18, see rules drawn up in accordance with Section 4, Act XX of 1865 (Pleaders and Muktear Act) for the qualification admission and enrollment of pleaders and *muktears* in mofussil courts.
85. BJP, January 1868, no. 128, Agnew to Under Secretary, Bengal, 18 September 1867.
86. BJP, March 1868, no. 3, Notification by Lieutenant Governor, 2 March 1868.
87. Ibid.
88. BJP, July 1869, no. 157, Peacock, Secretary, Committee of Examiners to the Secretary, Bengal, 5 July 1869.
89. Ibid., no. 158.
90. Ibid.
91. BJP, December 1868, no. 122, Thompson, Officiating Superintendent and Rememberence of Legal Affairs to the Officiating Secretary, Bengal, no. 1870, dated 31 October 1868.

APPENDIX 6.1
FORM OF NOMINATION OF *SADAR AMEEN* AND *MUNSIF*

1	Vacant Office
2	How Vacated
3	Name of the person nominated with the name of the father.
4	Age
5	Religion or Caste
6	Family residence, viz. Town or Village Paraganah and Zillah
7	Statement of past employment whether in the service of government or individual. If in the service of government by what office originally appointed and by whom subsequently promoted.
8	Statement of landed and other property belong to and where situated.
9	Propose residence and Jurisdiction.
10	Statement of qualification and knowledge of the Persian, English or the language of the province
11	Certificate that nominee is not disqualified by any Regulation and General Remarks.
12	Remark of the Assistant
13	Remark of the Commissioner

Source: BJP, 10 November 1834, no. 10.

APPENDIX 6.2

APPLICATION TO SIT IN THE EXAMINATION FOR THE OFFICE OF *MUNSIF* IN ASSAM

1	2	3	4	5	6	7	8
Name of the applicant and that of his father	Age	Religion Code	Family residence viz. Town or Village Paraganah and Zillah	Statement of past employment whether in the service of government or period of attendance at the government Schools and their names	Statement of landed or other property belonging to the nominee and where situated.	Statement whether the applicant is a debtor or creditor of other parties and if so the place of residence of his debtor or creditor.	Certificate of the assistant-in-charge or the district I do hereby certify that I have satisfied myself that the bearer of this certificate _____ is a man fully fitted by respectability and good character to fill the office of the *munsif* and from enquiries I have made, I have every reason to believe that he is qualified from his part conduct, and general information, to enjoy the privilege of examination for the office of *munsif* in Assam.

Source: BJP, 16 April 1851, no. 22.

APPENDIX 6.3

EXAMINATION FOR ENROLLMENT OF *MUNSIF* IN ASSAM

DIPLOMA CERTIFICATE

We hereby certify that _____was examined at the yearly examination held at _____ in the month of _____ 184 , and that we consider him duly qualified from his knowledge of the native language and laws and Rules of Practice for the guidance of the Courts of Civil Justice in Assam, to held the office of *munsif.*

Signature of the Members

Name of Candidate	Name of the Father	Age	Place of Residence

Source: BJP, 16 April 1851, no. 22.

APPENDIX 6.4

REGISTER OF AN APPLICATION FOR SUPERANNUATION PENSION FROM THE ESTABLISHMENT OF *MUNSIFS* PREFERRED UNDER THE RULES PASSED BY THE GOVERNMENT UNDER DATE 4 JANUARY 1831

1		Name of the person by whom pension is applied with the name of his father
2		No. of the Establishment
3		Identification of the applicant's person
4	Size	Feet
		Inches
5	Age	Years
		Month's
		Days
6		Religion, Cast or Tribe
7	Residing	Province
		Pargonah
		Village
8		Present Employment
9		Years
10		Months
11		Date of application to government
12		Average Salary. Authorised Official allowances per month for 5 years preceding to the date of application
13		Salary & authorised official allowances per month at the time of application.
14		Abstract of the grounds of Application
15		Remarks by the Head of the Office
16		Proposed amount per mensum
17		Treasury to which the party wishes to draw his pension

Source: BJP, 30 July 1845, no. 233.

APPENDIX 6.5

OATH FOR JURY MEN
(FPP, 19 March 1832, no. 81)

I AB solemnly swear that I will give my opinion on the evidence taken before me of the innocence or guilt of the Defendant or Defendants justly and honestly without fear and favour before God and men. So help me God.

JURY MEN

Source: FPP, 19 March 1832, no. 81.

CHAPTER 7

Police Administration

In 1832 when Robertson was the Commissioner of Assam, the *thana* or police station which had hitherto been confined to the headquarters of a district was extended gradually to the thickly populated areas. Each *thana* was placed under a *darogah* with a number of armed men under him to maintain peace and order in the locality. The *chowdhuris, patgiris* and other fiscal officers were now deprived of the power derived from police duties.[1] The village officials were, however, required to aid the police in the detection and seizure of criminals in their respective jurisdiction. In place of *chowdhuris* and other fiscal officers, Robertson recruited stipendiary officers to look after the mofussil police. *Thanas* were set up in almost all the areas of Lower and Central Assam. Thus five police stations were set up in Dehar, Kachree Mahal, Bajali, Barpeta and Kattah in Lower Assam and five in Central Assam, viz., Darrang and Chatgaree, Charduar, Nowgong, Raha and Jagee and Biswanath. Besides the *darogah, jamadar, mohurer, kakoti* and *barkandoz* or *teckela* were recruited in each police *thana* to help the officer-in-charge. The police establishment for Lower and Central Assam were given in Appendix 7.1.[2]

Definite rules were framed for the guidance of police officers. These rules were based on Regulation XX of 1817 which formed the basis of police law in Assam. This comprehensive rule consolidated the provisions of the existing police laws, and specified the details of the various kinds of duties to be performed by the police officers.

POWERS AND DUTIES OF POLICE *DAROGAHS*

Darogahs on receiving information upon oath or declaration of any crime cognizable by him was to enquire into the circumstances and examine without oath, publicly or privately, the witnesses to the fact. He was also to examine the sketch of the spot, which was to be transmitted under certain circumstances to the magistrate. He was not required to furnish details of evidence; only the substance was to be transmitted to the Magistrate. He was to make every endeavour to dispatch all evidence. He was to secure the attendance of witnesses in due time, so as to prevent delay in the enquiry. When the offenders could not be traced or apprehended, the witnesses to the local enquiry could not be sent to the magistrate or bound over to attend.[3] The *darogah* had to report if any person sent to the magistrate's court was apprehended earlier in any other case. In the report, the dates of the former cases were to be mentioned.

The persons and other particulars of known but absconding offenders had to be accurately described. A separate report was to be made when a person in the course of an enquiry, appeared to have been guilty of more than one offence. Similar report was to be made when the fiscal officers neglected to report. Principal persons in the villages were held responsible for the early communication of unnatural suspicious deaths under Regulation IX of 1807.[4]

The *darogah* moving to the spot of occurrence of any crime was to question the connections or the neighbours in the first instance. In case of murders, the instruments or weapons were to be procured if possible. If offenders could not be speedily detected, the *darogah*, or the police officer deputed by him was to ascertain whether any person in the neighbourhood bore enmity to the victim. If the victim was a stranger, it was to be ascertained where he was last seen. The *darogah* or the police officer was to procure assistance for any wounded person and not to remove him so long as risk attended it.

The *darogah* could not search the interior of any building, except by special order of the magistrate. The representation regarding, stolen property was to be sent to the magistrate for his orders. If the person, in whose house property alleged to be stolen was found, was unable to give a satisfactory account of the same, he had to be forwarded to the magistrate. All particulars regarding the property so found had to be carefully transmitted to the magistrate. All property claimed or suspected was to be removed and not to be restored without the magistrate's order. In heinous cases a list of property plundered was to be affixed in a conspicuous place and due notice was to be given. Proper enquiries were to be made about persons in whose possession the stolen properly might be found.

The *darogah* obtaining orders from the magistrate was to search the house of the persons accused upon credible information, and to transmit to the magistrate the coins, implements and accounts found in the offender's possession together with him.[5]

In case of an affray or intended affray, the police officer should was to all endeavours to induce the persons involved to disperse and to submit their dispute to arbitration. He was to proclaim aloud the consequences of a breach of peace and of certain measures to apprehend the guilty. *Darogahs* could not depute *barkandozes* to seize or protect the property of either party.

The police *darogahs* and Mohurers had to carefully preserve and promulgate all regulations of the government sent to their *thannahs*. The *darogah* had to enter every occurrence in their diaries including details of persons apprehended. A book was to be kept by the Darogah containing copies of all *urzies* (relief sought), *kyfeut* (reply), reports and returns to be transmitted to the Magistrate.[6] Another book was to be kept containing copies of *parwannahs* and orders. Besides a register containing a list of all heinous crimes and proclaimed offenders was to be maintained.

The system, however, did not work as desired. The police failed to check crime. In spite of it, crimes increased everywhere; robberies and murders were frequent and gangs of decoits roamed unchecked about the province. The *darogah* thus could not effectively check the forces of disorder and they themselves were often notoriously corrupt. There was no protection for life and property. In practice, the police in Assam were more a problem to the people than of benefit to them. It was said that whenever a theft was committed in a household, the family tried to conceal rather than report the same to the police, for it was known that the police would seize what the thieves had left.

The salaries of the police officers were grossly inadequate. The monthly emolument received by a *darogah* hardly exceeded Rs. 30. It was difficult to expect honesty, discipline and efficiency in such a low salary. While approving higher salary for the *darogah* of the Bengal Presidency, the President-in-Council observed, 'the necessity for removing as much as possible so evident a cause of corruption amongst this class of police officers by rendering their remuneration equal to their decent support'.[7] In spite of the Supreme government's clear instruction to enhance the salaries of police *darogahs*, the local authorities did not increase the salaries uniformly. In 1845 the salary of first, second and third grade darogahs were made Rs. 100, 75 and 50 respectively per month. Even the hike in their salaries was not fair considering the strenuous nature of their duties and this fact induced the police officers to find out alternative ways to make their fortune. 'Their love of gain', wrote A.J.M. Mills in his report,

Often leads them, actually, to sell justice for money and to lend their co-operation, in the perpetration of injury and oppression on the poor and helpless. The police *darogah* is the only authority to whom the ryots can at all times look up for protection. But the temptation offered by the wealth often induces those functionaries to wink at their proceedings. When poor ryot is put to duress or extortion, the wealth of his oppressor gains over the *darogah* to his side, and relief is not obtained. When murder, homicide, robbery occurs in a village, the villagers purchase their safety by levy of a general contribution. Even the occurrence of an unnatural death in a village and the inquisition that follows afford a fruitful field of extortion on the people. The trial and investigation in the first instance, of all criminal cases by the *darogah* and the exercise of partial judicial powers by them, are productive of no slight injury. The mercenary and biased proceedings in criminal trials held by them serve in various instances to convict the innocent and exculpate the guilty.[8]

The inconvenience and delay of prosecution in the criminal courts were so great and the chance of ultimate conviction of the heinous offenders was so small that strong temptations were held out to the police to conceal or misrepresent the character of crimes. Often the police were bribed by the guilty in an effort to evade the law. Sometimes, the police tried to safeguard the criminals or conceal the crime in consideration of bribe. If the crime could not be concealed, an innocent person was seized and was induced to confess by torture that he had committed the offence. The report of forcible confession was a matter of serious concern for the magistrate and his subordinates. The unlawful means practiced by police officers to extort confessions were notorious, inhuman, and oppressive.

Indiscriminate apprehension for the purpose of extortion was another evil deed of the police. If a murder was committed in a village the police would rush to the village, summon the headman and half of the villagers and would hint to them that it would be essential for them to appear before the magistrate. This produced a bribe from each of them to avoid such a calamity, as it were to the illiterate and ignorant rustics.

Table 7.1 shows the number of acquittals compared to convictions in three districts of Lower Assam from 1836 to 1838.

It can be reasonably inferred from Table 7.1 that there were unnecessary apprehensions and a large number of people were brought to trial without sufficient ground. The number of acquittals was very disproportionate to that of the convictions affording strong presumption that many innocent persons were needlessly apprehended and imprisoned.[9] The number of convictions to acquittals, including every description of offences in the said three districts of the province during the first half of 1837 was 439 to 673. 'No less than 673 persons were apprehended,' said Deputy Governor of

TABLE 7.1: THE NUMBER OF ACQUITTALS AND CONVICTIONS IN THREE DISTRICTS OF LOWER ASSAM

Year	District	Apprehended	Acquitted	Convicted
1836[10]	Kamrup	1,108	550	335
	Darrang	399	290	168
	Nowgong	962	601	207
1837[11]	Kamrup	937	425	354
	Darrang	482	227	180
	Nowgong	906	613	216
1838[12]	Kamrup	522	233	240
	Darrang	333	168	49
	Nowgong	533	274	204

Source: See endnotes 10, 11 and 12.

Bengal, 'most of them it may be presumed on insufficient grounds and subjected thereby to vexations and serious detention, a proportionate number of witnesses were also subjected to inconvenience and hardship.'[13] The crimes became a source of profit for the police. Instead of suppressing the crime by seizing the offenders they regarded it an opportunity to advance their evil motives. Sometimes the police refused to receive or record the reports of crime until those who came to report paid the prescribed illegal fees. The *darogah* of Jagee (present Jagiroad) in Nowgong district, it was reported in 1842 never summoned a witness for a defendant without extortion.[14]

It was felt that better salaries and amenities corresponding to their duties and responsibilities would help resist such temptations. The police officers, with two or three exceptions, were composed of Bengalis, who from their more intimate knowledge of the procedure, regulations and customs of the service were better qualified to hold these appointments. The Assamese were said to have been ill-suited for police duties as they could not properly understand the nature or meaning of the regulations and seemed to be very slow in comprehending their duties. On the other hand, the Assamese of rank and respectability were not interested in darogahship. It was believed that the appointment of Assamese would find favour with the people of the province at large and 'if the corruption is practiced at all by the police officers it will be considered more palatable in a countryman, than in foreigner and be inflicted less oppressively'.[15] The apathy of the local people to take up darogahship was seriously felt by the government when there was suspension or dismissal of police officers for corruption or misconduct. The magistrate had to face a dual problem—on the one hand persons of respectability of this province were reluctant to take up police duties and on the other hand, few persons of respectability came from outside the province who could be safely entrusted with police duties. 'The want of any respectable person', said the officiating Magistrate of Nowgong, 'to supply the place of those dismissed was the greatest difficulty a Magistrate had to contend with and few men of any respectability came up to this Country and those, who for the notoriety of their conduct, are unable in their own Country to procure service are perhaps only men he has to trust to supply the place of former occupants.'[16] Under such circumstances it was difficult to remove any *darogah* unless he was convicted of some serious offence.

A writer in the *Calcutta Review* (1846), while recommending better payment for darogahship (of Bengal Presidency) and recruitment from better classes, observed as follows:

> It is incumbent upon Government to change the name of *darogah*, because it is one with which the most odious associations are connected,—one, which is almost synonymous with dacoit—which carries terror in its very sound—which reminds the poor cultivator of him, over whom there is no control, of him who lives upon cruelty and extortion, and whose very vocation is corruption. No real native gentleman, however distressed his circumstances, will condescend to take a *Darogaship* as long as it bears its present designation.[17]

Little or no reliance could be placed by the magistrate on the proceedings conducted by the *darogahs*. The practice of censuring and occasionally dismissing police officers for not being able to trace offenders let them to have recourse to various means for convicting innocent parties. Such a practice was followed only to escape from censure or reprimand. The police officers were seriously deficient in their knowledge of duties. On the other hand, the jurisdiction of a single *thana* was so wide that its effective supervision was almost impossible. Some parts of the district were as far as 40 miles from the nearest police *thana* and still greater distance from the Sadar Station. As a result, the magistrate could not have a check on his police subordinates. It was not useful to send the police to make local investigation except when property of great value had been lost. To do otherwise was to increase the sufferings of those who had been robbed, besides giving room for plunder of number of other parties by somewhat different means.[18] The Sibsagar district occupied all the areas on the south bank of the river Brahmaputra between the Dhansiri River in the west and the Buridihing in the east with the great river island called Majuli; yet there were in it only two police stations, one at Sibsagar and the other at Jorhat. 'If it is expected', observed Matthie, 'all crimes that are committed are to be reported and the lives and properties of the people efficiently protected, it is manifest there ought to be an increase of police establishment of this division particularly for the eastern division'.[19] The extent of police jurisdiction of Raja Bijoynarayan similarly was extended over an area of 663 sq miles with a population of 1,29,492 which was too extensive to be managed by a single functionary. The district of Nowgong, which was the largest in the province in terms of area, had only three police *thanas* upto April 1839. Similarly the *thana* of Dhakuakhana in the district of Lakhimpore, with a *darogah* and six *barkandozes* had jurisdiction over Sisi-Dhemaji and all the villages from the river Subansiri to the mouth of Buridihing, and from the northern hills to the River Lohit. In a country of jungles and marshes, where mobility was exceedingly difficult, this extensive jurisdiction together with inadequate staff rendered the police utterly inefficient. 'But the real cause of the evil', observed, the Deputy Governor of Bengal, 'is to be found in the want of intelligence or in the want of honesty in the police establishment'.[20]

The Court of Directors provided detailed guidelines for a reorganization of the police all over the country in their dispatch of 24 September 1856, in which they said:

That the police in India has lamentably failed in accomplishing the ends for which it was established is a notorious fact; that it is all but useful for the prevention, and sadly inefficient for the detection of crime, is generally admitted, unable to check crime, it is with rare exceptions, unscrupulous as to its mode of wielding the authority with which it is armed for the functions which it fails to fulfill, and has a very general character for corruption and oppression.[21]

The inefficiency and misconduct of the police appeared over and again in the Magistrates' annual report on the police. The functioning of the police was almost universally condemned by officials and people alike. It was said that crime was bad, but the subsequent police enquiry was much worse.

Reorganization of the police system received due attention of the government and on 17 August 1860, the Government of India appointed a commission to investigate into police administration in India.[22] The main objectives of the commission were:

1. To propose a new system of police applicable to India in general, whereby economy and efficiency might be secured.
2. To propose for publication all available information regarding the best system of police organization.
3. To collect the most complete and comprehensive statistics obtainable, regarding the cost and establishment of police of all kinds throughout India.

The recommendations of this commission were embodied in the Police Act of 1861, which was extended to all the provinces comprised within the jurisdiction of the Lieutenant Governor of Bengal on 11 April 1862. In reorganizing the police system in Assam the provisions of this act were followed. On 29 April 1862, Major H. Raban was appointed Deputy Inspector-General of Civil Constabulary, Assam Circle, with the powers of Inspector-General in consideration of the great distance between Assam and the headquarters of the Inspector-General in Calcutta.[23]

Under the new Police Act, district superintendents were appointed in every district having headquarters at the Sadar Station of the magistrate. Assistant district superintendent at the headquarters of the deputy magistrate, who, under the general control of the district superintendent, administered the division or the subdivision, as might be allotted to him. A divisional station ordinarily consisted of one Inspector, one sub-inspector, one head constable, and 16-20 constables. A Sub-Divisional Station had one sub-inspector, one head constable, and from 12 to 16 constables. A police officer with the rank of a sub-inspector with requisite number of constables was always to be present in the magistrate's court. He was to receive and enter in a book kept for the purpose, all orders given by the magistrate, whose initials were to be attached to each order. No separate *parwannah* was issued; the orders were simply transmitted to the division for which they were intended. For warrants and other process a separate register was maintained.

All persons summoned to the criminal courts, whether witnesses or others, and all cases whether cognizable or not by the police were to be received by the inspector in attendance. He was to register their names in a book kept for the purpose and to hand over such persons to such officer as might be appointed by the magistrate, taking care that they were also to be registered by such officer. The responsibility of the detention of all witnesses and others, when once made over, rested with the magistrate. The inspector was also to take charge of and act as prosecutor in all cases sent up by the police. He was responsible for bringing all persons detained in custody pending trial, as well as for escorting to the jail such prisoners sentenced to imprisonment.[24]

The magistrate was to be accompanied by one Inspector while he was on tour within his district. All police reports were to be sent to the magistrate through the inspector in attendance while he was on tour. In the absence of the magistrate, the next superior officer would be empowered to deal with police cases and the reports were to be sent to that officer. Normally a copy of all reports had to be forwarded to the district superintendent and in his absence to the next superior police officer.[25]

The police officers were directed to conform strictly to the rules laid down in the new Criminal Procedure Code, specially chapters IV, V and VIII dealing with the mode in which the 'summon', 'warrant' and 'search warrant' were to be issued. They were further advised to follow Sections 69 to 72, 76, 77, 80, 115 and 116 in dealing with such questions. The police officer executing a warrant must inform the substance of that warrant to the person to be arrested and the officer must 'actually touch or confine body of the person to be arrested, unless there be submission to custody by word or action'.[26] The attention of subordinate police officers, inspectors, and others, should be especially called to Chapter VI of the Police Act, which detailed in what cases the police might interfere and even arrest without warrant from a magistrate. The police might arrest a person without a warrant, but such persons should, without any unnecessary delay, be taken before the magistrate having jurisdiction in the case.

The officer in-charge of a police station after receiving information about the commission of a crime might proceed in person or depute one of his subordinates to proceed to the spot to enquire into the facts and circumstances of the case and to take such measures as might be necessary for the discovery and apprehension of the offender. If the case be one demanding enquiry, the investigating officer should in no case detain an accused person beyond 24 hours. He was to produce the accused before the magistrate who would decide whether to keep the latter in custody or to release him on bail. He was to forward a charge-sheet without any expression of opinion as to the guilt of the accused person. But if it should appear to a police officer, on a complaint or information being preferred to him, that there was no sufficient ground for entering in an enquiry, or that the immediate apprehension of the accused was not necessary for the ends of justice, he should abstain from proceeding in the case and should report the substance of the complaint or information for the orders of the Magistrate.[27]

Cases of a very serious nature, such as murder, gang robbery, highway robbery and serious burglary had to be specially reported in Form E for the information of the Deputy Inspector-General with a copy to the Commissioner (Appendix 7.2). A diary had to be kept in every police station in which all complaints, charges, and so on had to be recorded. In addition to this, another diary was to be maintained and sent daily to the district superintendent, setting forth the ordinary routine of the station, such as the parading of the police party, the distribution of duty and also the extraordinary occurrences of the day. Further, all complaints and information, and the proceedings taken, the dispatch of information, etc., as briefly as possible, as well as any general matters that might come to the notice of the officer-in-charge of the station had to be recorded. A daily record of proceedings was to be forwarded to the district superintendent in every enquiry, extending beyond 24 hours. Monthly returns in Form 3 would henceforth to be submitted to the deputy inspector-general, the first being a return of crimes and the second the monthly state of the forces, including strength, causalities and punishments inflicted (Appendix 7.3).

District superintendents were required by law to administer the police under the general control and direction of the magistrate of the district. But the internal organization and discipline of the police force were exclusively in his hands. He was responsible for the efficient discharge of all duties devolving on the police. In was his duty to inform the magistrate immediately after receiving instruction to assume charge of the police of any district. All reports which had hitherto gone to the magistrate were to be received by the superintendent. All heinous offences had to be reported by the police to the magistrate in the division and deputy magistrate in the sub-division.

NOTES

1. *Assam in the Days of the Company*, p. 79.
2. Territorial Proceedings (Revenue), 12 August 1833, no. 2. Also see FPP, 30 May 1833, no. 94.
3. See Blunt and Shakespere, *Abstract of Regulation XX of 1817*. Also see M.N. Gupta, *Analytical Study of Bengal Regulations*, pp. 145, 154.
4. Ibid.
5. Ibid.
6. Ibid.
7. BJP (criminal), 19 June 1843, no. 3.
8. RPA, p. 114.
9. BJP (Criminal), 6 March 1838, no. 43.
10. BJP (Criminal), 6 March 1838, no. 39, see Police Report of 1836.
11. Ibid., no. 45, also see BJP (Criminal) 27 November 1838, nos. 77-9, see Police Report of 1837.
12. BJP (Criminal), 4 June 1839, nos. 33-4 also see 22 August, no. 24, see Police Report of 1838.
13. BJP (Criminal), 6 March 1838, no. 47, Secy. Bengal to Commmissioner of Assam, 6 March 1838.
14. BJP (Criminal), 7 November 1842, no. 24, Bigge to Jenkins, 4 September 1840.
15. BJP (Criminal), 14 July 1840, no. 12, Matthie to Halliday, 30 March 1840.
16. BJP (Criminal), 7 November 1840, no. 82, Bigee to Matthie, 14 August 1840.
17. R.C. Majumder, *British Paramountary and Indian Renaissance*, p. 378.
18. BJP (Criminal), 27 November 1838, no. 78.
19. BJP (Criminal), 14 July 1840, no. 12, Matthie to Halliday, 30 March 1840.

20. BJP (Criminal), 6 March 1838, no. 47.
21. Anandaswarup Gupta, *The Police in British India Introduction VII.*
22. Resolution Home Department (Judicial), dated 17 August 1860, quoted in *Final Report of the Police Commission of 1860.*
23. BJP, April 1862, no. 602.
24. BJP, November 1862, no. 39, see Police Act of 1861.
25. Ibid.
26. Ibid.
27. Ibid.

APPENDIX 7.1

LOWER ASSAM

SADAR POLICE AT GUWAHATI

Darogah	35
2 Mohurers @ 12	24
Jamadar	10
10 Barkandozes	50
Stationary and contingencies	8
Boat	10
	137

MOFUSSIL POLICE

Darogah	30
Mohurer	12
Jamadar	8
4 Barkandozes @ 5	20
6 Teckela @ 2/8	15
Contingencies	5
	90

DEHAR *THANA*

Darogah	30
2 Mohurer @ 12	24
Jamadar	8
6 Barkandozes @ 5	30
6 Teckela	15
Contingencies	6
	113

KACHAREE MOHAL *THANA*

Mohurer	20.00
Jamadar	8.00
Kakoti	3.00
4 Barkandozes @ 5	20.00
11 Teckelas @ 2/8	27.50
Contingencies	5.00
	83.50

BAJALEE THANA

Mohurer	20
Kakoti	3
Jamadar	8
4 Barkandozes @ 5	20
10 Teckelas @ 2/8	25
Contingencies	5
	81

KATTAH THANA

Darogah	30
Mohurer	12
Kakoti	3
Jamadar	8
4 Barkandozes @ 5	20
4 Teckela @ 2/8	10
Contingencies	5
Boat for 6 months at *thana*	600
	688

BARPETA THANA

Darogah	30
Mohurer	20
Jamadar	10
14 Barkandozes	56
Sarjamnee	5
Boat	8
	129

POLICE ESTABLISHMENT CENTRAL ASSAM

DARRANG AND CHATGARE

Superintendent	50
2 Mohurers @ 15	30
Borkandozes @ 2/8	25
Burra	25
Mohurer	12
20 Teckelas @ 2/8	50
Contingencies	10
Boat 3 men	18
	220

NOWGONG

1 Pharee Mohurer	25
1 Pharee Mohurer	12
Burra	4
10 Teckelas @ 2/8	25
8 Sepoys @ 2/8	20
2 Boat @ 9	18
Contingencies	8
	112

CHARDUAR

1 Pharee Mohurer	25
1 Burra	3
10 Teckelas @ 2/8	25
6 Sepoys @ 2/8	15
2 Boat @ 9	18
Contingencies	6
	92

RAHA AND JAGEE

1 Mohurer	25.00
1 Teckelas Burra	4.00
8 Teckelas @ 2/8	20.00
5 Sepoys @ 2/8	12.80
2 Boat @ 9	18.00
Contingencies	5
	84.80

Another police station was at Biswanath, i.e. in the headquarter of the Political Agent, Upper Assam at a monthly expense of Rs. 1,190.

Source: TP, (Revenue), 12 August 1833, no. 2. Also see FPP, 30 May 1833, no. 94.

APPENDIX 7.2

FORM E: SPECIAL REPORT OF CRIME

No................. District.................... Dated..................

Description of offences and name of parties	NUMBER OF PERSONS		Amount of plundered	Amount of property recovered	Statement of the nature of crime, the conduct of Police, and measures taken to arrest and bring offenders to punishment
	Supposed to have been concerned	Arrested			

Source: BJP, (Police), November 1862, no. 39.

APPENDIX 7.3

FORM 3: BENGAL POLICE

Return of Crimes in the................. District of................., the value of property sto and recovered, a number of persons committed for trial, and discharged in the month.................186

	Number of Causes	Value of property stolen	Value of property Recovered	Number of Causes in which no ultimate loss occurred	NUMBER OF PERSONS							Number of Cases not detect	Value of property not recovered	Remarks
					Concerned	Arrested	Brought before Magistrate	Convicted	Committed	Discharged			
Against Property { Murder with robbery, house-breaking or theft Murder of children for ornaments Murder Homicide Wounding with intent to kill Assaulting with wounding Rape Highway robbery with aggravating circumstances Highway robbery without aggravating circumstances		This is the property said to have been stolen unless the statements are evidently false		Cases in which property was at stake	This is reported or supposed to have been concerned	All 'arrested', whether sent in for trial or released on Bail							

APPENDIX 7.3 contd.

| | Number of Causes | Value of property stolen | Value of property Recovered | Number of Causes in which no ultimate loss occurred | NUMBER OF PERSONS ||||||| Number of Cases not detect | Value of property not recovered | Remarks |
					Concerned	Arrested	Brought before Magistrate	Convicted	Committed	Discharged			
Gang robbery with aggravating circustances													
Gang robbery without aggravating circumstances													
House-breaking with personal injury													
House-breaking, simple													
Theft by administering poison or drugs													
Theft, simple													
Cattle stealing													
Arson													
Various													
Total													

Source: BJP, (Police), November 1862, no. 39.

CHAPTER 8

Impact of the Administration of Justice on the Life of the People

The administration of civil and criminal justice in any country is intimately connected with its revenue and police administration. The civil courts would be affected if the laws and regulations governing the revenue administration are defective or vague. Likewise the criminal justice system would become ineffective without a strong police force to detect crimes and catch the criminals. Again a bad revenue system gives rise to poverty which, in turn, disturbs the peace and stability of the society. It is, therefore, desirable to examine the effects of revenue and police administration in order to ascertain the impact of the administration of justice on the life of the people for the period under review.

Reference has already been made to the effects of the revenue system in the early years of British rule (supra Chapter 3). Things, however, began to improve with the inauguration of radical reforms in the revenue administration in 1836, when taxes on house, hearth and head were abolished throwing the entire burden of revenue on land. The house tax, however, continued to levy in Gauhati. With the formation of Town Committee, it became a source of revenue for the Committee. This was followed by the proprietary right on land and the issue of *pattah* by the collector of the district after due measurement of land. The area of the land belonged to a particular ryot and the revenue to be paid on it was defined in the said *pattah*. But the measurement and classification of land were not carried out systematically and carefully. In practice, the settlements were conducted in the Sadar Station based on the report of petty officials leading to incorrect classification and false measurement. At the same time, there were frequent instances of fiscal officers engaged in the survey and measurement of land attempting 'transfer, on sinister motives, the land of one ryot to the possession of another, by laying down in the measurement papers lands occupied by one party in the name of another, and thereby imperceptibly depriving him of his possession'.[1] Allegations of causing an over-assessment, of illegal imposts, of concealment of terms and even of a secret pact on their personal account, were not uncommon. The only course open to a *ryot* under such circumstances was to seek justice in summary suit courts or civil courts. But as Anandaram Dhekial Phukan says:

Many insurmountable obstacles lie in their way to redress; that a civil or summary prosecution for damages, exactions, or dispossession, is actually beyond their means; and that they are obliged to submit to loss and privation rather than leave their cultivations and sojourn half a year at the distance of eighty miles to obtain an award for damages.[2]

Instances of *ryots* presenting petitions to the collector and the commissioner were, however, not uncommon after the settlement had been completed, complaining of false measurement and incorrect classification. The *ryots*, with their limited resources, also never failed to pursue their cause in civil courts seeking justice. This is corroborated by the innumerable suits that flooded the civil courts of the province.

With the introduction of land revenue, the *ryots* in Assam enjoyed proprietary rights over their possessions. At the same time, land was made saleable, mortgagable and alienable. The rent to be paid on land to the government solely depended upon the produce of the land. There was hardly any consideration for a crop failure due to flood or drought. The absence of trade and manufacturing rendered it difficult for the people to clear their rent in time, that too in cash. The system of transport and communication was also then in a very deplorable state, due to which the cultivators could not take their produce to trading centres or markets where they could obtain a fair price. As a result, there was a glut in the local markets. The *ryots*, therefore, had to sell their produce at a much lower rate as the 'prices fall when goods are in abundance or during harvest time'. The entire trade of the province was in the hands of the Kyahs and Bengalis. 'In the manner it has been managed', said Jenkins, 'the Assamese have had to pay maximum prices and received only minimum profits: for those experienced traders have usually taken advantage of the necessities of our Ryots and made them advance at an almost incredible interest for impossible returns and then ruined the defaulters in the civil court.'[3] The people preferred getting into debt by mortgaging their lands to a moneylender rather than losing them outright. But once in debt, they found it difficult to get out of it. The moneylender through cunning and deceitful means got the peasants deeper and deeper into debt till they parted with their land. As Robinson says:

> The great body of the cultivators are, in fact, mere servants of the merchants who engage them to pay their rent for them, whilst they in turn agree to surrender all the produce of their land to him—If the produce be more than the debts, the farmer keeps the surplus—if on the other hand, he should very unfortunate in his harvest, the poor cultivator, little all is sold by the merchant, and with this family he is turned out upon the cold unfeeling world, to beg his bread, or to perish.[4]

The moneylender was greatly assisted by the new administration of justice. While giving the *ryot* freedom to mortgage or sell his land in distress, it gave the creditor of the indebted *ryot* freedom to seize the latter's land. The literate and shrewd moneylender could easily take advantage of the ignorance and illiteracy of the *ryot* to twist the complicated process of law to get judicial decisions in his favour. The attention of the Government of Bengal was drawn in 1869 to the indebtedness of the Mikirs (Karbis) in the district of Nowgong and the impositions practised on them by the Kyahs (Marwaris) and other foreign traders taking advantage of civil laws. 'Almost all the cases instituted against the Mikirs in civil courts', Eden, Secretary, Bengal was constrained to remark, 'were of an extortionate character and that in the mode in which they were disposed of much injustice has been done to those simple and ignorant people under the cover of law'.[5]

Rural indebtedness, backward methods of cultivation, flood and drought resulted in pauperization of the rural masses. The poverty and distress led the people to criminal activities mainly to maintain their livelihood. They preferred to go to jail than to remain outside as freemen without food and shelter. 'There are so many of our convicts,' observed Lt. Charles Scott, Principal Assistant at Kamrup, 'who would rather be in than out of jail. They are well fed, well clothed, sheltered and taken care of in sickness as well as in health and have to undergo labour not at all in excess of which have most of our ryot to go through. They have certain hours of work and no thought and anarchy of their food and they have regular hours of sleep, the only difficulty is of leaving their families at home.'[6] Thus, the revenue administration, on the one hand, gave rise to civil suits concerning land and monetary transactions and, on the other, poverty arising out of this induced the people to commit crimes in order to save themselves from starvation.

Likewise the police were inefficient and corrupt as discussed above. Instead of protecting the poor inhabitants, the police officers inflicted far greater distress on them than the thieves and robbers. Their oppression and extortion crossed all limits. It was difficult to set the police in motion on the occurrence of any crime without bribing them. Even their enquiry sometimes brought harassment and hardship to the complainant. The people preferred to remain silent than to report the occurrence of a crime. The result was obvious, the criminals freely resorted to unlawful activities and there was hardly any security of life and property of the people.

PROCEDURAL LAW

The ignorant commoners of the province were hit hard by the cumbersome procedure which the court was required to follow. In all stages, from filing a suit to receiving the final judgement, there was need of doing a mass of writing. This system was hitherto unnecessary both to the people and to the public functionaries and hence they considered it very oppressive. The new practice of taking written deposition had appeared to Purandar Singha, former king of Assam, as an obstacle in the speedy adjustment of disputes. 'It was our system', said Purandar Singha, 'to hear all complaints viva voce, afterwards to summon the party complained against, and if his statement proved unsatisfactory, prompt punishment ensured, without further delay for witnesses'.[7] Both the people and the native officials, therefore, were amazed at the mass of writings, in which, they saw that even the most insignificant transactions of the government were recorded. Naturally, they proved themselves incapable of furnishing these voluminous and minute details required of them. The entire process of writing in pleadings and depositions was not intelligible to the people, more than 90 per cent of whom were illiterate. 'The system of having four written pleadings', admitted, Mills, 'drawn up and filed in every case, is ill-suited to the simple habits of the people of Assam.'[8] Consequently, they had little confidence in the justice of the decision.

Delay was the result of the new system. It also produced circumlocution and red-tape, which were major obstacles in the way of speedy justice. The parties to the suit had to cross several hurdles in each stage of the suit.

'Under the present judicial system' said Anandaram Dhekial Phukan,

a party, how trivial so ever may be nature of his complaint, can never obtain relief without submitting to vexations and a harassing course of procedure, extending from at least six months to an unlimited length of time, and even when he obtains an award in his favour, the execution of the same is attended with so many obstacles that he is in many instances, actually compelled to relinquish all hopes of recovering of his dues. Justice is thereby defeated and, the people prefer giving up their just dues rather than resort to so uncertain a course and throw away money to meet the costs of suit in pursuit of an object which they are never sure of securing.[9]

The numerous appeals and revisions, to which the decisions of courts were successively subjected to, were further impediments to speedy justice. Appeals were allowed in all cases irrespective of the nature of the suits, serious or trifling. Consequently petty suits of small value came up for appeal before the commissioner or deputy commissioner's (later judicial commissioner's) courts resulting in heavy expenses and harassment for the concerned parties. In criminal cases appeals from the decision of junior or subassistant were preferred to the commissioner's and later to the deputy commissioner's court. But in a province nearly 400 miles in length and 50 miles in breadth on an average, having an estimated population of 8,30,000 and where the postal communication by water was necessarily very slow, it was quite out of power of a person, sentenced to a short term of imprisonment, to prefer an appeal before the sentence expired. 'For instance', observed Mills:

in Lakhimpur or Dibrugarh a man be sentenced to one month's imprisonment, sent his petition by *dak*, before an order staying execution of the sentence could be received at either place, the sentence would unless the greatest dispatch be used, have expired.[10]

It was, in effect, as the old saying goes, 'justice delayed is justice denied'. The system of special appeal caused serious harm to the poor and downtrodden. It encouraged litigation and gave the rich an advantage to outbid their poor adversary in the expensive system of justice. The appellate judge did not have the advantage of a subordinate judge of having contact with the witnesses, yet he might reverse the findings, while those of his own were absolutely irreversible or immutable except on rare occasions. Every appellate court worked upon dead records, not having witnesses before it. These records or documents were prepared by corrupt *omlahs* to favour the appellant so as to get the verdict in the latter's favour. Sometimes the cases dragged on for years and it often happened that the final decision was made after the descendants in the second generation took the place of the original parties.

Considering the peculiar circumstances and customs of the people, Clause 5, Section II of the Assam Code (Civil) gave the assistant the power to make a summary enquiry into the merits of a case by confronting the parties. 'But the Assistants', said Mill, 'have no time to take up these cases themselves; while to require the attendance of parties, some two or three days journey from the station, would be extremely harassing to them.'[11]

LARGE JURISDICTION

The large extent of territory under the jurisdiction of a magistrate made his task extremely difficult. A magistrate could not keep in touch with the rural population and exercise effective supervision over his subordinates. The long distance which plaintiffs or a witnesses had to travel made them reluctant to attend the Magistrate's court. Most of the trifling crimes went undetected and the people were also apathetic to report about the occurrence of such crimes. Even if these were reported, the sufferers did not think it worthwhile to involve themselves in legal complications, as they could not very often leave their agricultural pursuits to come into the Sadar Station, braving great inconvenience and trouble. 'In my opinion the cause of sufferers being unwilling to prosecute in cases of theft arises from several circumstances, the principal of which are', observed, officiating Magistrate of Sibsagar, Lt. Brodie,

First, the want of proof against any particular individual, and the chance of prosecutors being detained from their homes for long time without being better off than if they never prosecuted, second, small amount of property stolen, and third the dislike of the people to go to the *thana* at all from the every gross oppression that were committed there.[12]

Section II of the Regulation 2 of 1832 prescribed that police officers should not enquire into cases of simple theft or burglary, unless a petition was presented by the sufferers or the magistrate ordered an enquiry. Everyone from the magistrate or the police to the common men took advantage of this regulation. While the former two considered prosecution a burden to their ever increasing business, the common people accepted it as a relief as they were no longer required to go to the police station or to the Sadar Station. 'The small amount of property stolen', remarked Lt. Vetch,

seldom exceeding a very few rupees the recovery of which would scarcely compensate for the trouble and loss of time upon prosecuting especially when the complainant lived at a distance of 30 or 40 miles from the nearest *thana* and at a still greater one from their Sadar Station.[13]

The inhabitants of Lakhimpore were the worst sufferers as the headquarter of the district was located in the south bank of the river Brahmaputra. It was extremely inconvenient for the people residing at the north bank of the river to seek justice in any wrong done to them. The sub-assistant, *sadar ameen* and *munsif* were stationed at Lakhimpore in the north bank, but all orders on petitions were to be issued from the Sadar Station at Dibrugarh on the south bank. In heinous offences, the sufferer had to attend the Sadar Station in person. The officer-in-charge of the district who was also the Political Agent of Upper Assam could not give immediate attention to the business of the division. As Matthie remarked, 'he had much more important duty to occupy time in the settlement and management of the Mattak and Sadiya division and our relation with border tribes, the Nagas, Singphos, Khamtis etc'.[14]

Likewise the officer-in-charge of Kamrup could not have any effective control over the proceedings either of the *munsifs* or police officers of the *parganas* in the north bank of the river Brahmaputra. In reality the people were deprived of having an enquiry even though they were interested to look into wrongs committed, which were not strictly cognizable by the police. 'As it is scarcely reasonable', said Matthie, 'to suppose that the people who have cause for complaint will unless, they have been very seriously injured indeed, undertake a journey from their house to Guwahati, which occupied six to seven days.'[15] The sub-assistant or *munsif* of Barpeta had no authority to receive petitions as they were to be presented to the assistant-in-charge of the district at Sadar Station. Subordinate officials were empowered only to try referred cases. 'Their usefulness', admitted Mills, 'when employed in the interior is much impaired by their not being able to receive petitions'.[16]

EXAMINATION OF WITNESSES

The system of examining witnesses in the courts of justice caused mischief and great injustice. It had facilitated the commission of perjury to an extent scarcely credible, and in fact, it had utterly defeated the ends of justice, and converted the public tribunals into engines of oppression rather than of protection.

Under the existing practice of the courts, witnesses were seldom or never examined personally by the judges. Provisions were made in 1837 that the ministerial officers might be empowered to record depositions in matters of minor importance, but in all instances in the presence of the presiding officer and a certificate to that effect was to be annexed thereto.[17] Section II, Clause 3, of the Assam

Code (Civil) enjoined the senior assistant to examine the witnesses themselves, or to delegate that duty to the junior assistant and only in case of necessity to the head *omlah*. But the native judges were not authorized to delegate that duty to any of their ministerial officers. The criminal rules, however, required the judges to record themselves the substance of the evidence in all petty criminal cases. Unfortunately, such provisions were followed sincerely neither by the assistants nor by the native judges. In contrast, they conducted their business contrary to these beneficial rules.

The assistant in-charge of the district being also the collector was often pre-occupied with revenue matters. He did not have enough time to devote to the Criminal Court's work, and therefore, clerks or omlahs were authorized to take down depositions. Even the examinations were made by the *omlahs* in the absence of the assistants. These court writers by means of bribery were made to lean on one side or the other, and deliberately wrote 'no' when the witness said 'yes' and vice versa. The plaints thus prepared were read over in a loud and hurried voice and then the evidence before each witness. Being written in Bengali language, the witnesses, confused and terrified by the official ambience of the place heard the account like dumb cattle. 'In ninety cases out of one hundred', writes Anandaram Dhekial Phukan,

The *Mohurer (Omlah)* is paid by the party at whose instance witnesses are summoned—In no instance has the examination of witnesses by the Mohurers admitted of such injury as the criminal cases. The evidence for the prosecution is generally, taken without the presence of the defendant or before he is summoned, and there is nobody to watch the examination. The *Mohurer* puts down whatever he thinks best conducive to the interest of the party who buys him over to his side.[18]

The *omlah* had, however, to procure a confirmation of the statements recorded (as is being done even now), but such a procedure was absolutely valueless when the very language in which the deposition was taken was not intelligible to the witness. Even if a clever person detected the forgery introduced into his written evidences, he was either not listened to or confronted with the threat of being prosecuted for perjury.[19]

COURT LANGUAGE

Perhaps the most damaging impact of the administration of justice, on the indigenous people of Assam for the period under review was on the question of court language. The British made Persian, the court language of the Presidency, to be the court language of Assam too. But owing to the difficulties in procuring persons having proficiency in Persian they were forced to substitute it by Bengali. By 1835, Bengali had become the language of the province used in the courts and also in the schools, which was formalized by Act XXIX of 1837.

Act XXIX of 1837 paved the way for the use of vernacular language in the judicial and revenue proceedings of the Company's administration in India. Unfortunately, the local authorities in Assam considered Bengali to be the vernacular of the province, and favoured the continuation of this language as the lingua franca.

The local authorities, however, failed to foresee the mischief of introducing Bengali as the court language of the province. It was only to the officers and other persons connected with the courts that Bengali was generally intelligible. The common people possessed no knowledge of that language. 'For want of our mother tongue in the Government offices', said the inhabitants of Tezpore in their memorandum of Lieutenant Governor, 'persons who have no means to appoint an agent, or do not know Bengali, are greatly deceived by the opposite party who knows Bengali, or have means to appoint Vakeels on behalf of them; because in such cases the ignorant plaintiff or defendant is misled by the opponent to think true what is said by the opponent, a written statement being made in one way, and its meaning as well as that of the Bengali rules, being explained in quite another way'.[20] Most litigants were unable to read and understand the judgement delivered in the courts. Further, the English officials had to be furnished with English translation of Bengali records. This process delayed dispensation of justice and made it costlier. The plaintiff or the defendants were unable to detect any incorrect statements recorded by the *mohurer* due to their total ignorance of the Bengali language. The parties to the suits were in no position to ascertain the arguments put forward by their vakeels. 'To me', observed Haughton, Commissioner of Assam, 'it appears certain that a native villager would not in a court of justice understand one word of his case, if the proceedings were recorded in Bengali, neither would a pure native of Bengal be able to understand the same if read out to him in Assamese.'[21] Even Commissioner Jenkins admitted as early as 1837 the difference between the Assamese and Bengali language. Still he encouraged Bengali, on the ground that it was the common language of the entire population of this wide province. According to him, the Assamese dialect is not the only current dialect of the province, there are several other dialects spoken though not written by the rude tribes within our frontiers, with them, there is daily increasing commerce with the merchants of Bengal and this intercourse will be materially furthered by the extended knowledge of the language of that country.[22] Thus, the motive was very clear: for the interest of commerce and for administrative convenience, the Company authorities in Assam desired the continuation of Bengali, sacrificing the interest of the indigenous people. In spite of Anandaram Dhekial Phukan's lengthy memorandum to Mill in 1853 and Mill's own view on the subject, the government did nothing till the year 1873 to undo the wrong done to the Assamese people.

The benefits that would be derived if the Assamese language was introduced in the courts can be judged from a memorial submitted by the inhabitants of Tezpore to the local authorities. They observed:

The parties to suits, who are quite ignorant of Bengali, and consequently obliged to incur more than double expense to institute a suit, will be able to write themselves their own plaints or statements, to express their ideas personally, and so to be satisfied by understanding what is recorded in the proceedings; and doubts will thus be removed from their minds in a less expensive manner than by waiting for another's assistance. It will no longer be necessary to appoint a clerk or Mohurer as an interpreter at the time of hearing or deciding a case to explain before some of the Bengali or European officers the verbal statements of Plaintiff, defendants or witnesses, as the Officers, who now give little heed to the Assamese language on account of its not being used in the proceedings, will try their best to be well up in it. The clerks or Mohurers who are appointed to interpret without taking a legal oath, and who are not well educated in English, sometimes, though not always, cause great harm to the parties to suits for want of exact translation of certain expressions, which is either owing to the interpreter's partiality or to his want of knowledge of English, and failing to confess his inability to interpret before the Judge for fear of shame or punishment.

It would no doubt remove the difficulties and inconveniences the ryots feel through not knowing what conversations are held between the Bengali Vakeels of both parties and Judges or Magistrate at the time of hearing or deciding a case. Besides this, certain common Bengali words, through difference of pronunciation, convey too shameful a meaning to the Assamese mind that they sometimes think it better to resign the case rather that hear such words.[23]

With Bengali being made the medium of instruction in the schools of Assam, the same problem was faced by the Assamese students. The objection to this injudicious act was first raised by the American Baptist Missionaries. In his petition to Halliday, Lt. Governor of Bengal, Dr. Miles Bronson remarked:

Bengali is not the vernacular of Assam. The Common people do not understand that language, written or spoken; we find people in almost every village who on being offered a book reply, we cannot read your books; but on being told that they are not Bengali but Assamese, receive and read them readily—This is the case with every school in the province. On the playground, in the family circle at home, on the religious assemblies when their shastras are explained, the first word the new born child hears from his mother, the first word he learns to lisp, the rude song of the boatman as he pulls the oar, or spreads his sail, the joyous song of the reaper, as he shouts the harvest home, always, and everywhere, the language used is Assamese, not Bengali; and in our humble opinion, the only way to render any plan of education popular in this province, is to give it to them in their own mother tongue.[24]

Anandaram Dhekial Phukan in his memorandum submitted to A.J. Moffatt Mills, Judge of the Sadar Court, on his visit to Assam in 1853 pleaded for the restoration of Assamese. Phukan observed:

It is only to the officers and other persons connected with the courts that Bengali is generally intelligible. The mass of the population and even private gentlemen possess no knowledge of the language. The native judges are less familiar with the Bengali than with their own tongue, and the European judges have always been found to understand the vernacular Assamese with greater facility than the Bengali; and they often speak the former with a degree of fluency much to be commended.[25]

These protests and resentments ultimately had the desired effect; in 1873, the Government of Bengal, under whose jurisdiction Assam was administered, restored Assamese as the court language of Assam.

CONCENTRATION OF POWER: JUSTICE UNITED WITH ADMINISTRATION AND REVENUE

The administration of justice was seriously undermined as a result of the concentration of all authority in a single individual. Under the existing system where the offices of the collector, magistrate and judge were united in the hands of a single person, it was utterly impossible for him, except by most unusual efforts, to do justice to the judicial department under him. Taking and recording evidence and conducting a trial to a successful conclusion demanded security from interruption, which could not be expected from the collector-cum-magistrate-cum-judge, as he would be bound by restrictions associated with other offices or there might cross-interests or prejudices. The Assistant having several offices under him had several masters to serve. As collector and magistrate he was to send extracts, viz., reports, returns, statements and accounts. He had to superintend all matters connected with revenue, police, *khas mahals*, roads, stamps, stationery, registration, acquisition of land for public purposes, and so on. As such, leisure available for him for judicial and police duties was very small. His prime concern was the office of the collector, because he was appreciated or discredited for his success or failure in realizing the revenue. Consequently the judicial business received little attention.

An assistant could not sit continuously for several days together on the trial of a serious criminal case. The practice of taking the examination of one or two witnesses on one day, and of the rest after a considerable interval of time not only delayed the process but put the judges into great disadvantage, depriving them of the convenience of conducting a trial by oral testimony.

In the regulation provinces, the administration of civil justice, with the important exception of rent suits, was in the hands of a body of officers who had little executive duties. In the superior level, the administration of criminal justice was, in like manner, taken entirely out of the hands of the officers doing executive duties. So also in some of the intermediate stages, the joint magistrate was employed almost exclusively in judicial duties. There was thus in the regulation provinces a considerable advance that allowed a move from concentration of power towards separation or diffusion.

In Assam, which was a non-regulation province, the situation was different. The same individual was the civil judge, magistrate, revenue officer and everything else. So he continued with gradually increasing powers throughout his service and such officers were burdened with incongruous duties. The magistrate, collector and judge were then a sort of local governor, and had a great advantage in this management from the combination of powers. Campbell observed, 'He (District Officer) exercises an extended superintendence over his district, a good deal beyond what his simple name implies, and the people look to him as their immediate ruler'.[26] The magistrate had become a despotic ruler in the district, both as head of the revenue collection and judge of civil cases. Neither the fiscal officers nor the *ryots* could regard him as an impartial judge in revenue cases. People whom he had wronged in the revenue court could never hope to obtain redress from him while he presided over the civil courts.

The conglomeration of powers of a magistrate with those of a Judge were truly anomalous in theory and mischievous in practice. District officers as a single functionary playing the roles of a thief catcher and thief trier received severe condemnation from all quarters even in regulation provinces. A writer in the *Calcutta Review* observed as follows:

> There is scarcely any principle in jurisprudence more important than the separation of these two offices. Their union is injurious to offenders, to the community, and to the Magistrate,—injurious to the offenders, because they are not tried by a unbiased judge,—but by one whose interest it is to convict them,—who will again get credit if they are convicted;—whose opinion has been formed before the trial by a previous knowledge of the

circumstance of the case, whose judgment has been influenced by collateral circumstances,—who has himself been advising the police officers how to conduct the case,—who unites in himself the offices of accuser, judge and jury.[27]

LEGISLATION

The people of the province were hit hard by the multiplicity of hastily enacted laws, some of which were badly drafted. The laws were made by the Governor-General in his executive capacity in consultation with local authorities. Of these laws, some were new and substantive pieces of legislation; others were merely explicit extensions of existing regulation or acts.

The rules for the administration of criminal justice in Assam contained no provision whatsoever regarding appeals to magistrates for the decision of their subordinates. It was neither enacted that the orders of these officers should be final or binding nor provided that the regulation was to be followed in such cases. Although there was a provision to refer to Bengal Regulations in civil cases when points might arise un-provided for in the rules for civil justice in the province, no similar latitude was extended to cases where like difficulties in connection to criminal matters arose. As a result, in cases of appeal, some magistrates followed regulation laws admitting appeals from their subordinates, and others followed local laws, and considered the decision of their subordinates final or binding unless appealed to the commissioner and later to the deputy commissioner at Guwahati. 'Unsatisfactory system of part Regulation law and part local law,' observed Agnew, 'so blinded and intermixed with each other as they are in practice, that it is difficult to say in many instances which should be adopted as one's guide.'[28] The officers of the province found the system an endless source of trouble and vexations. Likewise the suitors were not sure through which laws and regulations their case was to be determined.

With the introduction of Civil and Criminal Procedure Codes and the Indian Penal Code, which provided a uniform system of law and justice throughout India, the Assam Code ceased to exist.

Assam now had a well-organized system of courts and uniform system of law and procedure. But there were some initial difficulties. The Code of Civil Procedure for India provided the existence of a separate judiciary for dispensing civil justice, and a Bar of authorized pleaders. Under the Assam system, both these conditions were wanting. The civil judges in Assam acted as magistrates as well as collectors of revenue and thus one set of officers administered every department of government. The introduction of qualified pleaders in the court as provided for in the code was also not suited to the province. Further it took long time to adjust or define the powers and authority of different functionaries which were not similar to those in the Regulating provinces. The new codes, still untried, were sometime at variance with the principles evolved by judicial experience in Assam. However, the local authorities admitted that the new code was more scientific and comprehensive than the Assam Code, which had for several years been in force in Assam. Gradually, the new codes became fairly popular and the people availed themselves of the refined and published laws and procedures.

NOTES

1. Report on the Province of Assam, p. 98.
2. Ibid.
3. Ibid, p. 59, Appendix B.
4. William Robinson, *A Descriptive Account of Assam*, p. 218.
5. BJP, November 1870, no. 185, Eden, Secretary, Bengal to Register, High Court, 3 November 1870.
6. BJP, 30 July 1845, no. 247, see Police Statement of 1844.
7. *Anglo-Assamese Relations (1771-1826)*, p. 571.
8. RPA, p. 34.
9. Ibid., p. 119.
10. Ibid., p. 36.
11. Ibid., p. 33.
12. BJP (Criminal), 7 November 1842, no. 24, Brodie to Jenkins, 2 October 1840.
13. Ibid., no. to Indians to Jenkins, 6 October 1840.

14. BJP (Criminal), 7 November 1842, no. 38, Matthie to Jenkins, 1 March 1841.
15. Ibid., no. 37.
16. RPA, p. 36.
17. BJP, 1859, 24 February, no. 138, Butler to Junior Secretary, Bengal, 25 January 1859, see Extracts of Sadar Dewani Adalat's Resolution, 25 October 1858.
18. RPA, pp. 123-4.
19. BJP (Criminal), 4 July 1842, no. 62. See the Petition of Lawyers and Muktyars to the Deputy Commissioner Matthie about the nefarious activities of Court Omlahs.
20. General Proceedings, May 1872, no. 79.
21. General Proceedings, October 1865, no. 63. Major J.C. Haughten, Officiating Commissioner of Assam to Secretary, Bengal, 28 November 1862.
22. BJP (Civil), 9 June 1835, no. 10. Commissioner Jenkins to Register, Sadar Nizamat Adalat, 25 April 1835.
23. General Proceedings, May 1872, no. 79.
24. Selected Records of Government of Bengal, no. 22, Miles Bronson to James Halliday, Lieutenant Governor of Bengal, 13 November 1854.
25. RPA, p. 131.
26. George Campbell, *Modern India*, pp. 239-40.
27. *Calcutta Review* (1846), p. 150, quoted in R.G. Majumder, *British Paramountcy and Indian Renaissance*, p. 348.
28. BJP, April 1860, no. 336, Agnew Deputy Commissioner to Commissioner, 21 March 1860.

CHAPTER 9

Conclusion

The administration of justice in Assam described in the foregoing pages formed a subject of universal complaint and condemnation. 'From one extremity of the province to the other', observed Anandaram Dhekial Phukan in 1853:

> If the opinion of the lowliest clown be taken on the working of our judicial system, he would unhesitatingly declare, that the public courts of justice are exclusively for the benefit of the rich and powerful, that it is both imprudent and foolish for men in humble life to resort to them for relief, that cunning and deceit, falsehood and perjury beset the courts on all sides and that in the civil and criminal courts, truth is often transformed into falsehood, and falsehood into truth.[1]

The administration of justice is the discharge of the state's obligation to protect the people from any kind of injury. State's protection is a natural assumption, and anybody who disturbs it makes himself or herself liable to punishment. Both protection and punishment have to be defined so that the limits of the state's authority and the kind of punishment for different kinds of injuries may become known to the people. But for more than ten years after their occupation, the British East India Company could not provide a Code of Laws and Procedures either for the information of the people or for the guidance of the person who presided over the law courts.

Imperceptibly extending the non-regulation system, they tried to create an illusion that the province would be governed by a system that would be taking into consideration the traditional customs and habits of the people. The naming of native courts as panchayats was an attempt to give the impression that these courts were no innovations, but were a continuation of the indigenous institutions prevailing in the pre-British days, while in fact, the courts established by the Company were new institutions to be worked on the English laws and procedures.

Under the cover of non-regulation system, the province was governed by a mixed method of various Regulations, Acts of the Legislative Council and local laws. Maniram Dewan observed, 'the expenses incurred by Government for the establishment of Dewany Courts is quite useless, because neither are the Regulations nor the established customs of the country adhered to therein, but instead thereof a system is pursued which resembles *kicheree* or mixture to the great ruin of the people'.[2] Laws were replete with anomalies and justice depended largely on the whims of the dispensing officers. The apparatus of justice remained unorganized and arbitrary, more specifically in the first decade of the British rule. Neither the presiding officer nor the suitors or defendants were aware of the laws and procedure to be adopted in a particular suit.

It was only during the commissionership of Robertson that the administration of justice received its first footing and sincere patronage. But Robertson could not accomplish his objects because of his early departure to the Presidency. The issue of rules marked his short tenure as Commissioner for the Administration of Civil Justice for Lower Assam.

The task of setting up an ordered administration fell to Capt. Jenkins who succeeded Robertson. Jenkins was keen to reorganize the ill-equipped judicial machinery and to provide honest and speedy justice to the people. During his commissionership, the Rules for Administration of Civil and Criminal Justice (commonly known as Assam Code) were introduced in 1837. The rules were, however, respected more by violation than observance.[3] The provisions of examining witnesses by the principal assistant himself or by his juniors in civil cases and the recording of evidence by the presiding officer himself in criminal cases were not taken in true spirit by the European functionaries. In the same manner, the wise rule of viva voce examination for the speedy disposal of suits was not put into practice till the year 1852.

On the other hand, there was hardly any uniformity in following the provisions of the Assam Code amongst the assistants. Some of the assistants were keen to follow Regulation more closely than the Assam Code. Capt. Matthie, assistant at Darrang and Guwahati who later became the deputy commissioner, always advocated the adoption of Bengal Regulations in place of the inadequate Assam Code. He openly exposed the defects of the Assam Code and the superiority of the Bengal Regulations in his voluminous correspondence with the Government of Bengal. As a result, the Assam Code fell into disuse, it being an insufficient instrument for the honest and speedy dispensing of justice.

The administration of justice needed trained judges to administer the laws which the legislature had provided. A man cannot be a good judge unless he has some knowledge of the general administration of the country and of the manners and customs of the people. But the judges in Assam were mostly military men having little knowledge about the country and its people. Trained in the art of warfare, these men were directly brought in to administer justice without any training on law and procedure. The nomination of judges to the subordinate courts entirely depended upon choice, and upon personal acquaintance with a candidate. 'The necessary consequence of this rule is,' said Anandaram Dhekial Phukan, 'that the choice is sometimes misguided, and the estimate formed of the candidate's fitness proves either erroneous or based upon an imperfect knowledge of his character and attainments.'[4]

There was a want of aptness, or perfection in the conduct of the process of trial, which necessarily favoured the prolongation of litigation. 'The Judicial Officers as a body,' reported Mills, 'are persons of inferior ability, and seem to have been selected, some on account of their respectability of character, and others from political motives, more than on account of their superior sagacity.'[5] The capacity to perceive the points which distinguishes one case from another might be acquired in a measure by the study of books, but the best education in the art would be secured by the early acquaintance with the practice and procedure in the courts of justice and the experience gained by an early call to judicial work. Even the best of the laws in the world administered by inexperienced and unpractical judges can never be successful.

Nevertheless, the British built up a better system of jurisprudence than the one that existed just before their rule. The British laid the foundation of a new system of dispensing justice through a hierarchy of civil and criminal courts. They also established a new system of laws through the processes of enactment and codification of old laws. The traditional system of justice had been largely based on religion as well as on imperial authority. Where the administration of justice is regulated by religion, the law is bound to be considered static, not dynamic. Though the British largely continued to observe customary laws, they gradually evolved a new legal system. They introduced regulations, codified the existing laws, and often systematized and modernized them through judicial interpretations. The Code of Civil Procedure (1859), the Penal Code (1860) and the Code of Criminal Procedure (1861) laid down in clear, precise and exact language the law applicable to all inhabitants, high and low, irrespective of caste, creed or religion.

The principle of the rule of law was the most precious legacy of the British administration. The rule of law means that the administration was to be carried out, at least in theory, in obedience to laws, which clearly defined the rights, privileges and obligations of the subjects, and not according to the personal discretion of the ruler. A natural corollary to the principle of rule of law was the principle of equality before the law. This certainly was a novel feature in a caste-ridden society. The same law was applied to all persons and the administration of justice paid no heed to caste or religious consideration. Even government officials could be brought before a court of law for breach of official duty or for acts done in excess of one's official authority.

There were, however, departures from the excellent principle of rule of law. The Charter of 1661, the earliest of the kind to provide for the exercise of judicial powers in the English settlements in India, itself was a denial of this principle for it made the Governor and Council of Bombay and for that matter the executive government itself the highest judiciary of the island.

After providing separate laws for the rulers and the ruled, the British adopted means to distinguish or separate procedures. The king's court was reserved for British subjects and the courts set up by the Company under its own authority granted to it by its charters were reserved for the natives. The ruling class and the ruled were thus distinguished in justice and judicial administration. The object of the Company was to keep the Indian subjects out of English law and English courts and thus to deprive them from the benefit of the rule of law. The Company had understood that it was necessary, in the interest of revenue collection and administration, to keep this distinction; otherwise, the natives would use the law in their favour.

Until 1836 the British subjects were under the control of the Supreme Court both for civil and criminal matters. Macaulay observed, 'Till the passing of Act XI of 1836 an Englishman at Agra or Benares who owed a small debt to a native, who had beaten a native, who had come with a body of Bludgeon-men and ploughed up a native's land, if sued by the injured party for damages, was able to drag that party before the Supreme Court of Calcutta (a distance perhaps of 1,000 miles), a court which in one most important point—the character of the judges—stands as high as any court can stand, but which in every other respect I believe to be worst in India, the mostly dilatory, and the most ruinously expensive.'[6]

Macaulay's efforts to bring the European and British subjects under the full jurisdiction of the courts of the Company in civil and criminal matters was foiled by violent opposition of the Europeans. But he achieved partial success when Act XI of 1836 placed Englishmen under the jurisdiction of the Company's courts in civil matters, and distinctions of race were abolished in civil matters throughout India.

But the British subjects in India continued to enjoy the right to be tried in the Supreme Court in criminal cases. An attempt was made in 1849 to stop this glaring iniquity. A bill was drafted in order to abolish the exemption of British-born subjects from the jurisdiction of the criminal courts established by the East India Company. But this bill had to be withdrawn due to the stiff opposition of the European community. Ultimately in 1861, a compromise formula was evolved by which it was decided that in criminal cases the European subjects would be tried by European judges. Under this law even an Indian magistrate or judge holding a covenanted post could not try the humblest individual claiming British birth. Though in 1872, the Europeans were subjected to the jurisdiction of the mofussil courts, they were to be tried only by first-class Indian magistrates or judges of their own race. A first-class magistrate was competent only to inflict a sentence of three months imprisonment on Europeans whereas in the case of an Indian he could do it for two years. A Session Court that had full powers of sentence over Indians, but could only pass a sentence of one year's imprisonment on Europeans.

Many English officials and planters behaved in a haughty, harsh, and even brutal manner with Indians. When efforts were made to bring them to justice, they were given indirect and undue protection and consequently light or no punishment by many of the European judges before whom alone they could be tried. Innumerable instances are on record, which show how European subjects took advantage of the racial indulgence shown to them and abused the rule of law. Such lamentable lapses of law resulting in light punishment caused discontent and great resentment amongst the natives. A few instances are quoted below:

Stephen, a tea planter in the district of Nowgong shot a person dead. He escaped to Burmah. When he heard that his case had been decided in his absence and he was acquitted on the plea that he acted in self-defence, Stephen returned to Assam.[7] Mr. Todd, an Honorary Magistrate, brutally beat one Rosheswar Sarmah, a tea-seed seller, following a heated argument. Mr. Todd was tried by Lieutenant Gregory, Officiating Assistant Commissioner and received a very light sentence of a fine of Rs. 50.[8] On yet another occasion a planter beat a tailor in Sibsagar and was fined Rs. 50.[9] A court peon wrote a letter to the editor of *Hindu Patriot* from Sibsagar that

> It is a common phrase amongst the planters here that if he can pay fifty rupees he is allowed to beat a native.[10]

In 1866, one Mr. Hynes, an employee of North East Saw Mills Company had beaten to death a worker at Dibrugarh. Mr. Haynes was only fined for this serious crime.[11] The planters always took law into their own hands under the cover of various legislations that were in force in the province concerning labours and their wages. Under the Workmen's Breach of Contract Act of 1859, Section 490 and 492 of the Indian Penal Code (1860) and the Labour Act of 1863 as amended in 1865, 1870 and 1873, the government alone could punish runaway workers. Yet the planters generally 'disciplined' such workers inflicting upon them punitive tortures of all kinds, for labour was too precious to be sent out of their gardens to police and judicial custody.[12]

The principle of the rule of law was seriously abused during the period of the Revolt of 1857, or the First War of Indian Independence. Indiscriminate arrests were made and the people were detained without trial for a long time. It has been stated earlier that Raja Kandarpeswar was confined at Calcutta without a trial. Both Maniram Dewan and Peali Baruah were put to death after hasty trial without giving them any opportunity to defend themselves. Capt. Holroyd who ordered their execution acted both as prosecutor and judge.

The detailed account of the different organs of the administration of justice may be fittingly concluded with a general review based on the publicly expressed opinions of contemporary Assamese whose position and status lent great weight to their views. For whatever may be the degree of excellence claimed for it, the real merit of an administrative system depends, largely, upon the views and sentiments of the people affected by it.

The popular Assamese satirical literature depicting the socio-economic condition of Assam during the British rule made mockery of contemporary judicial system where the nuances of judicial proceedings required witnesses even for a established case to prosecute a guilty. *Sahitarathi* Lakshinath Bezbarua's play *Sikarpati Nikarpati* has a comic scene where the illiterate housewife expresses her utter surprise when the judicial officer asks her to produce witness in a case where the thief is caught red-handed. To the illiterate and ignorant subjects, procedures like oath-taking and cross-examination for even plaintiffs appeared not only unreasonable but also funny.

We have also the benefit of the views expressed by Anandaram Dhekial Phukan, both in his writing as well as in his memorandum submitted to A.J. Moffatt Mills in 1853, to which reference has been made above. Anandaram was a great admirer of the British government in Assam and he acknowledged with the feeling of gratitude, the expectations which the Assamese had formed of the happy and beneficial results from the Government of England.[13] But while Anandaram fully appreciated the 'degree of confidence in the safety of their lives and property' which they never had for ages past, he was equally alive to the defects and deficiencies of the administration of justice and made constructive suggestions with a view to removing them. One of his suggestions was the establishment of mofussil courts in each *thana* jurisdiction under a judicial officer styled either a *sadar ameen* or an assistant. This measure, he said, would serve to remove two of the most prominent defects in the administration of justice, viz., the inefficiency of the police and the paucity of the courts including their distance from the interior of the district. He spoke highly of the incalculable benefits that would result from the establishment of a mofussil court invested with powers to try all cases in each *thana* jurisdiction. 'We feel assured', Anandaram said:

that this is the only means by which life and property could be properly and effectually protected. The infliction of oppression and various other injuries by the rich on the poor with the connivance of a corrupt police, will be put an end to. The extortion of confession, the unlawful detention and restraint of witnesses and parties at the Thannah to extort money, the compulsion and, intimidation practiced on witnesses to deliver false testimony, and not infrequently the training up of witnesses to pass through cross-examinations without detection before the magistrate, and the extortions from the villagers in the prosecution of local inquiries, will be thoroughly done away with.[14]

Among other reforms suggested by him mention may be made of the substitution of Assamese for Bengali as the official language of the courts of law, creation of rural police, establishment of small causes courts and the appointment of regular vakeels.

The views of Anandaram Dhekial Phukan clearly show that while the British system of justice was highly appreciated as making a great improvement upon the earlier system, the enlightened public opinion in this province regarded it as outmoded, and demanded a more practicable and people-friendly system on the model of the British.

Liberal-minded Europeans and others also joined with the Assamese in condemning various aspects of the administration of justice introduced by the British government. This may be elucidated by quoting extracts form the views expressed by highly-placed Englishmen, who had intimate and personal knowledge about the affairs of the province.

Commenting upon the benefit of English law David Scott, the first commissioner and one of the most beloved Europeans of contemporary times remarked as follows:

> I fancy the people in this country, if they ever obtain what it is the fashion to call the benefits of the English law will find themselves in the situation of the frogs who prayed for a kings and at length got stork set over them.[15]

A writer in the *Calcutta Review*, presumably an Englishman (1853), observes as follows:

> There are numerous practitioners ever ready to encourage the fondness for litigation. The commonest quarrel will furnish occasion for a slow and vexatious case of assault, abduction or robbery, the case will be decided at last, then appealed, and fresh proceedings instituted in a civil court, (Holidays meanwhile keep intervening) until after the lapse perhaps of many years, and the use of much corruption and intrigue, both parties becoming exhausted, it may terminate in much the same state as it originally commenced.[16]

To these we may add the views of the Missionaries who had more acquaintance with the Assamese people than any other Englishman or other foreigner. The following extracts are taken from the Baptist Missionary Magazine of 1856:

> Justice was a luxury beyond the reach of people and they generally prefer to suffer patiently rather than carry cases into the court, especially against their superiors, who have the advantage of them in wealth and influence, and can bring against them an array of false witnesses and bribe the court people so that there is little chance of justice being obtained even before a European magistrate.[17]

In conclusion we may quote George Campbell, one of the best British administrators:

Our judicial system is inappropriate and inefficient. The natives in some respect prefer indifferent justice, easily procured, to the most perfect system if complicated and difficult to access.[18]

The contemporary views on the British administration of justice in Assam not by disaffected Assamese, or Indians but by well wishers of the empire, naturally carries some weight.

However, it must be admitted that the British rule brought to this country an entirely new concept of justice and law which took firm root even though political necessity, or defective legislation, incompetence of judges or complicated procedure often denied the people justice in the proper sense of the term. Even in eliminating a political enemy, an elaborate procedure of trial in an open court had to be followed. No Ahom king or official would have taken so much trouble to punish a person whom he regarded as a political suspect; a word from him would have pushed the political enemy to the executioner's grip.

In summing up, it may be said that the administration of justice introduced by the British government was immeasurably superior to that of its predecessor. This is evidenced by the fact that free India did not abolish the British judicial system but only restructured and modified it to suit its needs and interests. Contemporary Indian judicial system being thus largely a legacy of the British rule carries the evils inherent in British jurisprudence. Moreover, such a system was most undesirable in view of the prevailing socio-economic circumstances of the country. Ilbert spoke of the unregenerate English law—insular, technical, formless, tempered in its application to English circumstances by the quibbles of judges and the obstinacy of juries, capable of being an instrument of the most monstrous injustice when administered in an atmosphere different from that in which it had grown and such law as sought to be transplanted on Indian soil.[19] Therefore, the story of law in India has been a saga of betrayal of hopes and aspirations of the Indian people. Law is not Indian either in its spirit, in form, in contents or even in its language. There is no concord between the law and the people and as such, law today does not warrant compliance, obedience or reverence. Eminent jurist Palkivala observed:

Conclusion

The administration of justice has become so obsolescent that most people regard the law as an enemy rather than as a friend. The law may not be an ass but it is certainly a snail, the operation of our legal system is not merely slow but is susceptible to the most shameless delaying tactics, and resort to the courts has become a costly lottery which takes years in the drawing.[20]

Even after nearly seventy years of our Independence, no serious attempts have been made for thorough reforms of judicial procedure and law of evidence, which are entirely based on English law. Many countries, where the English systems of jurisprudence prevail, are making constructive reforms in their judiciary to suit their needs. For instance, the USA has passed legislation for the simplification of legal language by ridding statutes and documents of obfuscatory terms.[21] Its time India followed suit and made a determined attempt to eradicate the incredible fuzziness from its laws.

Almost all the eminent jurists of our country have stressed on administration of pure and speedy justice by the courts. Judiciary is attacked as an 'anti labour Block to social and economic advance and progress'.[22] 'What is needed' said Justice Bhagawati, 'is a drastic change, a new outlook, a fresh approach which takes into account the socio-economic realities and seeks to provide a cheap, expeditious and effective instrument for realization of justice by all sections of people.'[23] It is of imperative need to change the colonial system by an Indian legal system best suited to our circumstances and condition of our people.

As far back as 1925, the Civil Justice Committee recommended a revival of the ancient system and an enlargement of the jurisdiction of the village panchayat courts. Fortunately, this is now being done and legislation for this purpose has been undertaken in many states. The foundation of Lok Adalat is a progressive step in this direction. In recent times the judiciary has gone beyond its traditional role of interpreting the laws and regulations. Now the judiciary is interpreting existing laws according to the needs of time for the benefit of society at large. The development of a new class of legislation popularly known as Public Interest Litigation comes as an instrument of relief and remedy for the common people.

NOTES

1. Report on the Province of Assam, p. 113.
2. Ibid., p. 606. Appendix K.B. Petition presented by Maniram Baruah Dewan on account of Ghanakanta Singh Joobraj and others.
3. AIDC, p. 211.
4. RPA, p. 129.
5. Ibid, p. 38.
6. Sir John Strachey, *India: Its Administration & Progress*, pp. 116-17.
7. BJP, January 1863, no. 152.
8. BJP, June 1863, no. 155.
9. Ibid.
10. Ibid.
11. BJP, January 1867, no. 55, Hopkinson to Secretary Bengal, 20 December 1866.
12. N. Griffiths, 28, pp. 269-73, D. Chamanlal Collie, 'The Story of Labour and Capital in India', vol. 2, p. 5, quoted in A.Guha, *Planters Raj to Swaraj*, p. 18.
13. RPA, p. 93, Appendix K.
14. Ibid., p. 116.
15. *Asiatic Journal*, vol. 7, 1832, p. 137, quoted in *DSNEI*, p. 232.
16. 'Assam Since the Expulsion of the Burmese', *Calcutta Review*, vol. XIX (1853), *A Memoir of the Late David Scott*, pp. 221-2.
17. *The Baptist Missionary Magazine*, December 1856. See *Journal of Mr. Ward*, p. 459 quoted from AIDC, p. 213.
18. George Campbell, *India as it May be: An Outline of Proposed Government and Policy*, Preface, XIII.
19. Gobinda Das, *Justice in India*, p. 52.
20. Nani Palkivala, *We the People of India: The Largest Democracy*, p. 354.
21. Ibid., p. 353.
22. S.N. Bhattacharjee, *Administration of Law and Justice in India*, p. 135.
23. Ibid., p. 191.

ANNEXURE

Assam Code

Rules for the Administration of Civil Justice in Assam

SECTION I: ON JURISDICTION

Clause First: There are to be two classes of Native Judges in Assam; Moonsiffs with powers to try and decide on such suits as may be referred to them by the Commissioner or his Assistants for moveable and immovable property, (excepting suits for land claimed as Lakheraj) not exceeding in value the sum of one hundred rupees; and Sudder Ameens with similar powers in cases of original suits referred to them for property, either moveable or immovable, not exceeding in value the sum of one thousand rupees, and also in cases of appeals from the decisions of Moonsiffs. The Moonsiffs are to hold their Courts either at the Sudder Station of the division to which they belong, or in the interior, as the Commissioner of Assam may determine. On a vacancy occurring in a Moonsiffship, three persons shall be nominated for the office by the Assistant in charge of the district, of whom one shall be selected by the Commissioner. The Sudder Ameens are to be appointed by the Commissioner, subject to the confirmation of the Governor of Bengal, and except in special cases to be fully reported, the best qualified Moonsiff in the district or province shall be promoted to the higher grade.

Description of Native Judges to be employed in Assam; powers to be exercised by them.

Place where Moonsiffs are to hold their Courts, to be determined by the Commissioner.

Moonsiffs to be nominated by the Assistant and selected by the Commissioner.

Sudder Ameens to be appointed by the Commissioner, subject to the confirmation of Government.

Exception.

Second: The European functionaries ordinarily employed in the administration of Civil justice are to be the Assistants in charge of the several districts into which Assam is divided, and the Commissioner. The Assistant, to whom all petitions of plaint are in the first instance to be presented, is to retain on his own file suits for property moveable or immoveable of a value exceeding one thousand rupees, as well as all suits for land claimed as Lakheraj, but may refer suits for smaller amounts to the Sudder Ameen or Moonsiff.

<blockquote>The European functionaries are to be the Assistants in charge of the several districts into which Assam is divided, and the Commissioner.

All petitions of plaint to be presented to the Assistant, who may refer suits for small amounts to Native Judges.</blockquote>

Third: An appeal shall lie under the provisions stated in the sequel, from the decision of an Assistant to the Commissioner of Assam.

<blockquote>An appeal shall lie from the decision of an Assistant to the Commissioner.</blockquote>

Fourth: A special appeal shall lie from all decisions passed by the Commissioner of Assam, on suits originally tried by an Assistant, to the Court of Sudder Dewanny Adawlut at the Presidency of Fort William.

<blockquote>A special appeal shall lie from all decisions of the Commissioner on suits tried by an Assistant, to the Presidency Sudder Court.</blockquote>

Fifth: The Commissioner or Assistant, as the case may be, is competent to remove to his own or any other Court in the province, any cause that may be depending in a lower court recording his reasons for so doing.

<blockquote>Commissioner or Assistant competent to remove any cause pending in a lower Court to his own or any other Court.</blockquote>

Sixth: In suits for land the value is to be calculated at the amount of its gross annual proceeds. If the suit be for gardens or houses, their value is to be reckoned at their estimated prices.

<blockquote>In suits for land or houses, value how to be reckoned.</blockquote>

Seventh: No civil suit shall be cognizable in any Court in Assam in which the cause of action shall have originated at any period antecedent to the date of the treaty or Yendaboo, viz. the 24 February 1826. For suits arising subsequently to that date, twelve years is to be the period of limitation, within which from the date of the

<blockquote>Limitation of period for the institution of suits in Assam.

Exception</blockquote>

transaction wherein it originates a suit must be instituted; unless the complainant can shew by clear and positive proof, that he had demanded the money or matter in question, and that the defendant had admitted the truth of the demand, or promised to pay the money; or that he directly preferred his claim within the period for the matters in dispute to a Court of competent jurisdiction to try the demand, and shall assign satisfactory reasons to the Court why he did not proceed in the suit; or shall prove that either from minority or other good and sufficient cause he had been precluded from obtaining redress.

Eighth: A suit for money or personal property shall be instituted in the Court of the Assistant in charge of the division within the defendant resides as a fixed inhabitant. In the event of his having changed his residence subsequently to the date on which the cause of action may have arisen, it shall be optional with the plaintiff to commence his action in the Court of the district within which the defendant may actually reside, or in that of the district in which the cause of action may have arisen. Suits for damages on account of injury done to personal character are to be instituted, at the discretion of the party complaining, either in the Court of the district within which the defendant resides, or in that of the district in which the act complained of was committed. The amount of damages to be awarded is to be fixed by the Officer presiding over the Court in which such suit may be tried, who will, in all such cases, endeavour to obtain if possible the aid of a jury or of a few native assessors. A suit for land or other immoveable property shall be instituted in the Court of the division wherein such property is situated.

Suit for money or personal property to be instituted in the Court of the Assistant in charge of the division where the defendant resides; in the event of his having changed residence, either in the Court of the district where he may actually reside, or in that where the cause of action may have arisen.

Suits for damages on account of injury done to personal character in what Court to be instituted.

Amount of damages to be fixed by the Court in which the suit may be tried; the aid of jury or native assessors to be obtained if possible.

Suit for immoveable property to be instituted in the Court of the division where such property is situated.

Ninth: The Civil authorities of one division are to cause all legal processes issued by those of another division, which may be sent to them for the purpose of being carried into effect within their jurisdiction, to be duly executed, and the returns thereon are to be made and duly forwarded to the Officer by whom the process was issued within the term originally specified therein, or in the event of that being impossible, a full statements of the cause of the delay and of the probable time within which a full return may be expected, must be furnished by the authority receiving a process, to the Officer by whom it was issued. It is to be distinctly understood that, in such cases, it rests with the authority issuing a process to decide upon the admissibility of any excuses that may be urged against its being carried into execution.

Tenth: Moonsiffs and Sudder Ameens guilty of any act of misconduct, may be fined by the Assistant in charge of the district in a sum not exceeding the amount of one month's salary. If the offence be of a more serious nature, so as to require severer notice, the Assistant in charge of the district must report the case for the consideration of the Commissioner, who, if the party offending be a Moonsiff, may dismiss him from office; or if he be a Sudder Ameen, may suspend him from the exercise of his judicial functions, appointing another person to fill his place temporarily, and submitting a report on the subject for the consideration and orders of the Governor of Bengal.

Eleventh: Moonsiffs and Sudder Ameens are hereby declared competent to sentence any party guilty of a gross contempt of their lawful authority, or any of their subordinate officers guilty of gross contumacy or disrespect, to pay a fine not exceeding the amount of fifty rupees, commutable in the event of non-payment to imprisonment without labor for the term of one month; reporting fully the particulars of the case to their immediate superior, within twenty-four hours from the time of such sentence being passed.

Twelfth: The Commissioner, the Assistants in charge of districts, and the Junior and Sub-Assistants are declared competent to punish offences of the class alluded to in the preceding clause by imposing a fine not exceeding two hundred rupees, commutable to imprisonment without labor for a period not exceeding six months. Such cases must be reported to the Commissioner for revisal or confirmation.

European functionaries also competent to punish offences of the class above alluded to; reporting the cases to the Commissioner.

SECTION II: ON ORIGINAL SUITS

First: If the suit be for land, houses, or money due on a bond, agreement, or commercial transaction, (and the Assistant shall not see cause to reject the same as frivolous or vexatious, under the discretion allowed in the sequel of this section) a written notice must, after numbering the petition of plaint according to its place in the yearly list, be issued, calling upon the defendant to file a written reply within fifteen days. In the event of the reply not being filed within that period, a proclamation is to be affixed, if possible, to the abode of the defendant, and a copy of it to be affixed in the court-room, calling upon the defendant to file reply within fifteen days from its date. On the expiration of the second period, if no reply be filed, the case is to be tried exparte. On a reply being filed within the prescribed period, the plaintiff is to be asked if he wishes to rejoin, and on his answering in the affirmative, ten days are to be allowed for that purpose; and five days for a replication, in the event of the defendant wishing to file one.

If the suit be for land, houses or money, and the Assistant see no cause to reject it, a notice must be issued to the defendant to file a reply within fifteen days.

In the event of the reply not being filed within fifteen days, proclamation to be affixed to the abode of the defendant, calling upon him to file one within fifteen days.

On the expiration of the second period, case to be tried ex parte.

On a reply being filed, ten days to be allowed to the plaintiff to rejoin, and five to the defendant to file a replication.

Second: On the pleadings being completed in the manner above prescribed the parties are to produce their proofs. The parties are to be allowed an option of bringing up their own witnesses, or of having subpoenas served upon them by peadas. If the witnesses fail upon this process to attend, a proclamation fixing a term for their appearance is to be issued, at the expiration of which, if still absent, a fine is to be imposed, to be levied by the attachment and sale of their property. Parties applying for a process to enforce the attendance of witnesses shall, on doing so, declare that they are ready to indemnify the said witnesses for any necessary expenses to be incurred by them in attending before the Court; and the Court, in passing a final decision upon the case, shall include whatever sum, not exceeding the rate of three annas per diem, may be proved to have been paid to witnesses for their subsistence among the costs of suit.

Third: When the witnesses shall be in attendance, their depositions are to be taken down in writing in the Bengallee language, in the presence of the Assistant in charge of the district, if possible; but in the event of his other avocations rendering it impossible for him to attend to this duty, he is allowed to delegate it to a junior assistant, or to the head ministerial officer of his court, who is to attest the deposition by his signature and to be responsible for its authenticity. On the whole evidence, documentary and parole, being filed, the Assistant is to proceed to pass judgment in open court, recording the substance of his decision, immediately, in a book to be kept by him for that purpose, and attesting the entry therein made by his signature before he shall quit the court. The decision is afterwards to be drawn up in the usual form by the officers of the court, and attested copies of it are to be tendered to the parties or their agents.

Parties may bring up their own witnesses, or have subpoenas served upon them by peadas.

Witnesses failing to attend upon this process and proclamation to be find, and the fine levied by the sale of their property.

Parties to indemnify witnesses for expenses incurred by them.

Court passing final decision shall include whatever sum not exceeding the rate of three annas per diem may have been paid to witnesses among the costs of suit.

Depositions to be taken down in writing in the Bengallee language in the presence of the Assistant in charge.

Assistant allowed to delegate this duty to a junior assistant, or to the head ministerial officer of his court.

Assistant to pass judgment in open court, and record the substance of it in a book before he shall quit the court. Decision afterwards to be drawn up in the usual form, and copies tendered to parties.

Fourth: If the petition of plaint in an original suit presented to an Assistant in charge of a district shall appear to him to be prima facie inadmissible, or shall prove to be so after a summary enquiry into its merits, he is at liberty to reject the same, without bringing it on his regular file and without calling upon the defendant for a reply; but parties discontented with such order of rejection may appeal to the Commissioner, who may, after calling for the original petition and proceedings held upon it, direct the Assistant to admit and proceed upon the same as a regular suit.

Assistant in charge of a district at liberty to reject a petition of plaint. Parties dissatisfied with the order of rejection may appeal to the Commissioner, who may direct the Assistant to admit and proceed upon the same as a regular suit.

Fifth: If the subject matter of the petition of plaint relate to a question of caste or marriage, it shall not be incumbent on the Assistant to bring the case on his file of regular suits, or to hold more than a summary enquiry into its merits, the result of which alone shall briefly recorded on the back of the petition. It shall however be competent to the Commissioner to direct that any case, thus summarily disposed of, shall be brought on the file and tried as a regular suit.

If the petition of plaint relate to a question of caste or marriage, it shall not be incumbent on the Assistant to bring the case on his file, but he may summarily dispose of it.

Commissioner declared competent to direct that the case be tried as a regular suit.

Sixth: The Assistant may insist on the attendance, in person, both of the plaintiff and defendant in any original suit; and he is strongly enjoined, in all cases in which it shall be practicable, so to confront them as at once to elicit the truth, and abridge the necessity of further legal proceedings; and he may take their examination on oath; if he judge it necessary previously to bringing the suit on-his regular file; and in all cases in which such meeting of the parties can be effected, their depositions shall be recorded and taken to be the plaint and reply in the suit. But any party feeling aggrieved by such a requisition, may appeal to the Commissioner, who is hereby empowered to cause it to be withdrawn, recording his reasons for doing so at

Assistant may insist on the attendance both of the plaintiff and defendant, and examine them on oath before bringing the suit on his file.

In all cases in which the meeting of the parties can be effected their depositions shall be taken to be the plaint and reply.

Any party aggrieved may appeal to the Commissioner, and the execution of the order shall stayed pending the appeal.

length in his proceedings. It is also to be understood that the filing of a petition of appeal by a plaintiff against such a requisition shall bar its enforcement pending the reference to the Commissioner.

Seventh: The Sudder Ameens and Moonsiffs shall, in cases referred to them, be guided in their proceedings by the provisions contained in the three first clauses of this section; with this exception, that they are, in all instances, expected to cause the depositions of witnesses to be taken in their own presence, and are not empowered to delegate that duty to any of their ministerial officers.

	Sudder Ameens and Moonsiffs to be guided by the provisions contained in the three first clauses of this section.
	Exception

Eighth: The Sudder Ameens and Moonsiffs are not to try cases in which their own amlah, near relations, or spiritual instructors, are parties concerned. Should any such case be inadvertently referred to them, they are hereby required to return it, with a suitable representation, representation, to the Assistant, who will either try it himself, or refer it to another Sudder Ameen or Moonsiff, if he prefer that course, to the Junior or Sub-Assistant, from those decision thereon an appeal will lie, under the general rules regarding appeals from the decisions of a Sudder Ameen or Moonsiff, to the Assistant in charge of the district.

Sudder Ameens and Moonsiffs not to try cases in which their amlah, near relations, or spiritual instructors, are parties.

Ninth: Whenever a plaintiff may satisfy the Assistant within whose district he may have a suit pending, either in that officer's own court or in any of the inferior courts, that the defendant, against whom a suit has been brought, is about to abscond or withdraw himself from the jurisdiction of the district courts, the Assistant may either demand security for the appearance of the said defendant, or attach his property. If the defendant in such a case cannot produce security, or should not possess property, the

Assistant on being satisfied that the defendant is about to abscond or withdraw himself from the jurisdiction, may demand security from him, or attach his property; or commit him to jail.

Assistant may arrest and place him in the civil jail of his district, provided the plaintiff deposit money for his subsistence, according to the usual rates allowed to persons imprisoned in executing decrees. The Assistant, in such cases, is empowered to try the suit without reference to its order on the file, if it be pending in his own court; or to direct its speedy investigation, if it be pending before a Sudder Ameen or Moonsiff.

Tenth: The several courts in Assam are hereby authorized to use every proper means for inducting the parties in suits to refer their disputes to arbitration, either with a view of settling some particular issue; or of obtaining a complete and final adjustment of their differences. An agreement shall, in such cases, be taken from the parties, in which it shall be distinctly stated whether the award is to be partial, that is, confined to a particular issue; or final, as embracing the whole merits of the case. In the former case, the court will take the finding of the arbitrators as conclusive upon the particular point referred to them; in the latter case, the award of the arbitrators shall, if open to no just cause of impeachment on the score of flagrant and palpable partiality, be confirmed by the courts, and held of the same force and validity as a regular judgment.

The courts authorized to use every proper means for inducing parties to refer their disputes to arbitration.

Award of arbitrators, if open to no just cause of impeachment on the score of partiality, to be held by the courts of the same validity as a regular judgment.

Eleventh: Any party desirous of instituting an original suit as a pauper must appear in person before the Assistant in charge of the district, and present a petition containing a general statement of the nature and grounds of the demand, of the value of the thing claimed, the name of the person or persons to be sued, and a schedule of the whole real or personal property belonging to the petitioner, with the estimated value of such property. In special cases, the Assistant in charge may receive such petitions through an authorized

Any party desirous of instituting an original suit as a pauper, to appear in person and present his petition to the Assistant, who may, in special cases, receive it through an authorized agent.

agent or Mookhtar. On the receipt of such a petition the Assistant shall institute a summary enquiry with a view of ascertaining the accuracy of the petitioner's allegations regarding his own circumstances. If satisfied of their accuracy the Assistant is to admit the petitioner to sue as a pauper; but if the result of the enquiry shall not be satisfactory, the Assistant will at once refuse to admit his suit in that form, and will refer him to the general rules in force. All orders passed by an Assistant under the provisions of this clause are to be open to revision by the Commissioner, if appealed against within the term of three months from the date on which they are passed.

> Assistant may admit the petitioner to sue as a pauper or refuse to admit his suit in that form. Such orders declared open to revision by the Commissioner.

Twelfth: If a suit be instituted against a European or Native Officer or Soldier, a notice in the usual form shall be sent, with a copy of the plaint, to the Commanding Officer of the Corps to which the said Officer or Soldier may belong. The Commanding Officer shall return such notice, with the written acknowledgement of the party endorsed thereon, or a statement of the cause which has prevented the service of it; and the court before whom the suit may be pending may then proceed to dispose of the case under the general rules. Provided always that, in such cases, every process that may be issued is to be served through the Commanding Officer of the Corps to which the party may belong, and that such processes, if issuing from any of the inferior courts, are to be sent in the first instance to the Assistant in charge of the district, to be by him forwarded to the Commanding Officer.

> Form of proceeding to be adopted on a suit being instituted against a European or Native Officer or Soldier.

SECTION III: APPEALS

First: Parties discontented with the decision of a Moonsiff or Sudder Ameen may, within one month from the date thereof, present a petition of appeal to the Assistant in charge of the district.

> Petitions of appeals from the decision of Moonsiffs or Sudder Ameens to be presented within one month to the Assistant.

Second: The Assistant may refer for trial to a Sudder Ameen appeals from the decisions of Moonsiffs.

Third: Parties discontented with the decision of an Assistant in any suit tried in the first instance before him, may, within the period of two months from the date of such decision, present a petition of appeal to the Commissioner of Assam, or if they prefer it, to the Assistant himself, whose duty it will then be to forward, with the least possible loss of time, the said petition, with the copy of the decision appealed from, to the Commissioner.

Fourth: When it may appear necessary for the ends of justice, in consequence of a decision being at variance with some existing law or established custom of the country, or in consequence of the subsequent discovery of new evidence, or for any other good and sufficient reason to be fully detailed in the order for its admission, that a special appeal should be admitted, such appeal, if presented within three months from the date of the decision, may be received by the Assistant, from the judgment of a Sudder Ameen on an appeal from that of a Moonsiff; by the Commissioner, from the judgment of an Assistant on an appeal from the award of a Moonsiff or Sudder Ameen; and by the Sudder Dewanny Adawlut, from the decision of the Commissioner. It is to be distinctly understood also, that no second appeal is to be received on any but the special grounds alluded to in this section, whether the previous decisions of the two subordinate courts may have been concurrent, or the reverse. When however it shall appear that the judgment against which the appeal is preferred is clearly in opposition to, or inconsistent with, another decree of the same court, or of another court having jurisdiction in the

Assistant may refer Appeals from Moonsiffs to a Sudder Ameen.

Petitions of appeal from the decision of an Assistant to be presented within two months either to the Commissioner, or to the Assistant.

Special appeals, if presented within three months from the date of the decision, may be received by the Assistant from the judgment of Sudder Ameen on an appeal from that of a Moonsiff; by the Commissioner, from the decision of an Assistant on an appeal from the award of a Moonsiff or Sudder Ameen; and by the Sudder Dewany, from the decision of the Commissioner.

same suit; or in a suit founded on a similar cause of action, a second or special appeal shall in all cases be admitted.

Fifth: Whenever an appeal shall be preferred to the Assistant from a Sudder Ameen or Moonsiff's decision, or to the Commissioner from the Assistant's decision, it shall not be necessary to summon the respondent, in the first instance, but merely to call for the original record of the proceedings in the case; and if after the perusal of the same in the presence of the appellant or his agent, the Commissioner or Assistant, as the case may be, shall see no reason to alter the decision appealed from, it shall be competent to them to confirm the same, communicating the order for confirmation, through the Court from whose judgment the appeal was made, to the respondent, with a view to enabling him to take measures for carrying the decision in his favor into execution. Should an appeal be allowed, a notice must be issued to the respondent; at the expiration of the term assigned in which; the Sudder Ameen, Assistant or Commissioner, as the case may be, shall, after receiving the respondent's reply to the petition of appeal, proceed to try and decide the merits of the appeal, and shall pass a decision confirming, modifying or reversing the decision of the Moonsiff, Sudder Ameen or Assistant. If the respondent fail to attend within the period fixed in the notice, the appeal is to be tried ex parte.

On an appeal being preferred to the Assistant or Commissioner, they need not summon the respondent in the first instance; but merely may call for the proceedings; and on perusal of them, in the presence of the appellant or his agent, to confirm the decision appealed from, or allow an appeal.

If the Decision be conformed, respondent must be warned, that he may sue out execution.

If the appeal be allowed, notice must be given to the respondent, to defend the appeal.

If the respondent fail to attend within the period fixed in the notice, the appeal is to be tried ex parte.

Sixth: The Sudder Dewanny Adawlut, Commissioner, Assistant, or Sudder Ameen, as the case may be, are empowered to call for further evidence in a case appealed, or to refer the case back to the Moonsiff, Sudder Ameen, Assistant, or Commissioner for re-investigation, if it appear to have been imperfectly enquired into.

Appellate Courts empowered to call for further evidence in a case appealed, or to refer it back for re-investigation.

Seventh: The Sudder Dewanny Adawlut, Commissioner, or Assistant, may admit appeals after the expiration of the term above fixed for their presentation, on its being clearly shewn that the appellant was prevented by some insurmountable obstacle from presenting the same within the prescribed term.

> Appellate Courts may admit appeals after the expiration of the term fixed for their presentation on sufficient cause for the delay being shewn.

Eighth: The execution of a decree passed by a Moonsiff, Sudder Ameen, or Assistant shall not, excepting in the particular case provided for below, be stayed notwithstanding an appeal, unless the appellant give security for the due fulfillment of the decree. Should he fail in furnishing security, the respondent is at liberty to cause the decree to be carried into execution on giving security for performing the final order to be passed by the higher court.

> The execution of a decree shall not be stayed except in the particular case provided for below.

Ninth: It is however to be understood, that the superior court by whom the appeal is admitted is competent to stay the execution of a decree, pending the trial of such appeal, even without exacting security from the appellant. But the reasons for the exercise of this power are, in every instance, to be entered at large in the order issued to the inferior court.

> The superior court admitting an appeal declared competent to stay the execution of a decree without exacting security.
>
> Reasons for the exercise of this power to be recorded in the order issued to the inferior Court.

Tenth: Security for the costs of an appeal are to be lodged when the petition of regular appeal is presented. In cases of special appeal, the security bond for the costs is not to be exacted until after such special appeal shall have been admitted. Should the appellant fail to observe this condition, a notice is to be issued allowing him a term of six weeks, at the expiration of which, if the security be not furnished, his right of appeal is to be held to be forfeited, and the decision of the lower court to be put in force, if required by the opposite party.

> Security for the costs of a regular appeal to be lodged with the petition of appeal.
>
> In special appeals security not to be required till the appeal is admitted.
>
> Right of appeal forfeited by failure to furnish security after six weeks notice.

Eleventh: The rules laid down in Clauses 10, 11 and 12 of Section II, on the subject or arbitrators, paupers, and military defendants, in original suits, are to be held applicable to the case of appeals.

Rules laid down in clauses 10, 11 and 12 of Section II regarding arbitrators, paupers and military defendants in original suits, declared applicable to the case of appeals.

SECTION IV: VALUE OR PLEADERS

First: There are to be no regular Vakeels attached to any of the courts in Assam. Parties preferring to plead in person are to be permitted to do so; but if any party chooses to appoint a Vakeel, he may employ any person whom he may select to act for him in that capacity, and he and the Vakeel may make whatever terms they please as to the amount of remuneration to be allowed to the said Vakeel. Provided however that the Commissioner is to have the power to declare any individual incompetent to act in the capacity of Vakeel in any court in the province of Assam, recording his reasons for so doing in his proceedings, in order that, in the event of an appeal, the same may be revised by the Sudder Dewanny Adawlut. It shall also be competent to every court in the province to reject, for reasons to be recorded on its proceedings, any individual whom a party may wish to employ as a Vakeel in any particular suit. Such order may be summarily appealed from, and the superior court may cancel it, and direct that the person affected by it be permitted to act as Vakeel for the party wishing to employ him. In awarding costs against a party cast in any action, no larger sum shall be charged on account of fees of the Vakeel of the successful party than it has been hitherto customary in Assam to allow on that score; viz. 5 per cent on the value of the property litigated. Any further sum to which the Vakeel may be entitled, under the agreement concluded between him and his employer, must be recovered by him from his employer.

There are to be no regular Vakeels.

Parties may plead in person, or appoint any person to do so, making whatever terms they please with the Vakeel as to the amount of remuneration to be allowed to him.

Commissioner empowered to declare any individual incompetent to act as Vakeel. Sudder Dewanny Adawlut may revise such order.

Every court declared competent to reject any individual whom a party may wish to employ as a Vakeel.

Superior court may cancel such order.

In awarding costs against a party cast, 5 per cent, to be charged on the value of the property litigated on account of the successful party's Vakeel's fees.

Any further sum agreed upon, the Vakeel must recover from his employer.

SECTION V: EXECUTION OR DECREES

First: Every petitioner praying for a warrant to enforce a decree, whether given in the court of the Commissioner, the Assistant, the Sudder Ameens or Moonsiffs, is to present his petition to the Commissioner, (who may refer it to the Assistant for execution) or else to the Assistant, who will be guided in his proceedings by the following rules.

Petitions for the warrant to enforce a decree to be presented to the Commissioner or Assistant, who will be guided by the following rules.

Second. Petitions for the enforcement of decrees must be presented within the term of one year from the date on which such decree is passed. If it shall however appear to any Assistant to whom such a petition may be presented, after the expiration of the term above prescribed, that good and sufficient reason is shewn for the delay, he may state the case for the consideration of the Commissioner, who is competent to sanction such decree being under such circumstances put in force. If a similar petition be presented to the Commissioner regarding any decree passed in his own court, he must, in like manner, apply by a letter, in the English language, to the Sudder Dewanny Adawlut, for permission to execute it.

Petitions to be presented within one year from the date of the decree.

Exception

Third. In cases not in the predicament of those specially provided for in Clauses 8 and 9 of Section III, a dustuk for the arrest of the party cast. In the event of his not paying the amount awarded against him, is first to be issued. Should he absent himself, or fail to pay, the peada, entrusted with the enforcement of the process, shall attach all his moveable property, of which he will take an inventory and give it over in charge to some respectable person of the village, taking a receipt for the same, which is to be lodged in the Assistant's court. The property shall be sold as hereafter provided, and its proceeds applied to satisfying the demands of the claimant.

Dustok to be issued for the arrest of the party cast in cases not in the predicament of those mentioned in Clauses 8 and 9 of Section III. Should be absent himself or fail to pay, his property to be attached and sold, and the proceeds applied to satisfying the demands of the claimant.

Fourth: Should the amount thus realized not satisfy the decree, all the immovable and landed property of the party cast is to be attached by the Nazir in the presence of some of his neighbours; by the erection of a post or other mark that may be intelligible to the people; a communication being at the same time made to the Collector of the district, through whom, if it be deemed preferable, the attachment of landed property may in all instances be made. The Assistant is to send up to the court of the Commissioner, a list of all such property for authority to dispose of it. On the expiration of the period fixed by the Commissioner, the property is to be sold in the presence of the Collector, who will remit the proceeds to the Assistant to be applied to discharge the balance of the decree.

Or the landed property of the party cast is to be attached;

a communication to be made to the Collector, through whom landed property may be attached in all instances.

List of attached property to be sent to Commissioner for authority to dispose of it.

Property to be sold in the presence of the Collector who is to remit the proceeds to the Assistant.

Fifth: Order are to be given from the court of the Assistant to the Nazir to dispose of moveable property attached; on receipt of which the Nazir shall proclaim the sale, which is to take place in fifteen days; at the expiration of which period, should the property be near to the Sudder station of the district, it is to be sold in the Nazir's presence; if at a distance, he is required to send out a Mohurir to conduct the sale. If the claimant be present at the time, the amount of proceeds arising from the sale is to be paid over to him on his granting a receipt. If he be absent, the amount is to be deposited in the court of the Assistant, and a deduction of five percent to be made from the proceeds, which the Nazir is to be allowed to retain to cover the expenses of the sale.

Moveable property to be disposed of by the Nazir or a Mohurir.

Amount to be paid over to claimant, or deposited in the Assistant's Court.

A deduction of 5 per cent to be made, which the Nazir is to be allowed to retain.

Sixth: In the event of the proceeds arising from the sale of the debtor's moveable as well as immoveable property not satisfying the amount of the decree, and the claimant petitioning for the arrest of the debtor, he is to be required, at

Should the proceeds not satisfy the decree, and the claimant deposit cash for the substance of the debtor, he may be placed in jail.

the same time, to deposit money for his subsistence, when the debtor may be placed in jail. It is to be understood, that the debtor may in like manner be placed in jail, in the event of his arrest by the peada entrusted with the dustuk, which is in the first instance to be issued, provided the claimant lodge funds for his subsistence.

He may in like manner be placed in jail if arrested by the peada entrusted with the dustuk issued in the first instance.

Seventh: The party applying for the arrest of another for the amount of a decree is required to lodge with the Nazir for his subsistence, funds for two months. At the expiration of the first month, the claimant to be called on to lodge funds for two more months' subsistence. If he should fail to lodge the amount before the expiration of the first two months, the Nazir to report it to the Assistant who will release the debtor; and no debtor, so released, is to be liable to any further process of arrest, on the same matter at the instance of the same party, unless it be proved that he was guilty of dishonest conduct in the fraudulent concealment or transfer of any property that would otherwise have been available for the satisfaction of the decree or other demand, on account of which he may have been originally confined.

The party applying for the arrest of another required to lodge funds for his subsistence for two months.

At the expiration of the first, for two months more.

Should he fail to do so before the first two months expire, debtor to be released and not liable to any further process of arrest.

Except on proof of dishonest conduct.

Eighth: Rates for the subsistence of debtors shall not exceed three annas, or to be lower than one anna per diem, to be fixed by the Assistant according to the rank of the debtor.

Rates for debtor's subsistence not to exceed three annas, or to be lower than one anna per diem.

Ninth: The fraudulent concealment of property with a view to evading the execution of decrees, or of obtaining permission to sue as a pauper, as also any overt act of violent resistance to the enforcement of a decree or order of a Civil court, is to be accounted a misdemeanor, punishable on conviction by a fine not exceeding two hundred rupees, commutable to imprisonment,

Concealment of property to evade execution of a decree, or to sue as a pauper, as also any act of violent resistance to the enforcement of a decree declared a misdemeanor; punishable by a fine or imprisonment, with or without labor for one year, or by imprisonment alone.

with or without labor, for a term not exceeding one year, or by imprisonment alone for that period. The roobukaree of the Civil court before whom parties may be convicted of any of these offences is to be held by the Magistrate to be a sufficient proof of their guilt, and he is warranted to pass such sentence, on the prisoners being transferred to his authority, as under the circumstances set forth therein he may deem adequate.

Roobukaree of the Civil Court to be held by the Magistrate to be a sufficient proof.

Tenth: If the debtor or debtors in confinement shall give in a statement upon oath containing a full and fair disclosure of all property belonging, to them, the court enforcing a decree may cause enquiry to be made for the purpose of ascertaining the truth of such statement, or the validity of any objections thereto which may be offered by the party at whose instance the prisoner or prisoners may be in confinement, and if the result of such enquiry shall satisfy the court that the statement so delivered, is true and faithful, the Court may accept the surrender of the property included therein, and upon surrender thereof in satisfaction of the judgment passed, order the release of the person or persons in confinement.

The Court enforcing a decree may order the release of debtors in confinement upon their surrendering their property in satisfaction of the judgment passed.

Eleventh: Should a claimant, after the release of a debtor, give in a petition setting forth that he has discovered more of his property, the same may be attached by the Assistant and disposed of, as is already enjoined, to satisfy the balance of the decree.

Should a claimant discover more of a debtor's property after his release, the same may be attached and disposed of by the Assistant.

Twelfth: If the Assistant should see special cause for the release of a debtor, although the claimant may have lodged the funds for his subsistence, he is required to send up to the court of the Commissioner a detailed statement, on which the Commissioner, if he thinks proper, may order the release of the debtor.

If the Assistant see cause for the release of a debtor although funds for his substance are lodged, he is required to report to the Commissioner, who may order the release of the debtor.

Annexure

Thirteenth: No person shall be liable to personal confinement in satisfaction of a decree for any sum not exceeding fifty rupees, beyond a period of six months. If a decree be for a sum not exceeding three hundred rupees, the party cast may be detained for a term of six months on account of every fifty rupees demandable thereon, so that the whole term of imprisonment shall not exceed three years. If the decree be for a greater sum than three hundred rupees, the Commissioner is competent, on the expiration of the three years, to liberate the party in confinement. It is to be distinctly understood however, that liberation from personal restraint under this clause is to be no bar to such further process against the property of a person so discharged, as the party holding a decree against him may find occasion to resort to.

Fourteenth: Should any person or persons report to the Assistant that part of their property has been attached along with that of the debtors, he is required to enquire into the case; and should it appear to him that the allegation is correct, and that the act was committed from malicious motives, he is to make over the offenders to the Fouzdarry Court to be there punished for a misdemeanor.

Fifteenth: If at the time of passing or of executing a decree, it shall be proved that no property can be pointed out, from which the judgment can be immediately enforced, it shall be competent to the court passing, enforcing, or revising such decree, to accept an engagement from the party against whom it is passed, on his surety, (under sufficient mal zaminee or hazir zaminee security,) for the liquidation of the amount due by instalments, and to cause execution of the decree in conformity therewith. In such cases, if the party executing or delivering the engagement

Specification of period of personal confinement in satisfaction of a decree.

Liberation from personal restraint to be no bar to process against the property of a person discharged.

Persons causing the property of others to be attached along with that of the debtor declared liable to be punished for a misdemeanor.

Court passing or enforcing a decree declared competent, if no property can be pointed out, to take security for the liquidation of the amount due by installments.

If the party delivering the engagement be in custody, he shall be discharged, and not liable to further arrest, unless he fail to perform the terms of it: interest to be charged only according to the engagement.

shall have been taken into custody, he shall be immediately discharged, and shall not be liable to further arrest in execution of the judgment to which such engagement may refer, except on failure to perform the terms of it; nor shall any interest be chargeable in such instances beyond what may be provided for in the engagement.

Sixteenth: The amount paid for subsistence is to be repaid by the party in confinement on his release, when property may be forthcoming from which it may be realized; but when no property can be so pointed out, a party shall not be kept in confinement for the repayment of such money only.

No party shall be kept in confinement for the repayment of subsistence money only.

Seventeenth: The Assistants are empowered to make over applications for the execution of decrees to the Junior or Sub-Assistants, or to the Sudder Ameens, who, in acting upon the same, will be guided by the preceding rules.

Assistants empowered to make over applications for the execution of decree to the Junior or Sub-Assistants, or the Sudder Ameens.

SECTION VI: ON THE NAZIR AND HIS PEONS

First: The Nazir of the court of the Assistant is required to conduct the duties in the courts of the Sudder Ameens and Moonsiffs.

Nazir of the Assistant's Court to conduct the duties in those of the Sudder Ameen's and Moonsiff's

Second. A register of all peadas and teeklahs, who are to be employed in the courts of the Assistants, Sudder Ameens and Moonsiffs shall be kept in the court of the Assistant, and none other are to be employed. The allowances of those employed in all the courts is to be three annas per diem, and during the rainy season the persons, upon whose business they are employed, are required to furnish them with a conveyance, or two additional annas per diem as compensation. The Nazir to be remunerated with a fourth of the allowance lodged for peadas and teeklahs. The Commissioner may, if he thinks proper, direct

Register to be kept of Peadahs and Teeklahs

Their allowance to be three annas per diem; person on whose business they are employed to furnish them with conveyance, or pay two additional annas during the rainy season.

The Nazir to be remunerated with a fourth of such allowance. Commissioner may direct Peadas and Teeklahs to furnish security.

security for appearance when required to be furnished by each peada or teeklah on the establishment.

Third: Prior to the employment of any peada or teeklah, the person, on whose business they are to be employed, is required to lodge the amount of their allowances with the Nazir, who is required to endorse his receipt for the same, specifying the amount lodged, on the back of the warrant which the peada is to serve. The peada, on the process being executed, must sign a receipt on the reverse of the warrant for the amount of his allowance.

Allowances of Peadas or Teeklah, to be lodged by the person on whose business they are to be employed.

Fourth: The period to be allowed for warrants to be served by the peadas must be regulated hereafter by the Assistant, in communication with the Commissioner.

Period for the service of the warrants to be regulated by the Assistant in communication with the Commissioner.

SECTION VII: ON RECORDS

First: A register of all original suits, as well as of appeals, shall be kept by the Assistant, in which are to be distinctly set forth the date on which each case was referred, and to what court. The Sudder Ameens and Moonsiffs shall also keep a register.

Registers of all original suits and appeals to be kept by the Assistant, the Sudder Ameens and nd Moonsiffs.

Second: The Sudder Ameens and Moonsiffs shall furnish the Assistant with a monthly return, or copy of their register, of all suits disposed of in their courts during the preceding month.

A monthly return of suits disposed of to be furnished by Sudder Ameens and Moonsiffs to the Assistant.

Third. All decisions in the courts in Assam are to be written in the Bengallee language and character, and are to exhibit the names of plaintiffs and defendants, the amount sued for, as well as the number, date, and order of arrangement of the documents attached to the proceedings, with every other necessary particulars.

All decisions to be written in the Bengallee language and contain certain particulars.

Fourth: The Sudder Dewanny Adawlut are declared competent to fix the minimum number of suits to be decided monthly by the several courts in Assam.

Sudder Dewanny declared competent to fix the minimum number of suits to be decided monthly by the several courts.

SECTION VIII: ON MORTGAGES

First: If the property mortgaged has been held from the date of the mortgage by the mortgagee, the party who has mortgaged the same shall, on paying, or tendering, or depositing in court, the full amount due on the said deed, be entitled, on the expiration of the term specified in the mortgage deed to recover possession of the same.

Party who has mortgaged property declared entitled to recover possession of it on the expiration of the term of mortgage on tendering the amount due.

Second: Wherever it shall appear that the profits accruing from the usufruct of the property ought, under the conditions of the transaction, to be received in lieu of interest, the payment, tender, or deposit of the principal of the sum borrowed shall suffice to entitle the mortgager to recover possession of the property mortgaged.

When the usufruct of the property ought to be received in lieu of interest, the payment or tender or deposit of the principal sum shall entitle the mortgager to recover possession.

Third: In the event of any mortgagee refusing to receive the sum due to him, according to the conditions of the transaction, the mortgager may deposit the sum thus due in the court, and the Officer presiding over the same shall then cause a notification to be issued to the mortgagee, calling upon him within a given period to attend either in person or by representative, and receive the said money.

Should any mortgager refuse to receive the amount due to him it may be deposited in Court, by which he will be called upon to receive it within a given period.

Fourth: After the expiration of the period specified in the notification, the Assistant in charge of the district may either proceed to conduct the further enquiry himself, or may refer the case for trial to the Sudder Ameen; and on its being satisfactory established, that the transaction was a bona fide mortgage and that the party applying to the court has deposited

After the expiration of the period specified in the notification, the complainant may be replaced in the possession of the property mortgaged.

Annexure

the full amount of what is thereon due to the mortgagee, the complainant may forthwith and without further suit, be replaced in possession of the property mortgaged.

Fifth: When any person holding a deed of mortgage shall be desirous for foreclosing the same, he shall, after the expiration of the period specified in the deed, present, either in person or by representative, to the court, a petition with the original deed of mortgage appended to it, praying that the opposite party may be called upon to pay in the amount that may be due thereon.

Mortgage how to be foreclosed.

Sixth: The Officer presiding over the court shall then cause a notice to be served the mortgager and, in the event of his not being found, a proclamation shall be issued calling on the mortgager to attend and pay the stipulated amount into court within the term of one year from the date on which such notice may be issued.

Mortgager to be called upon to pay the stipulated amount into court within one year from the date of notice.

Seventh: In the event of the mortgager failing, when thus summoned, to attend or to pay in the sum required of him, on the expiration of the term above presented, the mortgage shall be held to have foreclosed. But it is hereby notified that no lapse of time shall suffice to foreclose a mortgage, or to convert a conditional into an absolute sale, until the provisions of the clauses 5 and 6 shall be complied with.

On the mortgager failing to attend or to pay, the mortgage shall be held to have foreclosed.

No lapse of time shall suffice to foreclose a mortgage or convert a conditional into an absolute sale, until the provisions of clauses 5 and 6 shall be complied with.

Eighth: It is further necessary to explain that the mortgagee thus applying to have his mortgage foreclosed is not, if he be not in possession before, to be put in possession in consequence of such application by a summary process, but must bring a regular suit in order to acquire possession against the mortgager.

Mortgagee must bring a regular suit in order to acquire possession.

Ninth: In every case of mortgage the court before which it may be tried shall enquire into the amount that may have accrued to the mortgagee from the proceeds of the estate, and make a corresponding deduction from the sum that must be paid in order to procure the redemption of the same; and whenever it shall appear that the sum originally lent with legal interest has been realized out of the profits derived from the possession of the property, then the mortgage shall be held to have been from that date redeemed, and the mortgagee shall be held liable to account to the mortgager for any surplus that he may thus have appropriated.

Whenever it shall appear that the sum lent, with legal interest, has been realized out of the profits derived from the possession of the property, the mortgage shall be held to have been redeemed; and the mortgagee liable to account to the mortgager for any surplus that he may thus have appropriated.

Tenth: In cases, such as obtain occasionally in Assam, in which no term is specified in the deed, the parties therein concerned may, at any period, take advantage of the provisions of this rule, either to redeem or foreclose the mortgage.

In case in which no term is specified in the deed, parties may take advantage of this regulation at any time.

Eleventh: To prevent the bad effects of a species of mortgage that has prevailed in Assam, in which money is lent upon the implied security of persons not actually parties to the transaction, it is to be held as a general rule, that a decree is never to pass, or to be enforced, against any individual not actually and severally indicated by name in the petition of plaint, and the processes thereon issued.

No decree shall pass or be enforced against any individual not indicated by name in the petition of plaint, and the processes issued thereon.

Twelfth: It being understood that many transactions partaking of the nature of a mortgage have been concluded in Assam, on the faith merely of a verbal agreement; it is hereby enacted, that the conditions of all existing contracts of that description are to be enforced in as far as possible in conformity with the provisions of this action. But that no mortgage, not supported by a written deed, is, after the promulgation of this rule, to be taken cognizance of by any civil court in the province.

Conditions of existing contracts, partaking of the nature of a mortgage, on a verbal agreement to be enforced. But no mortgage, not supported by a written deed, is after the promulgation of this rule, to be taken cognizance of.

SECTION IX: SUMMARY SUITS

First: The Assistant in charge of a district shall in general hold the summary suit court in his capacity of Collector. And it shall be competent to a Junior or Sub-Assistant to do so, with the sanction of the Commissioner.

Second: The Assistant may employ one of the Moonsiffs of his division to sit, and act with him as an assessor, in the summary suit court.

Third: All complaints relative to arrears, or undue exaction of rent, or disputed revenue accounts, shall be received by the Assistant in his capacity of Collector, and be heard and decided in the summary suit court.

Fourth. No suit for arrears, exactions of rent, or for the adjustment of revenue accounts, shall be received in the summary suit court, unless it be preferred within one month from the close of the year to which they relate.

Fifth: Parties convicted in the summary suit court of unduly exacting, or attempting to exact, money on the plea of revenue or tulubana, or of extorting on any pretext whatever, shall be liable to be fined in a sum not exceeding four times the value of the amount extorted or wrongfully demanded; a portion of which may, at the discretion of the summary suit court, be awarded as compensation the party aggrieved. In the event of the fine not being paid, the party convicted may be committed to the civil jail for a term not exceeding one year.

Sixth: Persons discontented with the decision of the summary suit court may appeal to the Commissioner, provided their petition of appeal be presented within six weeks from the date of the order complained of. The Commissioner, if he sees no good and sufficient reason for revising the decision of the summary suit court, may reject such petition of appeal, recording his reasons for doing so at length in his proceedings. If the Commissioner sees good cause for admitting the appeal, he may use his discretion as to staying the execution of the award of the summary suit court. After revising the proceedings, the Commissioner may amend, cancel or confirm, the decision passed by the summary suit court, and, in doing so, he may, if he thinks proper, refer the party complaining to a regular suit for redress.

Seventh: Parties, preferring that course, may, in the first instance, seek redress in matters connected with arrears, or undue exaction, or settlement of revenue accounts, by a regular suit in the Civil court; but no Civil court shall take cognizance of any matter pending before, or that has been adjudicated in, the summary suit court, unless the petition of plaint be accompanied by a copy of the order of the Commissioner by which the party is referred to a regular suit.

Parties may in the first instance seek redress in the civil court; but such court shall not take cognizance of the case, unless the plaint be accompanied by the order of the Commissioner referring the party to a regular suit.

Proviso

Eighth: A special appeal, if presented within the term of three months from the date of the final order of the Commissioner on the case, may, in all matters cognizable by the summary suit court, be received by the Sudder Board of Revenue.

A special appeal from the award of the Commissioner may be received by the Sudder Board of Revenue.

Ninth: Claims instituted by the Collector against any individuals, denominated Bhugguts, or descendants of persons attached in former times to any Shustree or temple, for revenue alleged to be due from them to Government, shall be cognizable in the summary suit court. And it is competent to that court to award revenue against any person or persons denominated Bhugguts, who may be attached to a temple, in excess to the number specified in the original grant from the former rulers of the country.

Claims instituted by the Collector against Bhugguts declared cognizable in the summary suit court.

SECTION X: RETURNS

Monthly returns, in such form as he shall direct, shall be made by the Assistants in charge of districts to the Commissioner, shewing the number of cases instituted and disposed of in the various courts during the preceding month; and an annual report on the administration of Civil justice shall be made by the Commissioner to the Sudder Dewanny Adawlut in such form as that Court shall direct.

Monthly returns shall be made by the Assistants to the Commissioner.

An annual report by the latter to the Sudder Dewanny Adawlut.

SECTION XI: REGISTRY OF DEEDS

An office for the registry of deeds shall be established in the several districts of the province of Assam, under the immediate charge of the Junior or the Sub-Assistant, as the Commissioner shall determine. A single book, to be made of paper of English manufacture, will for the present suffice. The pages of this book are to be numbered, and each leaf is to be signed with his initials by the Senior Assistant in charge of the district, who is to certify at the end of the book how many pages it contains, and to affix his signature at full length with the date to the certificate. A fee of one rupee is to be paid on the registry of any deed; and a fee of eight annas, on a copy being taken from the book. The fees are to be the perquisite of the Junior or Sub-Assistant having charge of the books, who is to defray the expense attending their purchase and preservation. It shall for the present be optional with parties to register deeds or not, as they think proper.

An office for the registry of deeds to be established in each district.

A fee of one rupee to be paid on the registry of a deed, and of eight annas on a copy being taken from the registry book.

The fees to be perquisite of the Junior or Sub-Assistant, who is to defray the expense of purchasing and preserving the books. Registering of deeds left optional with parties.

SECTION XII

In all cases not specially provided for in the preceeding rules, the Commissioner, his Assistants and native functionaries, shall endeavour to

In case not provided for, the Commissioner and other functionaries to conform to the conform, as nearly as the circum-stances of the province of Assam will permit, to the provision of the Regulations in force in the provinces subordinate to the Presidency of Fort William; applying, in all doubtful matters for instruction to the Court of Sudder Dewanny Adawlut, or to the Sudder Board of Revenue, according as the question at issue may be of a judicial or of a fiscal nature.

regulations in force in provinces subordinate to the presidency of Fort William; applying in doubtful matters to the Sudder Dewany or Board of Revenue.

Rules for the Administration of Criminal Justice in Assam

SECTION I: ON JURISDICTION

Clause First: There are to be five grade of functionaries employed in the administration of Criminal Justice in Assam, viz.

Number and description of functionaries to be employed in the administration of criminal justice

> The Commissioner,
> Senior Assistants,
> Junior Assistants,
> Sub-Assistants and
> Sudder Ameens

Second: The powers of the Sub-Assistants and Sudder Ameens are restricted to the trial of cases referred to them by the Assistant in charge of the district; and to passing sentence of fine not exceeding fifty rupees, commutable to imprisonment, with or without labor, for six months, or of imprisonment alone for that period. In all cases calling for a severer sentence they shall send up their proceedings to the Assistant in charge of the district.

Sub-Asssistants and Sudder Ameens empowered to try cases referred to them, and to sentence to a fine of 50 Rupees or imprisonment for six months with or without labor.

Third: The ordinary powers of Junior Assistants, when not in charge of a district or station, are restricted to the trial of cases referred to them by their immediate superior; in which they are

Junior Assistant, when not in charge of a district, empowered in try cases referred to them by their superior; and to sentence of fine of 100 competent to pass sentence of fine not exceeding one hundred rupees, commutable to imprisonment for a period not exceeding twelve months, (in both instances with or without labor, at his discretion,) in case of misdemeanor, petty theft or assault, for which such punishment may appear adequate. In all cases demanding a severer sentence, the Junior Assistant shall send up his proceedings, with his opinion recorded thereon, to the Senior Assistant.

Fourth: The powers of the Senior Assistants in charge of districts shall include, with the general charge of the police of the district, the trial, in the first instance, of all persons charged with offences.

Fifth: In cases of burglary or theft, unattended with aggravated personal violence, in which the property stolen may not exceed in value the sum of three hundred rupees, as also in all cases of gross misconduct on the part of officers of police; of bribery and extortion on the part of any native officer in the pay of Government in which the sum demanded or received may not exceed the amount of three hundred rupees; and, likewise, in cases of unaggravated perjury; and also in cases of burkundazes, teeklahs, or others, employed in guarding prisoners, who may be convicted of having by gross neglect permitted any prisoner under their custody to escape; the Senior Assistant may pass sentence of imprisonment with labour for two years, and of imprisonment with labour for the additional terms of one year in lieu of corporal punishment.

Sixth: In all cases of affray or assaults, unattended with serious wounding or loss of life; as also of unaggravated misdemeanors, such as open resistance of process, forcible release of duly attached property, or other act of open contempt, including a refusal to attend and give evidence

Rupees or imprisonment for twelve months, or imprisonment alone for that period.

Senior Assistants vested with the charge of the police, and the trial, in the first instance, of all persons charged with offences.

The Senior Assistant empowered, in certain cases, to pass sentence of imprisonment with labor for two years, and an additional period of one year in lieu of corporal punishment.

In cases of affrays or assaults unattended with serious wounding and other cases, the Senior Assistant may pass sentence of fine not exceeding 200 rupees, or imprisonment for one year.

when summoned either before the Senior Assistant himself or any of the inferior tribunals in the district; the Senior Assistant may pass sentence of fine not exceeding two hundred rupees, commutable to imprisonment for not a period not exceeding one year, or of imprisonment alone for that period.

Seventh: In all cases of more aggravated nature, the Senior Assistant shall refer his proceedings to the Commissioner in the manner hereinafter provided.

Cases of a more aggravated nature to be referred by the Senior Assistant to the Commissioner.

Eighth: The powers of the Commissioner shall extend to the trial of all cases referred to him by a Senior Assistant, and the revision of all proceedings which he may think fit to call for from any subordinate authority within the term of six months from the date on which a final order thereon may have been passed by such subordinate authority. It is not intended by this provision to limit the power of the Commissioner to call for any proceedings that he may require for inspection. Provided however that if, after the expiration of the term above indicated, he shall see cause for setting aside the decision of a subordinate authority he shall report the particulars of the case, in an English letter, to the Nizamut Adawlut, and obtain the sanction of that Court for proceeding to the revision of the case.

Commissioner empowered to try all cases referred by Senior Assistants, and to revise all proceedings of lower authorities within 6 months after sentence.

In cases in which more than 6 months have elapsed since sentence was passed, the Commissioner must apply to the Nizamut Adawlut for permission to revise.

Ninth: In all-cases of theft, burglary, and dacoity, unattended with murder; and of wounding with intent to commit murder, the Commissioner shall be competent to pass sentence of imprisonment with labor, in banishment or not at his discretion, for a term not exceeding fourteen years.

In heinous offences, Commissioner may pass sentence of imprisonment for fourteen years with labor in irons in banishment.

Tenth: In all cases of affrays, manslaughter and other offences, the Commissioner shall be

In cases of affrays and other offences, Commissioner may

competent to pass a sentence of fine not exceeding five hundred rupees, or of imprisonment, with or without labor, for a term not exceeding seven years.

Eleventh: In all cases demanding a more severe sentence that the Commissioner is competent under the preceding clauses to pass, he shall refer his proceedings, in the manner provided for in the sequel, to the Nizamut Adawlut.

Twelfth: It shall be competent to the Commissioner to invest any Junior Assistant, during the temporary absence, either from the district or station, of a Senior Assistant, with the powers defined in Clauses 4, 5, 6 and 7 of this Section.

Thirteenth: It shall also be competent to the Commissioner to invest any experienced Junior Assistant with the powers defined in Clauses 4, 5, 6 and 7 of this Section; or any well qualified Sub-Assistant with the powers defined in Clauses 3 of this Section; whenever, from the state of the business in the district, he may deem such a measure expedient. Provided that an immediate report shall, in every instance, be made to the Nizamut Adawlut, by whom, if they disapprove of the arrangement, a recommendation that it may be set aside will be submitted to Government.

pass a sentence of fine of 500 rupees, or of imprisonment with or without labor for seven years.

Cases demanding a severer sentence must be referred to the Nizamut Adawlut.

Commissioner competent, during the absence of a Senior Assistant, to invest any Junior Assistant with powers defined in Clauses 4 to 7.

Also to invest a Junior Assistant with the above powers; or a Sub-Assistant with those defined in Clause 3;

Reporting the same to the Nizamut Adawlut, who, if they disapprove of the arrangement, may recommend to Government that it be set aside.

SECTION II: RULES OF PROCEDURE

First: In cases which may appear on the face of the police report, or the complaint, to be of a description to render an eventual reference to the Commissioner probable, the Assistant in charge shall, if possible, cause the preliminary magisterial proceedings to be held by the Junior Assistant, Sub-Assistant or Sudder Ameen.

In cases likely to be referred to the Commissioner the preliminary magisterial proceedings to be held, if possible, by a Junior Assistant, Sub-assistant or, Sudder Ameen.

Second: Should circumstances render such delegation of the preliminary enquiry to a subordinate unadvisable, the Assistant in charge shall, in conducting it, confine himself, as far as practical, to taking down the reply of the party accused in the event of his wishing to confess, and to causing the sub-stance of the evidence to be recorded in writing, with a view to facilitating the proceedings on the trial, for which he shall in every instance fix the earliest possible day.

<small>Assistant how to act should circumstances render, such delegation of the preliminary inquiry to a subordinate unadvisable.</small>

Third: Confessions, which in heinous cases ought always to be taken before either the Senior, the Junior, or Sub-Assistant, and never before the Sudder Ameen, must be attested by two or more competent witnesses, (who shall in every instance be made to stand within hearing of the prisoner as he delivers his statement). All such confessions shall be superscribed as follows by the officer before whom it is made: "I.A.B., Senior "Assistant, (Junior or Sub-Assistant, as the case may be,) 'hereby certify that this confession of————was made by the 'said————, and taken down in writing, and attested by the 'subscribing witnesses, before me, and in my presence, on 'the —— between the hours of ——; that, to the best 'of my belief, the confession was voluntary, and that no 'interference, directly or indirectly, on the part of any 'person likely to influence or intimidate the prisoner, was 'permitted'.

<small>Confessions in heinous cases to be taken, before the Senior, Junior, or Sub-Assistant, and attested by witnesses;

And to bear a certificate in a prescribed form.</small>

Fourth: Upon the day being fixed for the trial, the Assistant in charge of the district shall empanel a jury to consist of not less than three members, before whom he will proceed to take the evidence for the prosecution and defence. At the close of the examinations, which shall all be taken down in writing in the Bengalle language,

<small>Cases tried by a jury how to be conducted.

In heinous cases examination to be taken down in writing in the Bengalle language.</small>

he shall call upon the jury, after time being allowed them to deliberate, to return a verdict which shall be taken down in writing in open court, and be attested by the signature of each member of the jury.

Fifth: In the event of a verdict of acquittal being returned by a majority of the jury, the Assistant, if he concurs in it, may direct the immediate release of the prisoner. But in the event of the verdict being for conviction, or of his disapproving of a verdict of acquittal, the Assistant shall forward his proceeding, with an English letter containing an abstract of the evidence and his own opinion upon the merits of the case, to the Commissioner; who will either pass sentence himself, or forward the case, with an English letter, detailing the circumstances of the case, and his opinion with respect to the guilt or innocence of the accused, to the Nizamut Adawlut, as the case may or may not be within his competence to decide on.

In the event of a verdict of acquittal the Assistant, if he concurs in it, may release the prisoner. If he disapprove, or the verdict before conviction, he shall submit the case to the Commissioner, who will either pass sentence, or refer it to the Nizamut Adawlut.

Sixth: In all petty criminal cases (viz. misdemeanors, theft to the amount of fifty rupees, and offences for which Magistrates in the regulation provinces are empowered to pass sentence of imprisonment not exceeding six months) evidence may be taken viva voce, and the substance merely be recorded, either in the English or Bengalle language, as the Commissioner may direct.

In petty criminal cases, the evidence may be taken viva voce, and the substance recorded in the English or Bengalle language.

Seventh: In issuing processes in cases of petty criminal charges the Assistant in charge of a district and his subordinates shall be guided by the rules drawn up in the native language and transmitted to them by the late Commissioner of Assam, with his letter bearing date the 19 August 1833.

In issuing processes in cases of petty criminal charges, the Assistant and subordinate officers shall be guided by the rules drawn up by the late Commissioner, and circulated with his letter of 19 August 1833.

Eighth: A register of all trials, held before the Assistant and his subordinates, shall be kept in such form as the Commissioner may, in communication with the Nizamut Adawlut, direct.

| | A register to be kept of trials held before the Assistant and his subordinates. |

Ninth: Monthly returns of trials referred to the Commissioner and disposed of by him, shall be made to the Nizamut Adawlut according to the annexed forms.

| | Monthly returns of trials shall be made by the Commissioner to the Nizamut Adawlut. |

Tenth: An annual report on the administration of criminal justice, shewing the aggregate number of trials held and prisoners punished in each division, and such other particulars as that court may require, shall be made to the Nizamut Adawlut.

| | An annual report on the administration of criminal justice shall be made to the Nizamut Adawlut. |

SECTION III: POLICE

First: The Regulation XX of 1817 of the Regulation Provinces is to be taken, with the following modifications, as the police law of Assam.

| | Regulation XX of 1817, with certain modifications, to be taken as the police law of Assam. |

Second: Darogahs are to be guided, in their general duties and in the control of their subordinates, by the provisions of Clause 1, Section IV of that Regulation.

| | Darogahs to be guided by Clause I, Section IV, of that Regulation. |

Third: Sections III, IV, V, VI, VII, VIII and IX of the above Regulations are to be observed, with this distinction, that the report required by the 12th clause of Section IX is to be made to the Commissioner of Assam.

| | Sections III to IX of that Regulation are to be observed; the report required by the 12th Clause of Section IX is to be made to the Com-missioner. |

Fourth: Such periodical reports are to be made to the Assistants in charge of districts, as the Commissioner in Assam may, in consideration of the circumstances of the province, direct.

| | Such periodical reports are to be made to the Assistants as the Commissioner may direct. |

Fifth: Sections XI, XII, XIII and XIV of the Regulation are to be particularly observed.

Sixth: Section XIII is to be enforced, but in cases of simple burglary or theft, unattended with violence, the darogah shall neither institute a local enquiry in person, or depute a subordinate for that purpose, excepting at the instance of the party injured.

Seventh: Of the remaining sections of Regulation XX of 1817, Sections XVI, XVII, XVIII, XIX and XX shall be strictly observed. Section XXI is not to be enforced. Sections XXII and XXIII are to be observed. Section XXIV is not to be acted upon. Sections XXV, XXVI and XXVII are to be enforced; but the subsequent Sections, being inapplicable to Assam, are not to be attended to.

Eighth: In the event of the Commissioner, or any of the Senior, Junior or Sub-Assistants in Assam deeming it necessary for any special reason to be personally present at the execution of any process of arrest or other judicial process, they shall be guided in their conduct on such occasions by the provisions of Regulation I of 1825 of the Regulation Provinces, which Regulation is to be in force in the province of Assam.

Sections XI to XIV of that Regulation are to be particularly observed.

Section XIII is to be enforced; but the Darogah in cases of simple burglary or theft, shall not institute a local enquiry, except at the instance of the party injured.

Sections XVI to XX, XXII, XXIII, XXV, XXVI and XXVII of Regulation XX of 1817 to be observed, but XXI and XXIV and remaining Sections not to be in force in Assam.

Regulation 1 of 1825 declared to be in force in Assam.

SECTION IV: PERJURY

First: The Assistants in their capacity of Magistrates, and all officers of police, are restricted from receiving or acting upon charges of perjury or subornation of perjury preferred by private parties. And it is hereby declared that no individual, whose attendance is required before any court or office shall be liable to any prosecution of this description, unless he shall be made over to the Assistant in his capacity of Magistrate by the officer presiding over the Court

Assistants and other officers of police restricted from receiving or acting upon charges of perjury preferred by private parties. No individual shall be liable to any prosecution for perjury unless made over to the Assistant in charge of a District, who may either pass sentence, or refer the trial to the Commissioner.

or office in which the imputed offence may have been committed. The proceedings held in the court or office in which the offence is alleged to have been committed shall, in all such cases, be transmitted to the Assistant in charge of the district in his capacity of Magistrate; and, if upon an inspection of the same, or after making such further enquiry as he may deem necessary, he shall be of opinion that the offence is proved, the Assistant may either pass sentence, or refer the trial to the Commissioner, according as the case is or is not one of an aggravated nature.

Source: BJP, (Civil), 6 July 1837, no. 2.

Glossary

Amlah or *Omlah*	The collective head native officer of a judicial or revenue court under a European judge or a collector
Amin or Ameen	A judge or arbitrator such as *sadar ameen* or principal *sadar ameen*
Barbaruah	An Ahom officer of rank, having control and supervision, ordinarily, over civil and revenue affairs
Barkandozes	An armed retainer or policman
Barpatra Gohain	One of the three Ahom cabinet ministers
Barphukan	The Viceroy of Guwahati under Ahom government
Baruah	An officer of the Ahom government of high rank
Bhisti	Water carrier
Borgohain	The second minister of the Ahom cabinet
Bundhbust	Agreement
Buragohain	The chief of the three ministers of the Ahom cabinet
Chaprasee/Chaprasi	A messenger or carrier wearing a *chapras* (badge), most usually a low-level public servant
Cutcherry/Kachari	A court, a hall, an office, the place where any public business is transacted
Daftar/Duftar	An office in which public records are kept
Daftari/Duftari	A record keeper, a registrar
Dak	Post
Dangariyas	Three top Ahom cabinet ministers
Darogah	A police officer in-charge of a police station.
Decree	A judgement or decision of a court, order given by a ruler of authority having the force of law

Deed	A written and signed instrument using words purporting to convey title to real property
Defendant	A person who is being used in a civil action or who is prosecuted in a criminal action.
Dewan	Chief executive
Dewani/ Dewani Adalat	The court of civil or revenue jurisdiction
Faree	Police outpost.
Fauzdari/ Nizamat Adalat	The court of criminal jurisdiction
Gangajolee/ Gangajoliya	Hindu religious officer
Goal	The English spelling of the word 'jail'; a prison
Gohain	A title applied to the three senior cabinet ministers, their sons, the frontier governors and also the princes of the royal blood
Hazarika	An officer in-charge of 1,000 *paiks*
Hajjut	Custody
Jamadar/Jumadar	An officer of police, custom or excise second to *darogah*
Kakoti	A writer, scribe, surveyor or accountant
Kanoogo/Kanungo	A village and district revenue officer, who under former governments recorded all circumstances within their sphere which concerned landed property and the realization of revenue, keeping registers of the value, tenure, extent and transfer of land, assisting in the measurement and survey of India, reporting deaths and succession of revenue payers
Khel	An organization of *paiks* to perform specific services to the Ahom government under the control of a Baruah
Kheldar	Officer-in-charge of *khel*
Koranee	Muslim religious officer
Kah/Keyah	A merchant from Marwar

Glossary 321

Kyfeut	Explanation
Lakhiraj	A rent-free grant *La* without and *khira*j tax
Lickshow/Lixsow	A labourer granted to an officer as remuneration in Ahom government
Mohal/Mohal	A province, a district/circle
Malgoozar/Mulguzars	One who pays rent or revenue
Mel	An estate consisting of land and *paiks*, administered by officers of Ahom government for the maintenance of the king's children, wives, and other near relatives; a royal banquet: any assembly of people; *paiks* or *ryots* of a *khel* or village, instituted to hold discussions on matters of common interest or to hold trials of persons according to local customs
Mofussil/Mofusil	Rural areas, semi-urban areas
Mouza	A fiscal unit
Muhafiz	A registrar or record keeper
Muharrir/Mohurer/Muharir	A permanent or regular clerk
Muktear/Mooktear	An agent, an attorney
Munshree/Munsree	Person well-versed in Arabic and Persian
Munsif	A native civil judge of the first or lowest rank
Naib	A deputy, a representative
Naik	The head of a small body of soldiers
Nakal/Nuqul	A copy, a transcript, any recorded written document, a register
Narayani rupee	Coin introduced in Cooch Behar by Maharaja Nara Narayan. The rate of exchange for 100 sicca rupees was Rs. 126-7-4 in Narayani rupee
Navis	A writer, a clerk
Nazir	An inspector, a supervisor; in ordinary use the officer of the court who is charged with the serving of process or who is sent to take deposition and make inquiry into any breach of law or peace
Nuzzur	Gift

Oath	A statement made by a witness in a trial with an adjuration to the Deity generally in the words: 'So help me God' to the effect that he will tell the truth, the whole truth, and nothing but the truth, an Oath may be made without any connection with an action at law; normally by officers of the government
Paik	An enrolled adult male subject of the Ahom government having to render specific duties to the state
Panchayat/*Panch*	A native court of arbitration, consisting of five members; people's court popular in villages
Paraganah	A revenue division
Parole	The release of a person from prison subject to his compliance with specified conditions
Pattah	Title dead on land
Parwannah	Warrant
Pauper	Poor man; this is the sense in which it is used in the phase *forma pauperis*
Peada	A footman, an armed servant; police or militia man serving on foot
Peon	Term commonly used by Europeans for the Hindustani *peada*—an inferior officer of police, custom or of court of justice, usually wearing a badge
Peskar	Native officer in a judge's or collector's office next in rank to *sheristadar*
Plaintiff	The person who brings an action at law by filing a declaration in the common law procedure
Prima facie	At the first view; the inference drawn about a thing by mere observance of it, or about an event by knowledge of its occurrence, without further investigation in either case

Pundit	A learned man
Rajkhowa	An officer under Ahom government having jurisdiction over a prescribed area or a unit of *paiks* not exceeding 3,000
Razanamah	A written testimonial given by a plaintiff, upon a cause being finally settled, that he is satisfied
Rubakari/Roobkari	A written record of a case, stating the particulars and the grounds of the decision drawn up and authenticated by the judge in a Company's Court, on passing sentence
Saikia	A supervisor over 100 *paiks*
Sanad	Government order or summons
Saristadar	A registrar, a record keeper, applied especially to the head native officer of a court of justice or collector's office, who has the general superintendence of the establishment and in-charge of public records and official documents
Sarrjamnee	Person who makes on-the-spot surveys
Session judge	Judicial officer holding session on goal delivery trying heinous offences
Sezwal	An officer employed for the collection of revenue
Sicca	A stamped coin, specially the designation of the silver currency of the king of Delhi, adopted by other Indian princes and eventually by the East India Company
Subpoena	A writ; a process or mandate issued to a person requiring him to be present at a court to give testimony in a certain case
Summary	Short brief without formal trial or proceeding
Surasuree panchayat	A tribunal for summary disposal of minor offences
Swargadeo	Literally god or heaven, the title of the Ahom kings
Tecklas/Teckelas	A messenger

Tahsildar/Tahseeldar	A revenue officer
Thana	A police station
Thanadar	An officer-in-charge of a police station
Witness	A person called in judicial or similar proceedings to give testimony under oath. He may appear voluntarily or be required to appear by sub-peon
Vakil/Vakeel	An advocate; Pleader

Bibliography

PRIMARY SOURCES

UNPUBLISHED DOCUMENTS

ENGLISH

State Archives, Government of West Bengal, Calcutta

Bengal Judicial Proceedings (Civil), 1830-1841.
Bengal Judicial Proceedings (Criminal), 1830-1841.
Bengal Judicial Proceedings (Criminal), 1830-1841.
General Department Miscellaneous Branch, 1859-1874.
General Proceedings, 1860-1874.
Judicial (Political) Consultations, 1870-1874.
Letters (General) to the Court of Directors (Select), 1825-1840.
Letters (General) from the Court of Directors (Select), 1825-1840.
Miscellaneous Records (Judicial Department), 1825-1830.
Revenue Proceedings, 1835-1840.
Sadar Board of Revenue Proceedings, 1829-1850.

National Archives of India, New Delhi

Foreign (Secret) Consultations, 1825-1834.
Foreign (Political) Consultations, 1825-1834.
Territorial Proceedings (Revenue), 1825-1834.

State Archives, Government of Assam, Dispur

Letters (Select) issued to the Government of Bengal.
Letters (Select) received from the Government of Bengal.
Letters (Select) issued to District Officers.

ASSAMESE

Baruah, Maniram, Buranji Viveka-Ratna, 1838; MSS No. 272, Transcript no. 108, preserved at the DHAS, Guwahati.

PUBLISHED

ENGLISH

Document, Reports, Work of Reference

Administrative Reports, Government of Bengal 1858-1874.

Blunt and Shakespeare, *Abstract of Regulation XX of 1817*, Calcutta, 1840 (?)

Clarke, Marshman John, *A Guide to the Civil Laws to the Presidency of Bengal*, Sreerampur Press, Calcutta, 1842.

Clarke, R., *The Regulations of the Government of Fortwillium in Bengal 1793-1853*, London, 1854.

Dutta, Sivanath, *A Handbook of the Assam Regulations*, Assam Secretariat, Shillong, 1896.

Mills A.J. Moffatt, Report on the Province of Assam, Publication Board, Assam, Gauhati, 2nd edn., April 1984. See *Observation on the Administration of the Province of Assam by Baboo Anundaram Dakeal Phookun*, Appendix J.

Pemberton, R.B., *Report on the Eastern Frontier of British India*, Calcutta, 1835, rpt., Guwahati, 1866.

Accounts, Memoirs, Journels

Buchanan, Hamilton Francis, *An Account of Assam 1807-1814*, London, 1820; rpt., Department of Historical and Antiquarian Studies, Gauhati, 1963.

Butler, John, *Travels and Adventures in the Province of Assam*, Smith, Elder, and Co. London, 1855.

Hunter, W.W. *A Statistical Account of Assam*, vols. I & II, Trubner & Co, London, 1879, rpt., New Delhi, 1975.

M'Cosh, J.N. *Topography of Assam*, Bengal Military Orphan Press, Calcutta, 1837.

Robinson, W. William, *A Descriptive Account of Assam*, Calcutta, 1st pub. 1841; rpt. Sanskaran Prakashan, Delhi, 1975.

Welsh, Thomas, *Report on Assam*, Calcutta, 1794; reproduced in Alexander Mackenzie's *History of the Relations of the Government with the Hill Tribes of The North-East Frontier of Bengal*, Home Department, Calcutta, 1884.

White, Adam, *A Memoir of the Late David Scott*, British Library, London, 1831, rpt., Department of Historical and Antiquarian Studies, Assam, Guwahati, 1988.

ASSAMESE

Bordoloi, K.C. (ed.), *Sadar Aminar Atmajdvani* by Harakanta Sarmah Baruah, North Guwahati, 1960.

Bibliography

Bhuyan, S.K. (ed.), *Asamar Padya Buranji*, consisting of two metrical chronicles, Kali Bharat Buranji (1679-1858) by Dutiram Hazarika and Belimar Buranji (1782-1819) by Bisweswar Baidydhipa, Guwahati, 1964.

Deodhai Assam Buronji, Department of Historical and Antiquarian Studies, Guwahati, 3rd edn., 1990.

Orunudoi, An Assamese monthly, printed at the American Beptist Mission Press, Sibsagar, 1846-80.

BENGALI

Dhekial Phukan, Anandaram, *Aain Aru Babastha Sangrah* (Notes on the Laws of Bengal), New Press, Calcutta, 1855.

Dhekial Phukan, Haliram, *Assam Buranji*, 1st published, Calcutta, 1929; rpt., ed. J.M. Bhattacharjee, Mokshada Pustakalaya, Gauhati, 1962.

SECONDARY WORKS

ENGLISH

Acharyya, Bijoy Kisor, *Codification in British India*, S.K. Banerji & Sons, Calcutta, 1914.

Banerjee, A.C., *The Eastern Frontier of British India*, A. Mukherjee & Co. Calcutta, 1946.

Barpujari, H.K., *Assam In the Days of the Company*, Spectrum Publications, Guwahati, 2nd edn., 1980.

—— (ed.), *Political History of Assam 1826-1919*, Government of Assam, Dispur, Guwahati, 1977.

Barooah, N.K., *David Scott in North East India, 1802-31: A Study of British Paternalism*, Munshiram Manoharlal, New Delhi, 1970.

Barooah, S.L., *A Comprehensive History of Assam*, Munshiram Manoharlal, New Delhi, 5th rpt., 2013.

Bhattacharjee, S.N., *Administration of Law and Justice in India*, The University of Burdwan, Burdwan, 1982.

Bhuyan, S.K. *Anglo-Assamese Relations 1771-1826*, Department of Historical and Antiquarian Studies, Guwahati, 1949; rpt. 1974.

——, *Studies in the History of Assam*, Omsons Publication, Guwahati, 1985.

Buckland, C.E., *Bengal under the Lt. Governors*, vol. I, S.K. Lahiri & Company, Calcutta, 1901.

Campbell, G., *Modern India*, John Murray, London, 1852.

——, *India as it May be: An Outline of Proposed Government and Policy*, John Murray, London, 1853.

Bibliography

Chailley, J., *The Administrative Problem of British India*, Macmillan & Co. Ltd., London, 1910.

Chandra, Bipan, *Modern India*, National Council for Educational Research and Training, New Delhi, 1971.

Chowdhury, Bhawani Sankar, *Studies in Judicial History of British India*, Eastern Law House, Calcutta, 1972.

Cowell, H., *History of the Constitution of Courts and Legislative Authorities in India*, Thacker Spink & Co., Calcutta, 1936.

Das, G., *Justice in India*, Shangon & Shangon, Cuttack, 1967.

Desai, A.R., *Social Background of Indian Nationalism*, Popular Prakashan, Bombay, 5th edn. 1976; rpt. 1987.

Dubey, H.P., *A Short History of the Judicial System of India and Some Foreign Countries*, N.M. Tripathy Pvt. Ltd., Bombay, 1968.

Dutt, K.N., *Landmarks of the Freedom Struggle in Assam*, Lawyer's Book Stall Guwahati, 1st pub. 1958; rpt. 1998.

Dutt, R., *The Economic History of India*, vol. II, 1st edn. 1960; 2nd rpt., Publication Division, Ministry of Information and Broadcasting, New Delhi, 1970.

Dutta, A.K. *Maniram Dewan and Contemporary Assamese Society*, Anuradha Dutta Neemati, Jorhat, 1990.

Fawcett, Sir Charles, *The First Century of British Justice in India*, published under the patronage of His Majesty's Secretary of State for India in Council, Oxford, London, 1934.

Gait, Sir Edward, *A History of Assam*, 3rd edn. (rpt.), LBS Publications, Gauhati, 1984.

Guha, A., *Planter-Raj to Swaraj: Freedom Struggle and Electoral Politics in Assam 1826-1947*, Peoples Publishing House, New Delhi, 1st pub. 1977, rpt., 1988.

Gupta, A., *The Police in India, 1861-1947*, Concept Publishing Company, New Delhi, 1979.

Gupta, M.N., *Analytical Survey of Bengal Regulations*, University of Calcutta, Calcutta, 1943.

Hazarika, B.B., *Political Life in Assam During the 19th Century*, Gyan Publishing House, New Delhi, 2006.

Kaye, J.W., *The Administration of the East India Company*, Richard Bentley, London, 1853; rpt. Kitab Mahal, Allahabad, 1966.

Keith, Arthur Berriedale, *A Constitutional History of India*, London, 1936; rpt., Central Book Depot, Allahabad, 1961.

Lahiri, Rebati Mohon, *The Annexation of Assam (1824-54)*; rpt., Firma KLM, Kolkata, 2003.

Bibliography

Majumdar, R.C. (ed.), *British Paramountcy and India Renaissance*, pt. I, Bharatiya Vidya Bhavan, Bombay, 1st edn. 1963; 2nd edn. 1970.

Mishra,B.B., *The Central Administration of East India Company*, Manchester University Press, Manchester, 1959.

——, *The Judicial Administration of the East India Company in Bengal 1765-1782*, Motilal Banarsidass, Delhi, 1961.

Morly, W.H., *The Administration of Justice in British India*, Metropolitan Book Co., New Delhi, rpt., 1976.

Palkivala, Nani, *We the People of India: The Largest Democracy*, Strand Book Stall, Bombay, 9th impression, 1991.

Sarma, Amulya Chandra, *Tai Ahom System of Government*, B.R. Publishing Corporation, New Delhi, 1986.

Srivastava, Ramesh Chandra, *Development of Judicial System in India under the East India Company, 1833-1858*, Lucknow Publishing House, Lucknow, 1971.

Ward, Mrs. S.R., *A Glimpse of Assam*, Thomas S. Smith, Calcutta, 1884.

Strachey, Sir John, *India: Its Administration & Progress*, Macmillan, London, 1911.

ASSAMESE

Barbaruah, H., *Ahomar Din*, Publication Board, Assam, Guwahati, 1981.

Barua, Harakanta, *Assam Buranji*, Department of Historical and Antiquarian Studies, Gauhati, 1990.

Baruah, Gunaviram, *Anandaram Dhekial Phukan Jivon Charita*, Publication Board, Assam, Guwahati, 2nd edn., 1992.

Bhuyan, S.K., *Deodhai Asam Buranji*, Department of Historical and Antiquarian Studies, Gauhati, 1962.

Sarma, A.C., *Satawan Sal Aru Piyali Baruah*, published by Pradip Adhyapak, Borkotoky & Company, Jorhat, 1988.

Sarma, Benudhar, *Maniram Dewan*, Asom Jyoti, Guwahati, 1950.

Sattar, A., *Bahadur Gaon Burha*, Dibrugarh, 1969.

Talukdar, N. (ed.), *Anandaram Dhekial Phukanar*, Rachana Sangrah, Lawer's Book Stall, Guwahati, 1977; 2nd edn., 1992.

Index

administration of justice, lamentable lapses of law resulting in light punishment 276; abolishment of the *munsif* court 182; Act VIII of 1859/Civil Procedure Code 178; appeals and revisions, impediments to speedy justice 258; badly drafted and hastily enacted laws 268; Bengal Civil Court Act (Act VI of 1871) 181; circumlocution and red-tape 258; Clause 5, Section II of the Assam Code (Civil) 259; Code of Civil Procedure for India 269; codes of civil and criminal procedure 178-82; conglomeration of powers of a magistrate 267; court language 263-6; Criminal Procedure Code (Act XXV of 1861) 178; examining witnesses in the courts of justice 261-2; impact on life of people 254-69; Indian High Courts Act, 6 August 1861 178; Indian Penal Code Act XLV of 1860 178; jurisdiction of a magistrate 259-61; justice united with 266-8; legislation 268-9; Mofussil courts in each *thana* jurisdiction 278; money-lender assisted by administration of justice 256; naming of native courts as panchayats 271-2; peasant uprising 182-7; principle of the rule of law 274, 277; procedural law 257-9; regulation provinces, administration of civil justice 267; revenue administration 257; rural masses, pauperization of 256-7; *ryots* enjoyed proprietary rights over their possessions 255; *ryots* presenting petitions to the collector and the commissioner 255; Section 66B, Criminal Procedure Code 180; Section CCLXXVI, Criminal Procedure Code 180; Section II of the Regulation 2 of 1832 260; Section XXXVIII Criminal Procedure Code 180; settlements were conducted in the Sadar Station 254-5; system of examination in the recruitment of assistants introduced 179; trained judges to administer laws which the legislature had provided 273; under the Crown till 1874 178-91

administrative re-organization 104-5; European officer designated as principal assistant to the Commissioner of Assam 104; Six-Parganas under Captain Bogle 104-5

Ahom administration 30-6; Barbaruas' court 31; Barphukan 31; Choladhara Phukan 33; complaints of minor nature 33; humanitarian value about justice 35; in Kamrup, *parganas* placed under a *chowdhury* 32; inflicting punishment to the guilty, method of 35; judicial system 33; Khargharia Phukan 33; king as the highest judicial authority 30; king's court 30-1; military in nature 35-6; no distinction between civil and criminal cases 32; Nyay Sodha Phukan 30, 31; occasional barbarity of the Ahom punishment 35; *paik* system 29-30; practice of releasing a person on bail or on sureties 32; *rajkhowas* 30; *roobkaris* of the Indian courts 33; *satra* institutions 32; *Siddhartha Patra* 32; *talukdars* 32; *teckela* or *chowdang* 32; three *dangariyas* 31; tribunals of justice 31; village assembly 31-2

Ahom government; *chamua* 29-30; *dangariyas* or cabinet ministers 29; Gohains 29; *hazarika* 30; *rajkhowas* 30

Ahom institution of law and justice 84

Ahom judicial system 30-6; influence of the Brahmanical religion 34; lack of judicial books 34; maintenance of law and imparted equal justice to all 34; shortcomings of 34

Ahom penal code 33-4; common punishments 33; death penalty 34; inflicting punishment to the guilty 35; penalty for rebellion 33-4; rigorous punishment, death and mutilation of limbs 33; severity and relation 33

Ahom period, functions of maintaining peace and order: *kheldars* 83

Ahoms; ideology of the Ahom government 29; *khels* 30; Khunlung 29; King Pratap Singha 29; monarchial and aristocratic government 29; Mughlas as formidable opponents 25-6; rebellion of the Moamaria (1769) 27; rulers described Assam as *Sonar Saphura* or 'casket of gold' 26-7; Sukapha, policy of peace and conciliation against the Morans and the Barahis 25; territorial expansion towards west 25

Assam Code, criminal justice, rules for the administration 132-40; Act of open contempt of court 137; Act XIX of 1853 135; affrays attended with homicide 139; appeal to courts 126-9; arbitration or compromise 129-32; assault and affrays 136; attendance of witness 135; Ayantia, annexation of 148; Bahadur Gaonburha, and Farmud Ali, charged of fomenting sedition among the Muslims of Jorhat 163; Barbora, Mayaram, trial of 161; Baruah, Dutiram, trial of 162-3; bribery and extortion on the part of any native officer 138; burglary or theft 136; Cachar, annexation of 146-8; Capt. Agnew as the principal assistant of Goalpara 130; Charles Holroyd, the principal assistant, Sibsagar 150; civil justice, administration of 118-32; 20 May 1846, passed by the Sadar Dewani Adalat 127-8; claims instituted by the collector against any individual 125-6; Clause 3 of Section III 127; Clause 6 of Section II of the Administration of Civil Justice 129; Clause 6, Section II of the Administration of Criminal Justice 140; Commissioner Jenkins planned annexation 145-6; confessions in heinous cases 132, 134; corporal punishment 140; Deputy Commissioner Capt. Vetch 141-2; deputy commissioner having powers of Civil and Session Judge 127; event of an acquittal 134; execution of

Index 333

decrees 120-2; forcible release of duly attached property 138; fraudulent concealment of property 122; great national upsurge and the Administration of justice 148-67; gross neglect of duty by the *barkandoz* or *teckelas* 137; house-breaking 137; judgement of a *sadar ameen* on an appeal from that of a *munsif* 126; Mallick, Madhu, trial of 162; Maniram Dutta Barbhandar Baruah Dewan/Maniram Dewan 148-9; Matak territory, annexation of 144-6; mortgages 123-4; neglect or ill-treatment of wife 138; Nizamat Adalat 134; offenders convicted of theft, burglary and decoity 139; Peali alias Mohesh Chandra Baruah 149; Penal Code of Assam 136; person guilty of wounding 139; persons conspiring against state, legal action and criminal proceedings 155-8; petty criminal cases 134; procedural law 118-20; procedure of submitting a complaint 141; prostitution 137; punishment for desertion by workmen 138; punishment for resistance of process 138; punishment for wilful murder 138-9; Purandar Singha ruled smoothly 143-4; revolt of 1857, alarm felt throughout Assam 149; *quabalah jowab* or *razenamah* 130; receivers of stolen property 136; recovering of debt without proper authority 137; registry of deeds 122-3; Regulation II of 1834 abolished corporal punishment 140; robbery 139; rules of procedure 132; Sadar Dewany Adalat 120; Sadiya, annexation of 146; Saring Raja joined his Dewan Maniram Dutta 148-9; Saring Raja Kandarpeswar Singha, detained as a state prisoner 163-6; Section II, Clause 10 of the Assam Civil Rules 131; Section III of the Rules for the Administration of Civil Justice 126-7; Section III, Clause 6 of the Assam Code (Civil) 135; Special appeal to the Sadar Dewani Adalat 126-7; special appeal, provisions of Act III of 1843 128; suit in forma pauperis, Clause XI of Section II 131-2; summary suit court 125-6; vakeels or pleaders 120; treason and complicity in Mutiny, trial of the persons accused of 152; trial of Maniram, prejudiced and biased 158-61; trial of the other convicts 161; Tularam ruled Cachar 147; unaggravated perjury 136; wilful perjury or forgery 139; Upper Assam, resumption of 143-4; *viva voce* examination 140-3; *viva voce* system, operation of 143

Assam, history of 23; Ahom, foundation of a kingdom by the Tai Shans 24, 25; Assam Range 24; hill tribes 24; invasions from the west led by the Turko-Afghan rulers of Bengal 24; kingdom of Kamrupa 23; Moamaria rebellion and the Burmese invasion 51; Naga hills 24; North Cachar and the Mikir hills (the Karbi Anglong) 24; Palas 23; Patkai range 24; right to dispense justice 25; rise of the Varmanas in the fourth century AD 23; Salastambha dynasty 23

authorized agent or *mukhtear* 131

Index

Bengal Act VI of 1868 191
Bentinck, William (Lord) 28
bhakats (bhugguts) 125
Brahmaputra valley, administering of 49-50; capitulation of Rangpur 49
British judicial administration, policy and organizational framework of 49-64; Brahmaputra valley, administering of 49-50; civil justice, administration of 54-9; criminal justice, administration of 59-64; Non-Regulation system into Assam, extension of 50-2

Campbell, A.L. 188
Central Assam, experimental division of 106-7
Charter Act of 1833 42-3; Section 53 of 43
Charter of 1661 274
Civil Justice Committee 281
civil justice, administration of 54-9; civil or *dewani* business in Upper Assam, courts of the Barphukan and the Barbaruah 55; civil suits in Lower Assam by 1832, gradation of courts dealing with 58-9; Lambodhar, Barphukan 55; Lower Assam, *chowdhury* of the *parganas* 55; Lower Assam, Senior Commissioner Scott empowered to try all civil suits 55; Mofussil Panchayat Court 56-7; Summary Suit Court at Guwahati 57; *tahsildar* 57
civil justice, reforms in 94-8; six *parganas* in Kamrup 97-8
Col. Richards 49, 54, 60
Commissioner Hopkinson 184, 187, 217, 218, 219
constitution of courts 93; institution fees 94; procedure to be followed 93; *vakeel*, appointment of 94

court language 263-6; Act XXIX of 1837 263
criminal justice, administration of 59-64, 75-89; Ahom institution of law and justice 84-5; authority of the Nizamat Adalat into Lower Assam 60-1; Bar Panchayat 60; British occupation of Lower Assam 59; British revenue policy impoverished the people 78; changes in 100-1; *chowdhury* employed the *kuruk sezwals* 81; *chowdhuryship* 81-2; civil courts, Assamese-speaking public officers of 76; Durrong trifling criminal cases 61; equality before law 88; extortion and oppression, complaints of 85-6; Haliram Dhekial Phukan 62-3; heinous offences, trial and punishment of 59-60; immoderate use of opium 82-3; important reforms made 76; in Darrang, police under Raja Bijoy Narayan 86; increase in litigations 89; indigenous courts 84; Lower Assam, cases 59-60; moneylenders exploited the provisions of the new legal system 79; native officers unfamiliar with the British method of administration 87; new revenue system 78-9; Nizamat Adalat, jurisdiction of 60; Nowgong, police under Ghinai Barphukan 86; *paraganas*, in Kamrup 81; peasantry, large-scale impoverishment of 79; people obliged to pay the *teckela* or *peada* 83-4; petty criminal cases 100; police establishments only nominally paid by the government 80; protection of an individual against arbitrary rule 88-9; punitive measure of

Index

imprisonment 82; Regulation IX of 1793 59; Regulation X of 1822 59; Regulation XII of 1818 100; Scott's policy of employing natives 85; selection of *chowdhury*, vested with the *ryots* themselves 81; system or machinery of collecting taxes 81; *thana* establishment 83; theft and other crimes of aggravated nature 100; trifling criminal cases in Upper Assam 61-2; unaggravated burglary 100; Upper Assam, criminal cases 59; Upper Assam, police duties in 86; Upper Assam, trifling criminal cases in 61-2

dustak 121

early years of British rule, growth and development of the administration of justice 70-107; civil justice, administration of 70-2; criminal justice, administration of 75-89; law and order, maintenance of 76; *lex-loci* or the local customs and prejudices 71; no proper police administration 83; panchayats or native courts, working of 71-5; uniform system of law 71

English law in India, evolution of 36-47; 1765 Shah Alam granted to the East India Company the Dewani of Bengal, Bihar and Orissa 39; 1771, Directors of the Company issued orders to the President and Council in Bengal 39; 1828, British retained Lower Assam permanently under their occupation 36; 1833, Upper Assam was assigned to an Ahom prince 36; 1838, Upper Assam annexed to British territories in India 36; Act of 1833, Governor-General-in-Council vested extensive powers of legislation 42; Assam administered by the same laws procedures prevailing in other parts of the British India 46; August 1861 Indian High Courts Act 45; Charter Act, 1833 42-3; Charter Act, 1861 41; Charter of 1726, Mayor's Court established 38; Charter of 1753 38; Code of Criminal Procedure of 1861 44-5; Company's legislative and judicial authority 37-8; Criminal Procedure Code 44; exercised power in accordance with laws, customs and administrative practices 37; exercised sovereign authority in Assam 37; First Law Commission 44; Hastings' Regulations of 1772 39-40; High Courts of Judicature 45; Indian Penal Code 44; Kings Court 40; law of the Company's settlements 37; legislative competence of subordinate presidencies 42; Legislative Council of India 44; Mofussil Dewani Adalats 39; Mofussil Foujdari Adalat 40; Nizamat Adalats 41; non-Regulation system got extended into Assam 46; parallel tribunals to administer justice in the Bengal Presidency 41; radical changes to the traditional administrative structure 37; Regulating Act of 1773 40; Regulating Act of 1781 41; Regulation X of 1822 46; Regulation XLI of 1793 42; Royal Charter April 1661 37-8; Sadar Dewani Adalat 39, 41;

Second Law Commission under the provisions of the Charter Act of 1853 44; series of Regulation promulgated on 1 May 1793 42; Supreme Court of judicature at Calcutta 40; Third Law Commission 44-5

First Panchayat Court 93
first-class magistrate 276

Gadadhar, rebellion of 91
Gohain, Indoo 205
Gohain, Maju 205
Gomdhar Konwar, rebellion of 89-90
government pleaders 224; Regulation VII of 1793 224

honorary magistrate 212-5; competent to take evidence in complaints or prosecution of felony or misdemeanor 213; powers enhanced under Criminal Procedure Code (Act X of 1872) 213

Jenkins, Francis (Captain) 97; appointment of 105-6; administrative reforms 106; agent to governor-general and commissioner for Assam and north-east Rangpur 106
Judicial Agencies 193-224; deputy commissioner 195; European functionaries commissioner 193-5; junior assistant 197-8; *lakhiraj* 196; native judges 200-7; principal assistants 195-6; sub-assistants in-charge of subdivisions, powers and duties of 198-200; subordinate assistant 198
Juggoram 205
jury trial 215-18; assistance of jurors obtained in Lower Assam 215; caste prejudice, influenced verdict of a jury 217; difficulties delay in trial 218; increasing influence of jurors in the proceedings 216-17; institution of jurors 215; jury list, imperfect and defective 217-18; not free from defects 217; statutory right under the Code of Criminal Procedure (Act XXV of 1861) 216

Kamal alias Nalliah Gohain 206
Kamrupa 23
kheldars 103
Khunlai 28
Khunlung 28, 29
Koch Hajo or Kamrupa 26

levying of *barangani* or extra cess 80
Lieutenant Singer 185-6
Lok Adalat 281
Lower Assam, administration of 52-3; organizational framework of the offices 53

Macaulay, Thomas Babington 43-4, 275
maulavis 40
Mofussil Panchayat courts 95
mohurer (omlah) 262
muftis 40
munsif 200-4; Assam Code laid down specific rules and procedure for appointment 200-1; method of examination and the procedure of appointment 204; monthly salary 208-9, 211, 212; preparation of a code of rules for the examination 201; reported all appointments to the Sadar Dewany Adalat 203
Munsif's Court 93; procedure to be followed 93

Index 337

native judges 200-7; allowances not at par with those prevailing in the Regulation Provinces 208-9; duties performed 212; monthly salary 210; *munsif* 200-4; powers and position of 207-12; powers made equal under the provisions of Regulation V of 1831 207-8; principal *sadar amen* 206-7; *sadar ameen* 205-6; salaries of judicial officers of the lower Provinces 210
nazir 121-2
Nizamat Adalat 40-1, 60-2, 106, 134
non-regulation system into Assam, extension of 50-2; native judges and *omlahs* gone to the Bengalis and north Indians 51; Regulation X of 1822 50-1; regulation provinces, all the revenue and judicial matters 52

omlahs 51, 86, 102, 103, 259, 262

paiks 29-30, 36, 55, 57, 81, 144
panchayats or native courts, working of 72-5: assistant-in-charge of a district 75; civil cases 74; Court of Directors 75; Governor-General's Agent 74; no trained judge, *omlah* or uniform laws and procedures 74; *Panchayats*, necessity for 74; *Sadar Panchayat* 75
parganas 32, 55, 97, 104, 105, 106, 261
pattah 254
peadas 121
Peali Barphukan and his associates, rebellion of 91-2; Dhanjoy Borgohain 91
peasant uprising 182-7; Act for imposing a duty on 'Arts, Trades and Dealings' 184; anti-colonial uprisings and Nowgong, in Assam 182; feasibility of a tax on betel nut and *pan* cultivation 183; high revenue assessment in different kinds of taxation 182; Income Tax Act 1861 184; Lieutenant Herbert Sconce, deputy commissioner of Nowgong 183-5, 187; local government deferred the decision in imposing License Tax 187; necessary to convey the unruly *ryots* to the *thana* 183; *Phulaguri Dhawa* 187; *ryots*, signs of dissatisfaction with the measure of taxation 183
Phukan, Anandaram Dhekial 200, 265-6
police administration 234-45; *chowdhuris* 234; *patgiris* 234; *thanas* 234
police *darogahs*, powers and duties of 234-45; affray or intended affray 236; carefully preserve and promulgate all regulations of government 236; cases of very serious nature, Form E 244; crimes as a source of profit for the police 239; criminal courts, inconvenience and delay of prosecution 237-8; Criminal Procedure Code, chapters IV, V and VIII 243; district superintendents 244-5; divisional station 242; indiscriminate apprehension for the purpose of extortion 238; inefficiency and misconduct of police 241; little or no reliance on proceedings conducted by the *darogahs* 240-1; Police Act of 1861 242; police failed to check crime 236; police officers, salaries of 236-7
Pragjyotishpur 23
principal *sadar ameen* 206-7; monthly salary 211, 212
professional pleaders 218-24; examination of candidates for the

338   Index

grades of pleaders 220-1; Government Examiners of Pleaders 220; no regularly appointed *vakeels* attached to the courts 218; provisions of Section 6, Act XX of 1865 219; qualifications to appear in the examination of pleaders and *mukhtears* 222

Public Interest Litigation 281

Raij Mel at Gobindapur 187-8; 1869, *rupit* and *non-rupit* lands, land revenue doubled 188; *ryots* in Kamrup district, protest against the increase of land revenue 187-8

Revolt of 1857/First War of Indian Independence 148

Robertson, T.C., appointed as Agent to the Governor-General 63-4, 92; civil code, preparation of 92-3; civil justice, reforms in 94-8; courts of *sadar ameen* and *munsif*, substitution of 97; experimental division of Central Assam 106; proposed to abolish the Moffussil Panchayat courts 95; recommendations of Capt. Bogle 96

sadar ameen 205-6; 1851, revised rules of appointment 206; monthly salary 208-9, 211, 212; post created by Bengal Regulation XLIX 205

sadar ameen and the *munsif*, powers of 98-9; Regulation VI of 1832 98; special appeal to the Sadar Dewani Adalat 99

Satya Yuga or Golden Age 29

Sconce, Lieutenant Herbert (Deputy Commissioner) 183-4, 185, 187

Scott, David 46, 49-52, 55-63; administration of civil justice, issued rules of practice 70-2; administration of criminal justice, important reforms made 76; introduction of trial by jury 215; Lower Assam, empowered to try all civil suits 55; ordered execution of both Peali and Jeuram 92; policies and programmes in Lower and Upper Assam 52-3; policy of employing natives in the administration of justice 85

Second Panchayat Court 93

Sein Bhandari Kakoti, first principal *sadar ameen* at Kamrup 206

Session Court 276

Sikarpati Nikarpati 277

Singha, Gaurinath 27; establishment of Burmese authority in Assam and in Cachar 27-8

Singha, Purandar 104

treaty of Yandabo 28

Upper Assam, administration of 53-4; Scott's policy 53; Ahom monarchy restored in 101-3; Court of *Gram Adhikars* or District Judges 102; Faujdari department 103; judicial machinery not working according to *raja's* expectation 103; *kheldars* empowered to try criminal cases 103; main provisions of the treaty 101-2; *omlahs* and the *darogahs* 103; Raja Purandar Singha, adequate efforts to improve the administration of justice 103